cinematography

screencraft

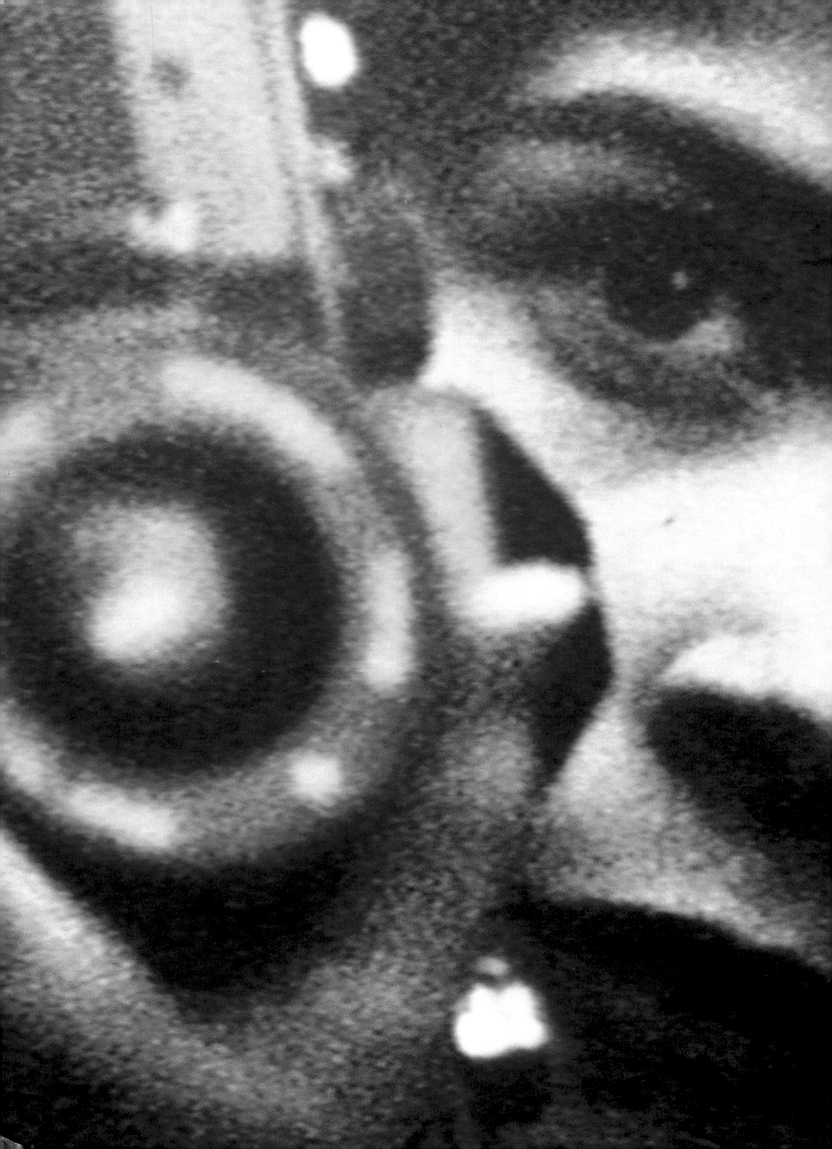

peter ettedgui

cinematography

screencraft

series devised by barbara mercer

**Focal
Press**

Boston Oxford Auckland Johannesburg Melbourne New Delhi

Focal Press is an imprint of

Butterworth-Heinemann

ℛ A member of the Reed-Elsevier Group

http://www.focalpress.com

The publisher offers special discounts on

bulk orders of this book. For information,

please contact:

Manager of Special Sales

Butterworth-Heinemann

225 Wildwood Avenue

Woburn, MA 01801-2041

Tel: 781-904-2500

Fax: 781-904-2620

ISBN 0-240-80382-5

10 9 8 7 6 5 4 3 2

Design Copyright © 1998 Morla Design, Inc., San Francisco

Layout by Artmedia, London

Illustrations by Peter Spells

Production and separations by ProVision Pte. Ltd., Singapore

Tel: +65 334 7720

Fax: +65 334 7721

contents

introduction

7

In the 1950s, the *auteur* theory championed the director as true author of a feature film. The notion was rapidly and widely accepted: for too long, particularly in the Hollywood studio system, the director had been regarded as little more than a technician. Now, however, directors increasingly provided the key impetus within the new, independent cinema movements that began to flourish internationally, following the example set by the French *nouvelle vague*. And with the emergence of film schools in the 1960s and 1970s largely replacing the system of apprenticeship that had existed previously in the film industry, the emphasis on the director's importance became ever more pronounced. Today, too often in film criticism and education, and even among many practising professionals, the cult surrounding the director means that the other arts and crafts which combine to produce a film are rarely sufficiently cherished or even acknowledged. Cinematographer Michael Chapman

comments: "In the 19th century, opera was the amalgamation of all the arts of the time; movies have taken on that mantle today."

The SCREENCRAFT series, of which this book is the first title, will focus in turn on each of the disciplines that make up the cinema and examine it through the eyes of some of its leading practitioners. In revealing their roles in the film-making process, they will shed light on the way films evolve through a fusion of forces which at first glance might appear to be incompatible: art and industry, vision and compromise, design and accident.

Apart from celebrating some of the creative artists and technicians whose work has been essential to the evolution of cinema, we hope that SCREENCRAFT will deepen understanding of a medium which is still so young – and yet so ubiquitous. Even within the film industry, rigid demarcation lines between different disciplines and departments mean that the full expressive potential of the medium in relation to a film's subject is all too rarely realised. It is hoped, therefore, that a book which features some of the world's finest cinematographers will be of inspiration not just to practising or aspiring cinematographers, but to professionals and students in all areas of the industry – as well as to all those who simply love the cinema.

SCREENCRAFT is not intended to be a series of 'how to' manuals; although the contributors who appear in the following pages may indeed reveal tricks of the trade and discuss technical issues, their contributions are more concerned with transmitting their individual, personal perspective on the language of film. "What makes a cinematographer put the camera here rather than over there?" asks Janusz Kaminski. "All one's experience of life subconsciously informs every creative decision one makes. That's what makes each individual cinematographer different."

The cinematographer (like the director) was regarded as a technician in the Hollywood studio system. This mentality still persists to some degree. Cinematographers are regarded as 'below the line' in film production parlance, along with the rest of the technical crew (the exclusive 'above the line' club consists of director, producer, writers and principal cast). Cinematographers are never accorded any rights in the images they generate. And they are rarely involved to the extent they should be in the preparation of a film; usually

their contracts only begin at a relatively advanced stage of pre-production. But read any of the contributors in the following pages, and it becomes immediately apparent that the cinematographer is so much more than a technician. Technical mastery of their craft may be the cornerstone of what they do, but it is the manipulation of light and shadow, colour and tone, space and movement, in order to create an emotionally charged visual arena for the action of a film which makes cinematography a vocation for so many. When practised by a master, the technical processes of this discipline are elevated to an art form. Michael Chapman recalls witnessing Boris Kaufman, the great Russian cinematographer, at work on a commercial in New York in the 1960s: "As you stood on the set and watched him, you realised this man was literally 'painting with light'; you couldn't help but be awed..."

The notion of painting with light – or sculpting it – is echoed by other cinematographers in this book, and it is a reminder that although their basic technical tools and procedures are directly related to those of the stills photographer, the work of the cinematographer often has deeper roots in the history of art. The Renaissance painters, striving for a greater sense of three-dimensional realism than had previously existed in painting, introduced the concept of source lighting, as well as many of the dramatic effects we see in feature films (such as chiaroscuro) – and their influence, as well as that of later painters and artistic movements, is acknowledged.

The cinematographer, working closely with the director, is the force behind the invisible character present in every film we see – the camera. The camera is always a participant in the drama, selecting not only what to reveal to us, the audience, but also subtly affecting how we respond emotionally to what we see. Actors may be the flesh and blood of a film, but the camera is its guiding spirit. Its significance within the dramatic context of a film is paralleled by the central, almost alchemical role it plays in the film's production. As Billy Williams points out: "The camera is the crucible for everyone's efforts." The screenplay, the director's vision, the creativity of production and costume designers, the actors' performances, the work of technicians in many disciplines, the complex logistics and myriad pressures of a film shoot – all these are as nothing without the magical moment when the camera turns over. Only then are all the hopes and dreams and hard graft transformed into photographic 'reality'. On the cinematographer's shoulders rests the burden of responsibility for this act of transformation – and all the attendant expectations that accompany it. Quite apart from technical and artistic considerations, the cinematographer must be a true communicator, able to understand and absorb the efforts of other key personnel on the film, and also to martial his own lighting and camera crews – abilities which are of critical importance in bringing a film in on schedule and on budget.

If the cinematographer's key relationship is with the director, then the reverse is also often true. Orson Welles famously shared his title card for directing and producing **Citizen Kane** with the visionary Gregg Toland – an all too rare

acknowledgement of just how important the director/cinematographer relationship is. Marriage metaphors abound when cinematographers talk about their collaborations with directors, for if the relationship is to succeed, a deep level of trust, understanding and joint commitment is required. But it's not a modern marriage of equals because, in the final analysis, there's no doubt that the director always holds the reins of power and is responsible for the overall vision of the film.

Most cinematographers readily accept this, especially when working with directors who respect and encourage their creativity. As Darius Khondji says: "I see my job as helping the director to visualise his film. This can be a very intense process, so my relationship with the directors I work with is never just professional; very often we become close friends during the course of our collaboration." If the camera is an invisible character in the film, then cinematographers can perhaps be likened to actors – with each film, they have to adapt their creative and technical abilities to the requirements of different dramatic subjects. Both acting and cinematography are interpretative arts, whereas the film director and screenwriter's role is closer to an act of origination. But this is not to demean the cinematographer's special importance, which lies in the simple fact that film is primarily a visual language, and the defining moments in its evolution – such as the example of **Citizen Kane** – have almost always come about as the result of the creative chemistry between director and cinematographer.

Such defining moments have played a part in determining the

selection of cinematographers who appear in this book. Many of our contributors, in the process of working with particular directors, have helped to expand and enhance the vocabulary and grammar of cinema language – Jack Cardiff with Michael Powell, Sven Nykvist with Ingmar Bergman, Raoul Coutard with Jean-Luc Godard and François Truffaut, Gordon Willis with Woody Allen and Francis Ford Coppola: these are just some examples included here. Similarly, we feature cinematographers who have been involved with the birth of new cinema movements (Coutard with the *nouvelle vague* in France, Robby Müller with the new German cinema in the 1970s), or the beginnings of a new studio adventure (Douglas Slocombe at Michael Balcon's Ealing in the 1940s) and even a fledgling film industry (Stuart Dryburgh in New Zealand). We also wanted our selection to reflect something of the diversity of world cinema. As a visual medium, film is able to cross international borders and transcend cultural divides. Of course, one can view this negatively – some might claim it's what opens cinema up to a dubious cultural imperialism by the film studios with the most corporate muscle, whose product is determined by the lowest common denominator and driven by the financial bottom line. But one can equally look at our film heritage today and see that the medium has enabled people of different nationalities, cultural or ethnic backgrounds to communicate and empathise with one another. As Darius Khondji points out in his chapter, if one loves film, one becomes part of a truly international family.

The third and last factor which informed the selection was that we wanted it to span three generations, so that the book might reach back towards the beginnings of the cinema and also look forward to its future. In the following pages, we will encounter a teenage Jack Cardiff working as a runner on silent films; and we will find contemporary cinematographers like Janusz Kaminski integrating computer-generated imagery into their cinematography.

Inevitably, there are those cinematographers notable by their absence. We could not hope to feature all the greats in a book of this size. Some declined our invitation to contribute to the book due to other commitments; others proved impossible to track down. The legendary Freddie Young, now in his 90s, sent us a kind note, saying that he felt that the time had come to stop giving interviews. Some readers may point to the absence of women cinematographers in the book. This is a regrettable reflection of the fact that, until very recently, the discipline has been almost exclusively a male preserve. With a number of women currently establishing themselves as feature film D.P.s (directors of photography) in Europe and the U.S., the status quo is only now beginning to change.

Omissions aside, we have been undoubtedly lucky and privileged to be able to include here so many wonderful artists, who freely gave of their time and contributed many of the memorable images and documents which appear in the book. When I met Haskell Wexler, he talked about cinematographers as a special group of people, intelligent, open-minded and generous: "Film is a dog-eat-dog world; but cinematographers take pleasure in appreciating one another and sharing any new discovery we make with one another." In putting this book together, I have repeatedly experienced this generosity and sense of camaraderie at first hand. It is most strongly manifested in the desire to transmit their own experience and love of the medium to the next generation of film-makers.

The basis for the text in each chapter was an interview conducted with the contributor. Subsequently, the material was structured and edited (and finally polished with the contributor) so that it would appear entirely in the contributor's own words. We felt that this approach could be more intimate and informal than an interview format – giving the impression of the contributor 'talking' directly to the reader.

As well as thanking our contributors for giving us such invaluable and inspiring insights into their lives and work, I would also like to thank the editorial team at RotoVision. Like a feature film, this book is the result of a collaborative effort. Books about film – oddly for a visual medium – are normally dominated by text. Senior Art Editor Barbara Mercer has had the vision to redress the balance and try to contribute something wholly original to the field of cinema literature. The design work of Morla Design in California and Artmedia in London has enabled this vision to be realised. Meanwhile, Natalia Price-Cabrera and Kate Noël-Paton have conducted a vast and complex research operation to supplement the visual material loaned to us by the contributors, locating many rare and fascinating images from production and distribution companies, picture libraries and

archives internationally – amongst which, our special thanks go to The Bridgeman Art Library, Hulton Getty Picture Library, The Kobal Collection, Ronald Grant Archive, the British Film Institute, The Movie Store Collection, Pictorial Press Ltd., Sygma, I.P.O.L., Magnum and the B.I.F.I. in Paris. To Natalia Price-Cabrera must also go the credit for persuading our dream-list of cinematographers to contribute, and then juggling with their hectic schedules and several time-zones across the world so that we would be able to feature them all. Our thanks in this respect also go to the cinematographers' agents, production assistants and partners who have all helped to make possible our access, as well as to guild organisations such as the American, British and French societies of cinematographers (A.S.C., B.S.C. and A.F.C.). For Sven Nykvist's chapter, our thanks go to his interpreter Annika Hagberg, and also to 'American Cinematographer', who kindly gave us permission to quote from articles by and about Mr Nykvist. Nick at the Cadillac Hotel in Los Angeles went out of his way to help us during our trip to meet and interview contributors living in California. Judith Burns at The Home Office in Brighton supplied immaculate transcriptions of the interviews with our contributors which have served us so well in preparing the book's text. My thanks also to Stella Bruzzi and George Tiffin who gave some invaluable advice when I first embarked on this project, and to Tessa Ettedgui who has provided constant encouragement, reading and discussing the evolving draft throughout what has been for me – and will I hope be for the reader – an inspiring journey of discovery.

PETER ETTEDGUI

biography

One of the great colourists, Jack Cardiff worked his way up from apprentice to camera operator in the 1930s, first in Freddie Young's camera department at Elstree studios, then at Denham Studios, where he worked under legendary Hollywood D.P.s such as Charles Rosher, Hal Rosson, Lee Garmes, Harry Stradling and Jimmy Wong Howe. Cardiff went on to photograph films by directors such as Alfred Hitchcock,

jack cardiff

King Vidor and John Huston, with stars including Ingrid Bergman, Vivien Leigh, James Mason, Ava Gardner, Bogart, Hepburn (Katherine and Audrey), Errol Flynn, Kirk Douglas, Orson Welles, Sophia Loren and Marilyn Monroe. But it was his collaboration with Michael Powell and Emeric Pressburger which secured his reputation as one of the great D.P.s. The films they made in the late 1940s (**A Matter of Life and Death**, **Black Narcissus** – for which Cardiff won an Oscar – and **The Red Shoes**) feature some of the greatest colour cinematography ever produced. As a director, Cardiff's 1960 film of **Sons and Lovers** remains one of the best screen adaptations of D.H. Lawrence. Honoured with Lifetime Achievement Awards by both the American and British Societies of Cinematographers, Cardiff published 'Magic Hour', his autobiography, in 1996.

interview

My parents both worked in vaudeville, so my whole young life was spent in the world of theatre, perpetually on the move, living in different digs, attending a new school every week. I learned nothing, but I was in a cocoon of happiness. Mum and Dad were intensely happy, very much in love. When they weren't on stage, they would fill in with film work, which was a lark. They worked as extras (a guinea a day) – and I started to get cast as a kid actor, mostly in bit parts, although I played the lead in one film. By the age of 14, I was a 'veteran'. Now too big for children's parts, I was still too young for older roles; but my father's health was failing, so I had to continue to work. I got a job as a tea-boy at Elstree Studios on a silent movie – **The Informer** (made in 1928). My main job was supplying the director with iced Vichy water to ease the indigestion from which he suffered. I had no thought of being a cameraman at this stage. As a boy, I'd taken snaps – I once got my father to dress up as a crook, and photographed him in a 'set' which I created in our outside toilet, dirtying the brick-work, pinning up a torn poster and putting a bit of broken wood on the window. That was just for fun; I had no great photographic ambition. But one day during the shoot of **The Informer**, a camera assistant called me over. "Listen, kid", he said, "you see these pencil marks on the lens? When I tell you, I want you to rotate the lens from that mark to that mark, okay?" He was winding the camera, and when he gave me the word, I turned the lens barrel as he'd ordered. When the shot was over, I asked what I had done. "Well, sonny", the assistant replied, "you followed focus…"

After that, I entered the camera department – mainly because I liked the idea that the camera boys got to travel abroad a lot! But very soon, I realised the film camera was to be my life. I became a 'numbers boy' – chalking up the shot identification on the board – then a 'clapper boy' when sound came in. Then one day, my big break came – on a film called **Harmony Heaven**. It was a musical, and we had six cameras for one sequence, and were short of an operator. "You'll have to do it", I was told. So there I was, 15 years of age, having to compose the shot through an upside-down viewfinder. Working as an operator, I was now able to watch the work of the lighting cameraman. For the first time, I realised there was a connection between cinematography and the great love of my life – painting.

When I was about nine, one of the schools I attended while accompanying my parents on tour organised a trip to a provincial art gallery. I had never seen a painting before, and suddenly I was in this vast chamber filled with these wondrous colour dreams. That really got to me, and thereafter, wherever I travelled with my parents, I went to as many museums as I could. Painters were my childhood heroes, and as I studied their work, I began to realise that it was all about light. The light always came from a certain direction and created shadows. Caravaggio, for example, was a 'one-light man' – he'd have a sweeping light from a side-angle. Vermeer's lighting was incredibly pure and simple; he paid infinite attention to the way light reflected and caressed whatever it fell on. Rembrandt used a high north light and took huge risks – whereas his contemporaries 'lit' their subjects to show them off to their best advantage, the people in a painting like 'The Nightwatch' were partly obscured in shadow. These masters taught me to study light and it became a habit – I analysed how the light fell wherever I went; in rooms, on buses or trains. I watched the subtle tricks light plays, how diverse lighting conditions reveal people's faces in different ways.

So, as my career in the camera department progressed, I was able to equate this private obsession with my job. Technicolor were about to set up a European operation, and I went for an interview to become their resident trainee. As I waited for my interview, other candidates staggered out, dazed by the highly technical interrogation they had just experienced. When my turn came, I told the panel I was a mathematical dunce. I was asked how on earth I expected to become a cameraman. I told them about my love of light and painting. Silence. Then I was asked, which side of the face did Rembrandt light from? From the right, I replied. The questions continued in this vein. Next day I learned I had been selected.

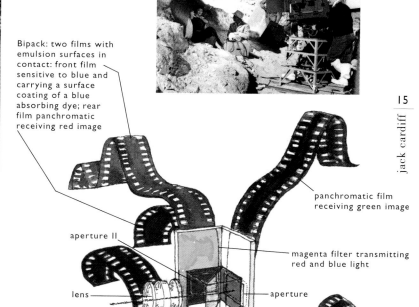

Bipack: two films with emulsion surfaces in contact: front film sensitive to blue and carrying a surface coating of a blue absorbing dye; rear film panchromatic receiving red image

panchromatic film receiving green image

aperture II

magenta filter transmitting red and blue light

lens

aperture

green filter transmitting green light only

sputtered gold mirror (between prisms) which divides light between the two apertures

jack cardiff

(top left) Shooting **Pandora and the Flying Dutchman** (1958): the muslin cage contains butterflies to flutter in shot foreground. *(centre left)* Prelit set, **Scott of the Antarctic** (1948): "A normal ceiling lamp could never throw fringed shadows on the wall, so I hung fringed material in front of my film light." *(lower left)* Shooting **The Vikings** in Norway (1958): "The locals thought we were mad — using firehoses while it was raining; but normal rain won't photograph on its own." *(right)* "The Rolls Royce of movie cameras" — Technicolor runs three films simultaneously. One behind the lens in a normal film gate; the other two in a second gate at right angles. Behind the lens is a square prism with a partial mirror set at 45° which allows 25 per cent of the light to pass through to the single gate, reflecting 75 per cent to the second gate. Filters separate the three primary colours.

Cardiff's study of colour in painting made him aware of the subtlest effects produced by light which he would then integrate into his cinematography, for example, distance revealed as blue in early Renaissance paintings such as Da Vinci's 'The Virgin of the Rocks' *(above left)*. In Caravaggio's 'The Supper at Emmaus' *(top right)*, "one source of light produces the dramatic chiaroscuro effect." In Rembrandt's 'The Nightwatch' *(above, centre)*, many of the subjects melt into the shadows: "a daring, realist painting – not popular in its time". Cardiff was inspired by Rembrandt's example to rebel against Technicolor diktats that every image should be brightly and evenly lit. *(right)* Rembrandt's 'Self Portrait', 1629.

'Lady writing a letter with her Maid', (1671) by Vermeer *(top left)*: "a wonderful richness achieved with the most simple light source. Of course he cheats a little – like all cameramen! When the light is obviously coming from a leaded window inscribed with colour decorations, Vermeer refrains – rightly – from indicating the shadows that would fall on the face." Preparing his 'colour palette' for **Black Narcissus**, Cardiff followed Gauguin's example, exaggerating the colours in his lighting (the vegetation in Gauguin's 'Nave Nave Moe (Sacred Spring)', (1894) *(above)* gives the shadows on the faces a green tint). Meanwhile, Van Gogh's juxtaposition of green and red in 'The Night Café', (1888) *(top right)* struck Cardiff as "an uncomfortable contrast of colours, suggestive of tragedy", inspiring his depiction of Sister Ruth's insanity in the film's climax.

At Technicolor, I was assigned to be camera operator on films using the revolutionary three-strip colour process. I also worked as an odd-job man at the newly-opened labs, and gradually I was given the opportunity to make short promotional films as the company's sole in-house cameraman. Although they had very strict diktats about how you were supposed to set the lighting for Technicolor – no hard shadows, soft light rather than high contrast, for example – I constantly broke the rules, experimenting with colour and exposure in order to find out what I could achieve. I devised a short film called **This Is Colour**, creating colour effects by such devices as pouring gallons of paint of one primary colour into a whirlpool of another. I became known as an *enfant terrible*, but when my employers saw the results I was getting, they tolerated my rebelliousness. The films I shot while at Technicolor – including a series of travelogues in Europe and Asia – enabled me to see what the process could do in every conceivable type of lighting condition.

When I subsequently became a lighting cameraman, this experience and my love of painterly effects helped me to strive for a heightened realism in colour that hadn't really been attempted previously. I was particularly influenced by the work of the Impressionists. Gauguin was quoted as saying, if you see something that is green, don't muck about, paint it green – as green as you can. For instance, if a subject was sitting on grass, the reflection on the face would come up green in the painting. An exaggerated effect – but one rooted in realism. Following this example, if I was shooting a scene in candlelight, which the eye perceives as yellow, I'd use

yellow filters. I'd put colours in my shadows to reflect the time of day. Combining pink and lemon filters could evoke dawn or sunrise or sunset very subtly. Palette seems like a pretentious word, but on any film I'd always have a wide range of coloured filters.

However, the big difference between a painter – or a photographer – and a lighting cameraman is that, although the cinematographer can help to develop an aesthetic approach for a film, you don't have the same control as with a static image. The actors are always on the move, and so is your camera. You also have to bear in mind that the camera should always serve the story and the characters. The cinematography must never draw attention to itself. If someone asked, "what did you think of the photography?" and the reply was, "I don't know – I didn't notice it," – then I would feel I had succeeded. It irritates me when you're aware of the camera moving about like mad, desperate to grab your attention. I learned how to operate by watching cartoons, where the movement of the frame in relation to the subject is always perfect. Because it's drawn, the timing is never jerky or sudden. That's how I like my camera to be – no violent or distracting movement (unless it is dramatically appropriate), just float up or ease down between positions.

If you are an artistically-inclined cameraman, then it is essential to find the right director to collaborate with. A director who plays safe can cripple your ambitions, but one who is too conscious of technique and effects will miss the most essential element of a film – the characterisation.

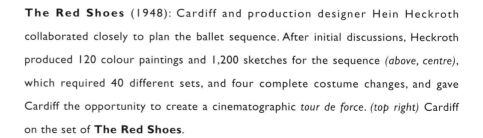

The Red Shoes (1948): Cardiff and production designer Hein Heckroth collaborated closely to plan the ballet sequence. After initial discussions, Heckroth produced 120 colour paintings and 1,200 sketches for the sequence *(above, centre)*, which required 40 different sets, and four complete costume changes, and gave Cardiff the opportunity to create a cinematographic *tour de force. (top right)* Cardiff on the set of **The Red Shoes**.

For me, Michael Powell was the ideal director. We were kindred spirits – both of us loved taking risks. When I started to work with him on **A Matter of Life and Death**, I said, "I suppose the scenes in heaven will be in colour, and those on earth in black-and-white?" "No", he replied, "that's what everyone will expect – so we'll do it the other way around." These sequences were shot with a conventional black-and-white camera, but for the penultimate shot we'd use the Technicolor three-strip camera so we could fade the colour dyes back into the monochrome image. This would enable us to make the transition from heaven (where, as one character put it, one was "starved for Technicolor") back to earth.

Michael would always respond positively to my suggestions, no matter how radical. For example, on **Black Narcissus** he wanted to shoot the final scene of Deborah Kerr on the bell-tower at dawn. We had a perfect early morning light, and I thought the shot would be enhanced by the use of a fog filter (at a time when no one was using them). He said, "great, let's do it." Next day, the lab report came back saying the material was ruined because of the fog filter. I was sick, because the cost to get Deborah to come back for a re-shoot would have been prohibitive (her contract had ended). But when we saw the rushes, Mickey turned to me and said, "Wonderful! That's exactly what I wanted..." The people from the labs protested that the image wasn't clear enough to play on American drive-in screens; Mickey said, "rubbish".

Photographing a film requires a balance of sound preparation and ability to improvise. As a rule, I don't like working from storyboards. You often find the draughtsman has drawn a strong light in the wrong direction, and that although the perspective is fine for the drawing, it is wrong for the actual camera set-up. However, drawings become necessary when you have a very complex scene to shoot. On **The Red Shoes**, I collaborated with the art director, Hein Heckroth, to storyboard the ballet sequence. We would have dinner and discuss how we saw it, and then he made colour sketches from our ideas. In addition, Michael Powell let me work with a dozen real ballet dancers over two days to do some tests in order to see how we could interpret ballet on film. I had been told how Nijinsky seemed to hover in the air at the top of a leap, and I wanted to try to achieve a similar effect in the film. So we devised a special motor that would make the camera speed up to about 48 fps (frames per second) and then return to normal speed within the shot. It was very rare at the time to have the opportunity to do such tests, but they were invaluable.

More usually, tests are run to make sure the costume, hair and make-up look right. Such tests provide the cameraman with an opportunity to think about how you're going to light the actors. Few people are blessed with the kind of flawless features of Ingrid Bergman (who I photographed on Hitchcock's **Under Capricorn**). One of the first things I look for is a certain firmness or lack of firmness either side of the mouth, which is caused by the *levator labi* muscle in the cheeks. If this is prominent in the actor's face, sharp cross-lighting will cause a deep shadow, so you have to light the actor more from the front. It is essential to make your principal actors feel secure about how they are being photographed. I never went as far as some who pandered to

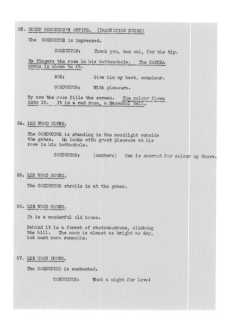

(top right) **Black Narcissus** (1957): Cardiff made up a fog filter (similar to the one shown here from **The Vikings**) to give a dawn effect for the film's climax. Despite Technicolor's objections ("that the image wasn't clear enough to play on American drive-in screens"), the diffusion gave the scene the appropriate eerie atmosphere. *(centre, right)* Michael Powell and Cardiff in front of a giant propeller used to whip up "the Himalayan wind" present throughout the film to help evoke the disturbing psychological effect of the natural environment on the nuns in the monastery. *(above, centre & left)* An extract from Emeric Pressburger's screenplay for **A Matter of Life and Death** (1946) shows the film's two worlds. Heaven was depicted in monochrome, with lighting inspired by the Vorticist painting movement, and earth in glorious colour. Notice the Conductor's line about being starved for colour in heaven; this was eventually amended to, "Up there, one is starved for Technicolor".

cinematography

(left) **War and Peace** (1956, King Vidor) with Henry Fonda, Mel Ferrer and Audrey Hepburn. Exterior snowscapes were recreated in Rome's Cinecitta studios. To photograph the duel scene in wide shot (and avoid revealing the top of the cyclorama), Cardiff had to make up his own glass matte. Coloured filters and diffusion evoked dawn. *(centre)* **African Queen** (1951, John Huston): an arduous shoot with Bogart and Hepburn in Africa. "The perfect film: a compelling story, brilliantly cast." *(right)* **The Prince and the Showgirl** (1957, Laurence Olivier): Marilyn Monroe later wrote to Cardiff, "if only I could be the way you created me". *(far right)* A tracking shot on Hitchcock's **Under Capricorn**: "We wanted Ingrid Bergman to be lit with a single beautiful light on her face as she crossed the crowded room. I customised a crane so the keylight could move with her during the track."

their leading ladies in order to become their regular camera-men – but it's important to acknowledge that actors are often insecure and need to be nurtured in order to achieve the best possible performance.

Sometimes, it doesn't matter how well prepared you are for a film, because the accidents and hazards you encounter while shooting can be overwhelming. On **African Queen**, the whole crew contracted dysentery or malaria because – unbeknown to us – our water filter wasn't working and we were drinking contaminated river water (John Huston and Humphrey Bogart, who drank only whiskey, never water, were the sole exceptions). Apart from having to cope with illness, we had to shoot in dangerous conditions, on white water, when we risked crashing into logs. One shot in a whirlpool on the river was a disaster. I suddenly realised all my lights and reflectors were spinning around – but once we'd got out of the turbulence, there was no way we were going to re-shoot. With a straight face, I told Huston it was fine to print the take – and no one ever seemed to notice the defect. In these circum-stances, the cameraman can't afford to be a perfectionist. You have to adapt, and take it on the chin. I thrive on this kind of experience, because it bonds the crew and draws out extra effort (in contrast to shooting in the placid comfort of a studio). For the same reason, it can also be very stimulating to work on films where the money is tight. Because you don't have access to the best equipment and the ideal conditions, you have to be that extra bit more creative.

Since ordinary photography has progressed over the last

hundred years, it has become indisputably acknowledged as an art form. Then came another miracle; using a succession of still pictures to simulate real, life-like movement – the film camera. And today, this magic box is able to articulate all the creative thoughts and actions of any subject and show it to billions of people all over the world. So can we also call this an art form? Of course we can! The cinema is surely a synthesis of all the arts – literature, music, poetry, sculpture – and of course the glory of painting. I urge aspiring cinematographers to study painting extensively. It's a thrilling exercise, because you see how the masters through the centuries have so expertly composed light and shadow to such wonderful effect. And you will, I hope, learn to do the same thing with your camera.

Fabled as one of the great photographers of leading actresses, Slocombe shot over 30 features at Ealing Studios, including classics like **Hue and Cry** (1947), **Kind Hearts and Coronets** (1949), **The Lavender Hill Mob** (1951) and **The Man In The White Suit** (1951) – photographed in luminous, atmospheric black and white. After Ealing folded, he worked with directors such as John Huston (**Freud: The**

douglas slocombe

Secret Passion, 1962), George Cukor (**Travels With My Aunt**, 1972; **Love Among The Ruins**, 1975), Jack Clayton (**The Great Gatsby**, 1974) and Fred Zinnemann (**Julia**, 1977) – who considered Slocombe "one of the finest cameramen in the world". He also worked with some of the finest British and American directors emerging in the '60s and '70s including Joseph Losey (**The Servant**, 1963; **Boom**, 1968), Roman Polanski (**Dance of the Vampires**, 1968), Ken Russell (**The Music Lovers**, 1971), Peter Yates (**Murphy's War**, 1971), Norman Jewison (**Jesus Christ, Superstar**, 1973; **Rollerball**, 1975) and Steven Spielberg (the Indian sequences for **Close Encounters of the Third Kind** were followed by the **Indiana Jones** trilogy). If his filmography is indicative of the romantic he claims to be, it also shows him as a cinematographer able to adapt his approach not only to the demands of very different directors, but also to changing times in the history of cinema. His work has been awarded with a quartet of BAFTAs and a trio of Oscar nominations.

When I was 13, I was sent to an international boarding school near Versailles. My father was diplomatic and foreign correspondent in the Paris office of British newspapers such as 'The Daily Express' and 'The Evening Standard', and when I went home for weekends, the family apartment would be filled by my father's friends – artists and writers, amongst whom were Sinclair Lewis, James Joyce (who played on our piano) and Ernest Hemingway. I developed a passion for photography and film at an early age. During the summer holidays I would experiment with my box brownie and my 9.5mm Pathé-Baby. I'd set up the slow box camera in the medieval church overlooking our country house in Normandy and leave the shutter open for an hour at a time while the sun crept around the stained glass windows, bathing the interior in a glowing light. At school, I filmed the sports events and ran a film club. Later, after finishing my education at the Sorbonne and seeking an opening in films, I was offered a job by Alexander Korda, who was then shooting at the Joinville studios outside

Ealing Studios: Slocombe's home for 17 years, where he collaborated with most of the directors who worked under the aegis of the 'headmaster' Michael Balcon: Charles Chrichton (**Hue and Cry**, *second & third shots from top left*; **The Lavender Hill Mob**, *fourth & fifth left*; **The Titfield Thunderbolt**, *lower left*); Alexander Mackendrick (**The Man In The White Suit**, *above centre, top two shots*); Basil Dearden (**Saraband for Dead Lovers**, *above, top right* – the first film Slocombe shot in colour, for which he broke all Technicolor's rules by illuminating the set with different levels of light, as opposed to maintaining a consistent level throughout); Robert Hamer (**Kind Hearts and Coronets**, *above centre, bottom still & right, centre still*). He photographed most of Ealing's regulars (Alec Guiness, Joan Greenwood, Stanley Holloway, Valerie Hobson, Michael Gough, Googie Withers, Dennis Price, Miles Malleson, Alfie Bass, Sid James, Flora Robson) and 'guest stars' like Audrey Hepburn and Stewart Granger.

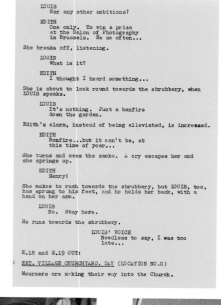

```
                    LOUIS' VOICE
                The funeral service was held in the
                village Church at Chalfont, prior
                to interment in the family vault.

E.21  EXT. CHURCHYARD GATE. DAY  (LOCATION NO. O)

A closed carriage drives up.  LOUIS descends from within
and helps out EDITH, in widow's weeds.

                    LOUIS' VOICE
                Mrs. D'Ascoyne, who had discerned
                in me a man of delicate sensibility
                and high purpose, asked me to
                accompany her on the cross-country
                journey.

E.22  INT. CHURCH. DAY  (SET NO. 21)

It is full of monuments to D'Ascoynes already departed,
including two busts of the First Duke and Duchess.  The
VERGER shows EDITH into the D'Ascoyne family pew.

                    LOUIS' VOICE
                I did so, but not as far as the
                family pew, since I did not feel
                this a propitious moment to stress
                my blood relationship.

LOUIS takes a seat in one of the side pews, facing the
nave.

                    LOUIS' VOICE
                The occasion was interesting in
                that it provided me with my first
                view of the D'Ascoynes en masse.
                Interesting and somewhat depressing,
                for it emphasised how far I had
                yet to travel.

The CAMERA takes in the members of the family as he
enumerates them.

                    LOUIS' VOICE
                There was the Duke.  There was my
                employer, Lord Ascoyne D'Ascoyne,
                there was General Lord Rufus
                D'Ascoyne, there was Admiral Lord
                Horatio D'Ascoyne, there was Lady
                Agatha D'Ascoyne, and in the pulpit
                talking interminable nonsense, the
                Reverend Lord Henry D'Ascoyne.

LOUIS yawns discreetly behind his hand.

                    LOUIS' VOICE
                The D'Ascoynes certainly appeared
                to have accorded with the tradition
                of the landed gentry and sent the
                fool of the family into the Church.

E.23  EXT. CHURCHYARD GATE. DAY  (LOCATION NO. O)

At the churchyard gate, afterwards, EDITH is waiting with
LOUIS for their carriage, when the Duke, ETHELRED, comes
up.
```

```
                    LOUIS
                Nor any other ambitions?

                    EDITH
                One only.  To win a prize
                at the Salon of Photography
                in Brussels.  He so often...

She breaks off, listening.

                    LOUIS
                What is it?

                    EDITH
                I thought I heard something...

She is about to look round towards the shrubbery, when
LOUIS speaks.

                    LOUIS
                It's nothing.  Just a bonfire
                down the garden.

Edith's alarm, instead of being alleviated, is increased.

                    EDITH
                Bonfire...but it can't be, at
                this time of year...

She turns and sees the smoke.  A cry escapes her and
she springs up.

                    EDITH
                Henry!

She makes to rush towards the shrubbery, but LOUIS, too,
has sprung to his feet, and he holds her back, with a
hand on her arm.

                    LOUIS
                No.  Stay here.

He runs towards the shrubbery.

                    LOUIS' VOICE
                Needless to say, I was too
                late...

E.18 and E.19 OUT:

EXT. VILLAGE CHURCHYARD. DAY  (LOCATION NO.O)

Mourners are making their way into the Church.
```

In script form, the scene from **Kind Hearts and Coronets** (1949) *(above left & top right)* seems straightforward: seven family members attend a funeral. But all seven were to be played by one actor: Alec Guiness. "I didn't want to use a printing process to achieve the effect – dupes in those days were very poor quality. I decided to do it in-camera. The image was divided into seven parts, which we shot one at a time, while keeping the other 6/7 blacked out. After each shot, the film had to be rewound to the first frame. Each of Alec Guiness's make-up changes took three hours, so the scene was shot over two days. Of course the camera had to be locked off – if even the studio cat had tripped over the tripod, we'd have been knocked for six. I slept overnight beside the camera…" *(right, top)* Slocombe on location: **Jesus Christ, Superstar** (1973), *(below)* shooting **The Blue Max** (the plane, urged to fly lower by director John Guillermin, clipped Slocombe's head).

cinematography

Freud (1962): "John Huston urged me to shoot the film (which he'd rewritten from a 700-page script by Satre) in several styles: a conventional approach for narrative scenes from Freud's life; one for the psychoanalysis scenes; another for the patients' flashbacks; and a fourth style for the dreams. I did tests and came up with a number of styles in terms of lighting, composition, using different film stocks and getting the laboratory to develop at different gammas." Slocombe believes he did some of his best work on the film. However, the studio refused to release Huston's full three-hour cut and the film was butchered into 90 minutes – "a heartbreaking experience". *(above)* Slocombe in front of glass smeared with vaseline, through which he shot the flashbacks. *(below)* Painting of Freud's teacher Charcot giving a demonstration of hypnosis, which Huston and Slocombe reproduced in the film *(below, right)*.

Paris. But my Kafkaesque journey through French bureaucracy, in order to obtain the necessary *permis de travail*, proved to be fruitless, and I decided to go back to London. I put my vocation on hold and followed in my father's footsteps by going to work for two years on the news desk of the British United Press (taking over from James Robertson Justice, who also started his pre-film days there!). Meanwhile, I was having some success with photographs I was taking (I always carried a Leica) which were published worldwide in 'Life', 'Picture Post' and 'Paris-Match'.

As the clouds of the Second World War gathered, I was able to get some money from 'Picture Post' to travel to Danzig on the border of Germany and Poland – labelled the danger-spot of Europe. I found myself in an absolute hornet's nest of Nazism – brown-shirted Storm Troopers, black-shirted SS, windows of Jewish-owned shops being smashed, people beaten up in the streets. I took photographs of all this, and when I returned to London, I was contacted by Herbert Klein, an American documentary director who was making a film entitled, **Lights Out In Europe**. The script, as he put it, was being written daily by Hitler, Mussolini and Chamberlain. Would I like to go back to Danzig – this time with a 35mm film camera? At last, my chance to break into films.

I had a day being taught how to use the Bell & Howell 'Eyemo', and then I went back to Danzig. I'd only been away a few weeks, but the situation had hotted up. I was able to record on film everything I had photographed previously; I shot Nazi rallies with huge crowds; and after filching the

press ticket of a journalist whom I drank under the table (the nastiest thing I've ever done), I got into a meeting of SS Storm Troopers, presided over by the visiting Goebbels. As he harangued his black- and brown-shirted audience, I plucked up the courage to begin shooting. The machine-gun racket of the camera stopped Goebbels in mid-flow, while his retinue visibly marked me out. I didn't dare shoot any more after that, and sat wondering how to get out unscathed. Then, when everyone rose to shout, "Heil Hitler!", I too got to my feet and crouching low, swiftly made my way out beneath their outstretched arms. The next night, noticing the sky was red, I took my camera and found that the synagogue had been set on fire. I was arrested filming the scene and frogmarched off to the Gestapo headquarters and thrown into a cell. I was interrogated, and was fortunately able to talk my way out. The Polish embassy, which had been smuggling my footage back to London, suggested I leave the 'Frei Stadt' of Danzig immediately and helped me cross the border into Poland.

In Warsaw, I was joined by the director Herbert Klein, and we began to film the pathetic Polish preparations for the imminent Nazi invasion. A few nights later, the aerial bombardment of the capital began. Klein and I joined the thousands of refugees fleeing the city, but our train was scarcely 30 kilometres out of Warsaw before it was bombed. We witnessed horrific scenes – people dying and villages being burned to the ground – the most harrowing material I've ever had to shoot. Subsequently we purchased a horse and cart, and slowly made our way out of Poland, avoiding the Russian invasion literally by hours. Eventually we reached

Riga in Latvia, where the French embassy agreed to send our rushes back in the diplomatic bag (the British refused any help) and also arranged for us to be flown back home via Stockholm.

In London, my work on **Lights Out In Europe** came to the attention of Alberto Cavalcanti, the great Brazilian director then based at Ealing Studios, which were making films for the Ministry of Information. As a result of our meeting, I got assigned to make morale-boosting films and spent the next four years on destroyers on the Atlantic convoys, on an aircraft carrier with the Fleet Air Arm, and with the Royal Air Force; some of the action which I shot found its way into dramatic propaganda films made by Ealing, such as **The Big Blockade**. By the end of the war, my duties for the Ministry were winding down – but I now had a foot in the door at Ealing. I was taken on, very conscious of the fact that I didn't have the background of the average cameraman who had worked his way up from junior assistant and learned the tricks of the trade by watching other cameramen at work (there were no film schools then).

But despite my anxiety, I was embarking on 17 of the happiest years of my working life. Ealing Studios – relatively small and self-contained – produced on average five pictures a year. The stages were well-designed and well-equipped, and the producers, directors, writers and technicians – all under contract – were presided over by Michael Balcon. He wanted Ealing to produce 'clean' films, expressive of the British way of life, and he encouraged the gentle satire for which the

studios became renowned. We employees were a tightly-knit family: there was a terrific excitement about film, and after work we would all retire to the 'Red Lion', the pub opposite the studios, to discuss the day's work and argue passionately about the cinema, often until closing time. Often, these animated discussions might have some direct impact on our future work; a story of mine, for instance, suggested to Tibby Clarke – writer of some of Ealing's greatest comedies – was filtered down into a sequence on the open staircases of the Eiffel Tower for his **The Lavender Hill Mob** screenplay. One of the marvellous things about Ealing was that we weren't limited by our own particular professional roles; we all trespassed into each other's spheres and made suggestions.

As I came to bridge the gulf between documentary (where you're photographing real events as they unfold in real settings and natural lighting conditions) and drama (where everything, including the climate, is artificially created), I remembered the first lesson I'd learned in Fleet Street: that you had to find the salient point of any story and make sure it got over. I would know exactly what the camera should focus on as well as the mood I would be required to create. Light played the key part in all this; I learned how to manipulate it, how to vary its intensity. I learned the countless ways to 'bend' light, cut the rays, make hard or soft shadows leaving more or less detail to peep through. In time, light came to feel like dough in my hands. I came to love the moment when you had decided the set-up with the director, and you'd be left alone in the set with your gaffer and 'sparks' and your lights to create the scene – like a painter in his studio. I also came

(left) **Julia** (1977): "I tried to strike a balance between depicting the harsh reality of the story's Nazi background, and a more romantic style for the scenes between Jane Fonda and Jason Robards." *(above, centre)* **The Great Gatsby** (1974): "I wanted a lush look to evoke the lives of these terribly spoiled people. I lit it very luxuriantly and used a lot of diffusion." *(above, right)* **The Servant** (1963): "Joe Losey loved long takes with complicated camera moves, so the challenge was to light so the camera wouldn't see one's lamps, while maintaining the overall, dramatic mood of the film. Joe was also fond of mirror shots. This mirror reflected everything – we had to disguise the camera so it would melt into some black set dressing."

Slocombe has worked with directors from Hollywood's golden age – John Huston (*top left*, with daughter Anjelica), George Cukor, Fred Zinnemann *(bottom, right)*: "great traditional film-makers, masters of their art, but mostly concerned with story and actors. They were happy to leave the film's look entirely to me." Directors like Joseph Losey *(above)* and Norman Jewison *(with viewfinder)*, "would be very involved in the film's overall look, but usually left the detail to me". Roman Polanski *(top right)* and Steven Spielberg *(right, second still from the top)* are "born film-makers: everything comes so naturally to them, like breathing. Both can talk lenses and get involved with every aspect of the camerawork."

to think of the human face as the cameraman's canvas. Each one demands to be treated in a different way. Cameramen have always been obliged to make the leading actresses as beautiful as possible (actually the male leads also). This can create problems because sometimes the ideal lighting for the actress might mean spilling unwanted light over other parts of the set, compromising the mood you are trying to create. So you have to weigh up what is more important. I generally favour mood over actors' looks in wider shots, and then concentrate on the face in the close-ups.

When I'm preparing to shoot a picture, I'll study the script and sketch out some ideas and pinpoint any potential problems. Then I talk to the director and liaise with the art director, who will nearly always arrange to cater for any set-lighting requirements in his designs. I've worked with (rather than from) storyboards a number of times, and have nothing against them as long as they do not have to be rigidly adhered to, and do not preclude any spontaneous invention on the set. (They can be an important security blanket for directors, and they are essential when there are a lot of different elements to co-ordinate in a scene – as on the **Indiana Jones** films). I like to walk on to a set, look for the important detail and start designing the cinematography from there – always bearing in mind a preconceived overall mood. When I started working as a cameraman, there was a tradition that comedy should be treated with high key photography but personally I did not necessarily treat comedy and drama any differently. For instance, **The Man In The White Suit**, ostensibly a comedy, had elements of drama – set in the industrial north, with

heavy political overtones, it demanded to be lit dramatically. When I first began to work in colour, on Ealing's **Saraband for Dead Lovers**, the Technicolor experts had all kinds of rules – your level of light had to be bright and uniform over the whole frame – which meant that everything would look flat. I had no desire to do this whatsoever, so I treated colour exactly as I treated black-and-white. I aimed for the same use of contrast and tone to create mood – but multiplied the intensity of the light, high and low, by ten (the slower film needed that much more to register an image). Sometimes I would go to the National Gallery to see how the Old Masters used colour. They would suggest an environment that might be full of rich colours but drew your eye, through their own lighting and shadow effects, to what they wanted you to see – part of a face illuminated by a flickering candle, for example.

I photographed some 30–40 pictures at Ealing, and have been director of photography on over 50 since. The pictures that have given me the most pleasure – and possibly inspiration – have always been those with some literary content. In the early days: **Kind Hearts and Coronets, The Man In The White Suit, It Always Rains on Sunday, Saraband for Dead Lovers**, and later **The Servant, The Lion in Winter, Travels with My Aunt, The Great Gatsby** and **Julia**. I also enjoyed the challenge of large-scale productions, such as **The Blue Max, Rollerball** and the **Indiana Jones** trilogy, usually shot in Cinemascope and other anamorphic formats to do justice to their vast settings. These were in the days when the image on the screen was almost entirely the work of the cameraman, including carefully lit shots involving

Raiders of the Lost Ark (1981): "If something wasn't working as planned in the storyboards, Steven would just improvise another solution. The scene *(below)* was to have featured an elaborately choreographed fight between Jones with his whip and a 'heavy' wielding a scimitar, but the light was fading as we set up. My heart was in my mouth – one often feels quite sick when one sees a magical natural light effect disappear – and Steven suddenly said, 'OK Harrison, we haven't got the time to do the fight so why don't you just get out a revolver and shoot the guy'. The continuity woman asked, 'where did he get the revolver?' but Steven didn't worry about that. And it's one of the funniest moments in the picture."

foreground miniatures, perspective backgrounds, super-impositions, and front and back projection. Now the advent of digital imaging often obscures what the cameraman himself has done, but as with every new innovation in the art of film-making, it nonetheless could open up new creative possibilities for him too.

To any aspiring cinematographer, I'd say learn the rules before you try to bend or break them. The terrible thing about so-called art today is that no one learns to draw any more. You need a foundation on which to build.

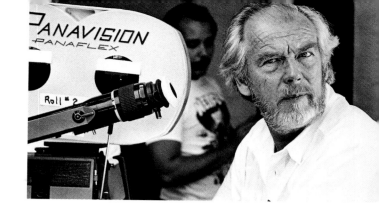

biography

Ingmar Bergman wrote: "I do mourn the fact that I no longer make films... Most of all I miss working with Sven Nykvist, perhaps because we are both utterly captivated by the problems of light..." Nykvist's collaboration with Bergman began with **Sawdust and Tinsel** (1953) and spanned three decades, producing 22 films, including **Through a Glass Darkly** (1961), **Winter Light** (1962), **The Silence** (1963),

sven nykvist

Persona (1966), **The Passion of Anna** (1969), **Cries and Whispers** (1973); the six films Nykvist cites as critical to the evolution of his understanding of light. Nykvist has shot many films elsewhere in Europe and the U.S., including **The Tenant** (Roman Polanski, 1976), **Pretty Baby** (Louis Malle, 1978), **Starting Over** (Alan Pakula, 1979), **Swann In Love** (Volker Schlöndorff, 1984), **Agnes of God** (Norman Jewison, 1985), **The Sacrifice** (Andrey Tarkovsky, 1986), **The Unbearable Lightness of Being** (Philip Kaufman, 1988), **Sleepless In Seattle** (Nora Ephron, 1992), **Another Woman** (Woody Allen, 1988), **Crimes and Misdemeanors** (Allen, 1989), **Chaplin** (Richard Attenborough, 1992), and **What's Eating Gilbert Grape?** (Lasse Hallström, 1993). He has also directed **The Vine Bridge** (1965) and **The Ox** (1991). He won Academy Awards for **Cries and Whispers** and **Fanny and Alexander**, and received the American Society of Cinematographers' Lifetime Achievement Award in 1996.

interview

My parents were missionaries in the Congo and one of my very early memories is of looking at images from Africa captured on a wind-up film camera. They showed African men building a church with my father, and they captivated me. Later, when my parents returned to Africa, I was sent to live with my aunt and she gave me my first stills camera. Apart from photography, I also loved sport as a boy. When I was 16, I worked as a newspaper delivery boy in order to earn the money to buy a Keystone 8mm camera, which I could use to film the athletes in slow motion during a competition in order to understand a new high-jump technique being used by American athletes to improve their scores. That experience got me interested in shooting film, but my parents didn't want me to go into the cinema because, to them, it was sinful. However, my stills photography earned me a place in a school of photography in Stockholm.

Once in the city, I was free to go to the movies every night. I decided to become a cinematographer, and soon I got my first job as an assistant cameraman. I worked for many different cinematographers, and also had the opportunity to travel to Rome, where I was employed at Cinecitta as an interpreter as well as an assistant. Shortly after my return to Sweden, a cameraman for whom I was working suddenly became sick and I was asked to take over. I underexposed the entire first day's work; fortunately, the director shouldered part of the blame, otherwise my career as a cinematographer would have ended then and there.

Through another stroke of luck, I met Ingmar Bergman. Göran Strindberg was to have shot **Sawdust and Tinsel**, but he decided to accept an invitation to go to Hollywood, and the film was offered to me. Initially, I was quite apprehensive; Ingmar was known as the 'demonic' director. But from the first day, we worked well together. Perhaps we understood each other because we were both the sons of pastors. There was a good atmosphere on those early films. We had very low budgets – there were around ten people in the crew and a cast of four or five actors. Everyone did everything. Everyone helped everyone else. When I came to make **The Virgin Spring**, my second film for Ingmar, I remember we had an exterior night shoot. I added some artificial light to the scene because I thought the natural light was boring and I wanted to see the actor's shadows dancing against a wall. The next day, when we saw the rushes, Ingmar screamed, "God damn it! How can there be shadows when the sun has gone down?" This incident marked the beginning of our journey together into light. Because Ingmar had worked in the theatre, he was

fascinated by light and how it can be applied to creating a mood. Had I not met him, in all probability I would have remained just another technician with no great awareness of the infinite possibilities of light.

Sufficient time is rarely taken to study light. It is as important as the lines the actors speak, or the direction given to them. It is an integral part of the story and that is why such close co-ordination is needed between director and cinematographer. Light is a treasure chest: once properly understood, it can bring another dimension to the medium. In his autobiography, Ingmar wrote about how we both became utterly captivated by light: "*The gentle, dangerous, dreamlike, living, dead, clear, misty, hot, violent, bare, sudden, dark, spring-like, falling, straight, slanting, sensual, subdued, limited, poisonous, calming, pale light.*" Gentle light is what you might use if you're photographing a woman and you want her to look very beautiful and soft. Dreamlike light is also very soft. I prefer to achieve this with light rather than low-contrast filters. Living light has more contrast and vitality, while dead light is very flat with no shadows. Clear light is more con-trasty, but not too much. Misty light might involve the use of smoke. Violent light is contrastier than living – such subtle distinctions influence how an audience perceives and reacts to the images on screen. Spring-like light is a little warmer. Falling light is when the angle is very low and you get elongated shadows. Sensual light is for love scenes. As I worked with Ingmar, I learned how to express in light the words in the script, and make it reflect the nuances of the drama. Light became a passion which has dominated my life.

Nykvist's voyage of discovery of light with Ingmar Bergman — the b&w films: **Through a Glass Darkly** (1961, *above, top two stills*), **Winter Light** (1962, *above*), **The Silence** (1963, *below*) and **Persona** (1966, *right*).

Nykvist's voyage of discovery of light with Bergman – the colour films: *(top left)* **The Passion of Anna** (1969), *(above)* **Cries and Whispers** (1973) and *(right)* **Fanny and Alexander** (1983), which was their last collaboration together before Bergman retired from cinema.

Generally, there is never enough time in the preparation of a film to explore properly the availability and possibilities of natural light. Ingmar, however, insisted on two months preparation for any film, during which time we would make an extensive study of the beautiful, sparse northern light we have in Sweden and discuss how to apply it to the story of each film. Before we shot **Through a Glass Darkly**, we would go out in the early, grey morning light and note down the values that were to be had and how these values changed as new light patterns and effects were created whenever the sun broke through. We wanted a graphite tone, one without extreme contrasts, and we determined the exact hours when this mood could be obtained naturally. At this time, we came to believe that artificial studio lighting was absolutely wrong – it had no logic. Logical light, by contrast, was light which appeared real, and it became our shared obsession. A naturalistic light can only be created with fewer lights – sometimes none at all (at times, I have used only kerosene lamps or candles).

Light was to play a vital role in **Winter Light**, which was set in a church on a Sunday over three hours. Although the church was to be built in a studio, Ingmar and I went to a real church during our preparation and took photos every five minutes to study how the winter light changed over a similar time period. The bad weather outside the church during the story meant that there should never be any shadows inside, and we promised ourselves that we would re-shoot every time there was a shadow in the rushes (and we did). Then, towards the end of the film, there is a vital scene between the teacher

(played by Ingrid Thulin) and her priest (Gunnar Björnstrand), where we planned for the sun to come out for about 30 seconds. That is light which was thought about and meant something in the story. But otherwise, we did not stray from the indirect, shadowless winter light. Since then, I have tried to avoid using direct light, working mainly with bounced light in my quest to stop a film looking lit. I was helped in this by developments in the sensitivity of raw stock, which enabled us to follow the example of the French new wave and shoot increasingly on location.

When we came to film **Persona**, we virtually discarded the medium shot. We went from wide shots to close-ups and vice versa. Ingmar had seen a certain resemblance between Liv Ullmann and Bibi Andersson, and the idea had dawned of making a film about identification between two people who come close together and start to think the same thoughts. The film gave me the opportunity to explore my fascination with the face, which has earned me my nickname, 'two faces and a teacup'. One of the more difficult tasks for me on **Persona** was to light the close-ups because they involved such incredible nuance. I like to see reflections in the eyes – which irritates some directors, but is true to life. Capturing these reflections helps to give the impression of a human being thinking. It's very important to me to light so that you can sense what lies behind a character's eyes. I always aim to catch the light in the eyes, because I feel they are the mirror of the soul. Truth is in the actor's eyes and very small changes in expression can reveal more than a thousand words.

One of the unique privileges of working with Ingmar was that there were a few actors who were always in his films. I came to know their faces intimately, and learned how to photograph every detail. It takes time to learn how a face will take light. For me, the actor is and will always be the most important instrument in a film. My ability to capture the subtleties of a performance depends on using very little light and giving the actor as much freedom as I possibly can, and also on treating him or her in such a way that they never feel manipulated or exploited. I make a point of not annoying actors with light meters or by shining light in their eyes, and I will always tell them what I am doing. When I worked with Ingrid Bergman on **Autumn Sonata**, I wasn't used to working with stand-ins. The first day, Ingrid said to me, "Sven, how can you work without stand-ins?" For a moment I wasn't sure what to say. I didn't want to admit that it was mostly for economic reasons; nevertheless, what I replied was also true: "It's different to light with the stand-in, because the actors give me inspiration, if I can light them." She said, "I will sit behind the camera the whole time, and whenever you want, I'll come up and stand where you need me." She was wonderful to work with. People often forget the personality connection between the cinematographer and the actor is so important. Good actors react to their lighting.

Making the transition from black-and-white to colour was not easy for Ingmar and me. We felt that colour raw stock was technically too perfect; it was difficult not to make it look beautiful. When we came to shoot **The Passion of Anna**, we wanted to control the colour palette so it would reflect the mood of the story. We managed to find a location with very little colour, and everything in the film's design was intended to simplify the colours in front of the camera. I wanted to avoid warm skin tones, and after exhaustive testing, I learned to use very little make-up and to drain some of the colour in the labs. (I used a similar technique on **The Sacrifice** for Tarkovsky, where we took out the red and the blue, giving us a look that was neither black-and-white nor colour – it was 'monocolour'.) **Cries and Whispers** marked another important step in my appreciation of how to use coloured light for dramatic effect. We developed a colour scheme for the interiors based on the colour red – every room was a different shade of red. Audiences watching the film might not realise this consciously – but they feel it. My experience has taught me that people are held spellbound by the mood created through proper utilisation and integration of light and design.

I'm not really a very technical person. I don't measure the highlight and shadows, for example; I decide such things by eye. I like to draw from experience and from my feelings when I shoot. Sometimes I feel ashamed at my lack of interest in all the new techniques of modern film-making, but I prefer to work with as little equipment as possible. If I have a good lens and a steady camera, that's all I need. **Fanny and Alexander** was shot with the same zoom lens throughout the entire six hours of its running time – except for a handful of shots where we didn't have enough light. With a zoom, you have all the possibilities at your fingertips (and the image quality is now so good). I use very little filtration on the lens. I have spent my whole working life learning to trust

47   (cont'd)

TEREZA runs toward the main street. TANKS and CROWDS are ahead of her. TOMAS is alone with SABINA.

              TOMAS
         Where are you going?

              SABINA
         To Switzerland. Want to come?

              TOMAS
         (looks at her, but
          thinks of Tereza)
         It's strange...but I've never seen
         her so happy.

              SABINA
         (understanding all)
         See you. Goodbye, monster.

She kisses TOMAS'S cheek and drives away.

48   EXT. ANOTHER CROWDED PRAGUE STREET. DAY.

TOMAS runs onto the MAIN STREET. HE SEES: TRUCKLOADS OF YOUNG CZECHS, banners aloft, rousing the crowds, challenging the tanks (stock). And on one of the trucks -- TEREZA, riding with the others.

CLOSE ON TOMAS. Her image is reflected in his sunglasses.

(Stock) People pierce a hole in the gastank of a tank. A young Czech boy drops a burning paper into the gastank. Tank bursts into flames. Russians jump from tank and try to beat out fire with coats.

ANOTHER TANK bursts into flames. BLACK SMOKE RISES (stock). ANOTHER ANGLE THROUGH SMOKE -- TEREZA in the crowd, photographing.

TOMAS WATCHES HER, separated by black smoke and tanks.

CROWD is screaming out of joy. People hold hands, form a circle, dance and sing around the tank through the black smoke. It's a drunken carnival of hate!

Russian soldiers holding their weapons are together in the middle of the circle. They just watch, not knowing what to do, perplexed.

TEREZA snaps one picture after another.

                                                      56

48   (cont'd)

Suddenly VERY LOUD DETONATIONS are heard.

Another Russian tank has begun to fire at the facades of the buildings. Huge pieces of stone and glass tumble to the ground. The whole crowd lies down on the pavement. TEREZA still stands photographing.

TOMAS sees her. He runs to her, pulls her down. TEREZA lying there is so exultant that she struggles, freeing herself from TOMAS. She keeps taking pictures lying down.

The tank stops firing. A STRANGE SILENCE hangs over the street. The people of Prague lying on the ground of their own city slowly look up.

A YOUNG GIRL rises and walks slowly toward the tank, its gun still smoking, turning right at her. She stands before the tank, places her hands on her hips. CLOSE ON GIRL'S FACE: Tears roll down her cheeks.

49   EXT. PRAGUE. NIGHT.

Stock footage from night. People hurling objects at trucks and tanks.

Fires rage at night.

LIGHTS FLASH ACROSS FACES OF TEREZA, TOMAS (and stock footage) giving weird, eerie effect.

(Another song rises: Jo! Jo! Jo!)

50   EXT. STREET OF PRAGUE. ANOTHER DAY.

All the buildings are surrounded and there are tanks everywhere.

Russian soldiers are trying to paint over the slogans; among these slogans are: "IVAN GO HOME, Moscow 1,500 km," "1938-1968," etc.

A group of young men sneak behind a tank and paint a swastika on it. WE HEAR: Russian voices screaming. The young people run away. GUN SHOTS. One of them falls.

TEREZA, among other people, is attracted by the gun shots. All run in one direction.

TEREZA SEES: People lifting the body of a young man onto their shoulders. She takes pictures.

                                                      57

50 (contd)

-BODIES LYING IN A DOORWAY (stock).

A young girl dips a Czech flag in the blood on the ground. She brandishes the blood-splattered flag and waves it in the air.

She runs after the young people carrying the body. A mass of people forms, surrounding a tank. The cannon of the tank turns ominously following them.

-A RUSSIAN TANK COMMANDER HAS HIS GUN OUT.

TEREZA MOVES CLOSER, bravely trying to photograph him.

-TANK COMMANDER TURNS AND POINTS HIS GUN AT HER.

-TEREZA LIFTS HER CAMERA, POINTS IT AT THE GUN, AND SHOOTS.

51 INT. POLICE STATION. DAY.

TEREZA is being interrogated by a RUSSIAN INTERROGATOR (all interrogators here are Russian) surrounded by several Russian soldiers. It's a small room jammed full of people. Most of the people are young and several are wounded. TEREZA is pulled through the crowd and pushed down to sit before a table. Her camera is violently ripped from her hands. (In the background other young people are being forcibly pulled to other rooms: commotion; lots of activity. Also some Czech officials in suits from Nightclub scene, including CZECH ASS KISSER).

              INTERROGATOR
         Have you gone mad? Don't you
         realize that we love you? That
         we've always loved you? That we
         came to protect you?

              TEREZA
         To protect us from what?

              INTERROGATOR
         Did you give your pictures to
         foreigners?

              TEREZA
         (with a kind of proud
          feeling)
         Yes. Yes, I did.

              INTERROGATOR
         Did you know that you could be
         shot for that?

"For **The Unbearable Lightness of Being** (1988), we had to match grainy, scratched 8mm archive footage we had from the Prague uprising. We shot footage of Daniel Day-Lewis and Juliette Binoche in Lyon on 35mm, making sure to keep the background blurry. We then transferred the footage to 8mm, mishandled it so it got scratched, and blew it back up to 35mm with visible edges. The authentic 8mm material was also blown up to 35mm. The result was quite convincing. The sequence is six minutes long and feels improvised but it was the most planned sequence in the film (it took a month to shoot). A story-board artist made drawings to indicate exactly how the new images had to be shot to match the archive footage." *(right)* Script for the sequence with images from the film; *(below)* Nykvist with director Philip Kaufman.

"It's very important for me to change my style for every picture. I start by asking myself how I can help the audience to look at the right thing: is it the actors, or the dialogue, or the mood, and so on." *(left)* **The Postman Always Rings Twice** (1981, directed by Bob Rafelson). *(above)* **Sleepless in Seattle** (1992, directed by Nora Ephron).

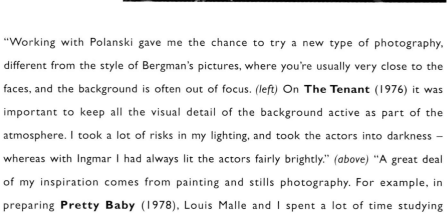

"Working with Polanski gave me the chance to try a new type of photography, different from the style of Bergman's pictures, where you're usually very close to the faces, and the background is often out of focus. *(left)* On **The Tenant** (1976) it was important to keep all the visual detail of the background active as part of the atmosphere. I took a lot of risks in my lighting, and took the actors into darkness — whereas with Ingmar I had always lit the actors fairly brightly." *(above)* "A great deal of my inspiration comes from painting and stills photography. For example, in preparing **Pretty Baby** (1978), Louis Malle and I spent a lot of time studying Vermeer's paintings, specifically the way he uses light."

A great fan of Bergman's films, Woody Allen began to work with Nykvist on **Another Woman** (1988, *above*) and their collaboration continued with **Crimes and Misdemeanors** (1989, *left*), **New York Stories** (1989) and **Celebrity** (1998), Shooting **The Sacrifice** (1986, *far right*), Andrey Tarkovsky's last film, gave Nykvist the opportunity to return to Sweden and also to a more visually-based cinema than American films with their emphasis on dialogue and conventional narrative structure.

simplicity. I've seen what happens on big pictures: people start filling the screen with a lot of perfectly placed and calculated light. There is nothing that can ruin an atmosphere so easily as too much light. Sometimes, I think having less money can lead to more artistry. Above all else, the cinematographer must be an absolute slave to the screenplay; this means being able to change one's style for every picture. Each time I start working on a film, I ask myself how I can help the audience to look at the right thing. Is it the actors? Or is it the mood? Or is it the dialogue? I have to confess that dialogue-rich films are not my favourites, and this is why I have a little difficulty with American scripts. They don't mention mood or atmosphere or how it looks. You just read dialogue. With Ingmar, how the scene should look and feel, even the weather, was written into the script. An overemphasis on dialogue can limit the cinematographer's potential to be creative – it becomes like photographing words. The films of Eisenstein and the great Swedish silent directors, Sjöström and Stiller, are so much more visual than anything we see today.

A handful of principles have defined my life as a cinematographer. Be true to the script. Be loyal to the director. Be able to adapt and change one's style. Learn simplicity. I would also say that a cinematographer should direct at least one film. As a cameraman, it is very easy to become a technical freak. The experience of writing and editing a film enables one to understand the whole creative process of film-making.

Page 37, 38 62 words (pp 229) from 'The Magic Lantern: An Autobiography' by Ingmar Bergman, translated by Joan Tate (Hamish Hamilton 1987, first published as 'Laterna Magica', by Norstedts Forlag, Sweden, 1987). Copyright © Ingmar Bergman, 1987. This translation copyright © Joan Tate, 1988. Territory: UK and Commonwealth excluding Canada. Extract taken from 'The Magic Lantern' by Ingmar Bergman, translated by Joan Tate. Translation copyright © 1988 by Joan Tate. Original copyright © 1987 by Ignmar Bergman. Used by permission of Viking Penguin, a division of Penguin Putman, Inc. Territory: US Canada P.I. Open.

Pages 37–47 Extracts from April 1972 article by Sven Nykvist, 'A Passion for Light'; January 1993, 'Nykvist Continues Storied Career with Chaplin', by David Heuring; and February 1996, 'ASC Salutes Sven Nykvist', by Bob Fisher have all been reprinted by permission of the publisher of 'American Cinematographer' and the American Society of Cinematographers. For further information about the American Society of Cinematographers and 'American Cinematographer' magazine, please visit the ASC website at
www.cinematographer.com or call +1 212 969 4333. The ASC is located at 1782 North Orange Drive, Hollywood, CA 90028, USA.

Born into a middle-class Bengali family in 1930, Subrata Mitra's beginnings in cinema were like a fairy tale: aged 21, with no formal film education or apprenticeship, he shot a film which became a landmark in world cinema. **Pather Panchali** (1955) began a collaboration with Satyajit Ray which produced ten films over 15 years (including **Aparajito**, **Apur Sansar**, **Jalsaghar**, **Devi**, **Kanchenjungha**,

subrata mitra

Charulata and **Nayak**). Just as Ray helped to create a new identity for Indian cinema, so Mitra revolutionised prevailing aesthetics in Indian cinematography with innovations designed to make light in film both more realistic and poetic (he was perhaps the first cinematographer to use bounce lighting consistently – ahead of Raoul Coutard in France and Sven Nykvist in Sweden). In the '60s, he shot four films for Merchant Ivory Productions – **The Householder**, **Shakespeare Wallah**, **The Guru** and **Bombay Talkie**. He has worked with other important Indian directors such as Basu Bhattacharya (**Teesi Kasam**, 1965) and Shyam Benegal (**Nehru**, 1984). In 1985, he shot **New Delhi Times** for Ramesh Sharma, winning the National Award for Best Cinematography – one of an array of international awards his work has garnered (including the Eastman Kodak Lifetime Achievement Award for Excellence in Cinematography in 1992). Mitra also composed music and played the sitar for Jean Renoir's **The River** and **Pather Panchali**.

interview

Little did I know that my habitual cycling down with schoolmates to a nearby cinema for the Sunday morning shows, to watch the British and Hollywood films from our lowest-priced seats, would secretly decide my fate. I was discovering the magic of film and was fascinated by the dramatic images with low-key lighting in Guy Greene's photography for **Great Expectations** and **Oliver Twist**, or Robert Krasker's for **The Third Man**. I became aware of the medium of cinematography and the urge to become a cameraman was sown. While in college, I had decided to become either an architect or a cinematographer. But failing to find work as a camera assistant, I reluctantly continued studying for my science degree. Then Jean Renoir came to my rescue. The Master arrived in Calcutta in 1950 to shoot **The River**. I tried to get a job on the film but was turned away. My parents were always supportive of my creative pursuits, and my father stepped in like an anxious parent trying to get his child admitted into a school. He took me to the producer, the director and his cinematographer-cousin Claude Renoir. I was given permission to watch the shooting. Every day, I travelled two hours by bus across the city to the shooting of **The River**. I made extensive notes and meticulous diagrams detailing the lighting, the movement of camera and actors. To my great delight, Claude one day asked if he could refer to them to check lighting continuity before doing a retake. However, I don't think I learned much about film-making as such. But I did come to realize that film-making was like a religion to Jean and Claude Renoir. And as I watched these two masters at work, I got initiated into that religion.

Meanwhile, Satyajit Ray, at the time a graphic designer and a friend of the film's art director, would visit the set on Sundays and holidays to watch the shooting. We became friends, and I would visit him every day, describe in great detail what I had witnessed and also show him the stills I had taken on the shooting. One day he told me, "You have the perfect eye now." He was already planning **Pather Panchali**, and promised to take me on as an assistant. As the shooting approached, he suddenly suggested, "Why don't you photograph the film?" "Me? I don't know a thing!" I replied. "What is there to know?" he asked. "There's a switch on the camera. You press it, the camera runs, and everything else is the same as with your stills camera." There was a lot of scepticism among relations and friends, not to speak of the sarcasm of the film world, but Ray stuck to his choice, perhaps prompted partly by his own apprehensions about having to work with established professionals. And so, at 21, I became a director of photography, without ever having touched a camera before.

However, I soon realised that one cannot be a D.P. by just switching the camera on. The responsibility of shooting **Pather Panchali** weighed heavy; I spent sleepless nights struggling with my worries, anxieties, doubts and fears.

When I started watching films in the 1940s and '50s, Indian cinematography was completely under the influence of Hollywood aesthetics, which mostly insisted on the 'ideal light' for the face, using heavy diffusion and strong back-light. I came to resent the complete disregard of the actual source of light and the clichéd use of back-light. Using back-light all the time is like putting chilli powder in whatever you cook. But Hollywood also had rebels like James Wong Howe, who was able to separate the foreground and the background with careful lighting in films like **Come Back, Little Sheba** and **The Rose Tattoo**, without using the back-light at all. I tried to follow him. And there were other films that inspired me and opened out new ways of seeing things. Carlo Montuori's work on **Bicycle Thieves** – like Cartier-Bresson in motion; the mood and atmosphere created by trees and foliage delicately photographed by Richard Leacock in Flaherty's **Louisiana Story**; rich tonality and crystal clarity in **People in the City** by Arne Sucksdorff; Kazuo Matsuyama's exquisite, haunting photography in Kurosawa's **Rashomon**; night scenes with grey-black sky in the Russian film **Mussorgsky**, contrary to Hollywood's convention of offensive blue cast all over for night scenes; lessons learnt from the apparently unobtrusive simplicity of Robert Burks' work in Hitchcock's **I Confess**; Boris Kaufman's photography of **On the Waterfront** – you could feel the wetness in the

Mitra's influences include: *(from top left)* Richard Leacock's photography of **Louisiana Story**, Kazuo Matsuyama's of **Rashomon**, Claude Renoir's of **Monsieur Vincent** – featuring dark faces against lighter backgrounds – and Guy Greene's photography of **Oliver Twist**. Renoir also shot **The River** *(lower left)* in Calcutta, giving Mitra his first taste of film-making. *(from top right)* Silvana Mangano's casually revealed under-arm hair in **Bitter Rice** was a revelation to Mitra, brought up on idealised images of female sensuality as depicted in Hollywood films and Indian cinema. Carlo Montuori's photography of **Bicycle Thieves** *(middle right)* was "like Cartier-Bresson in motion", while James Wong Howe's work on **The Rose Tattoo** *(lower right)* offered an example of how to avoid clichéd back-lighting.

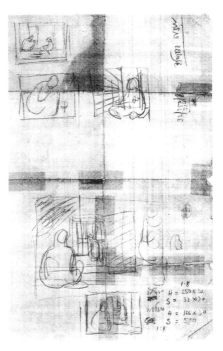

Pather Panchali – shot over four years, in chunks, whenever Ray was able to find funds. For 18 months, production shut down entirely – until Ray's mother talked to a friend of a friend of the chief minister of West Bengal who agreed to finance the film's completion. *(left)* Ray gave Mitra these hurried sketches for camera set-ups the night before shooting the scene with Indir and little Durga (the scribbled notes for lighting are Mitra's). The still above relates to the first sketch *(above left)*. *(far right)* Sketches for the scene where Apu's mother brings water back from the well, discovering little Durga with Indir. The sketch *(below, left)* relates to the stills *(below, right)* – Indir catching her breath prior to the sequence leading to her death in the bamboo grove. Silent movie actress Chunibala Devi was persuaded out of retirement to play Indir.

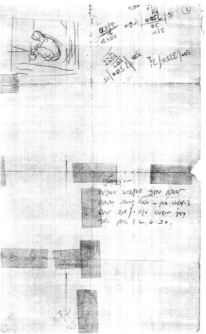

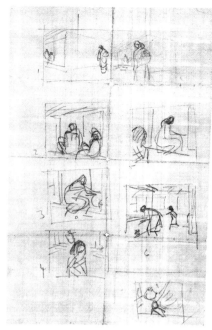

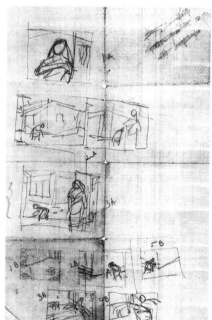

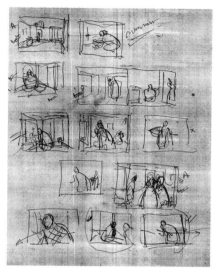

Pather Panchali was the first hands-on experience of film-making for most of the cast and crew. Working outside the rigid hierarchical studio system, the unit functioned like a close-knit family – with none of the usual divisions between different jobs, an atmosphere sustained on **Aparajito**, the second Apu film. For example *(second still from top, centre)*, art director Bansi Chandragupta is holding a reflector on his shoulder for Mitra (behind the camera). Below this shot, we see Mitra preparing another set-up on **Pather Panchali** (with Ray looking on), and Apu beside a Mitchell camera with 'camera coolie' Pagla ("extremely poor and yet passionately dedicated to the camera, dearer to him than his own life"). *(above right)* Sketches and still for the saree scene, where Durga is accused of theft.

subrata mitra

53

Waiting for the sun.

Waiting for the rain.

cinematography

air around the docks exuding from the texture of the images; darker faces against lighter backgrounds in exterior scenes in Claude Renoir's work on **Monsieur Vincent** – a revelation to me which held sway my style permanently, as Indian cinema did just the opposite as a rule. Today this practice has crept into the photography of interior scenes in Indian films – I wonder whether I was a catalyst in this breakthrough.

I have mostly tried to use lighting in such a way as if there has been no lighting done as such. I had to make my first technical innovation during the shooting of **Aparajito** – dictated by the effort to create an 'unlit' feeling. The fear of monsoon rain forced the art director, Bansi Chandragupta, to abandon our original plan to build the inner courtyard of a typical Benaras house in the open to get the same type of diffused available light from a patch of sky above. He insisted on building the set in the interior of a Calcutta studio. This came as a thunderbolt to me, as I could visualise undesirable multiple shadows floating all over the set, created by the conventional studio lights. I argued in vain with Chandragupta and Ray about the impossibility of simulating shadowless diffused skylight. I felt extremely helpless, but it was a blessing in disguise, as I was forced to innovate something that subsequently became one of my most important tools. It was bounce lighting, achieved by placing a framed, painted white cloth over the set, resembling that patch of sky – the only natural source of light in a Benares courtyard – and arranging studio lights below to bounce off the fake sky. The resulting light was soft, diffused and shadowless. The meticulous authenticity of the set helped the light to appear so real

that nobody, including a veteran cinematographer, could distinguish between the shots on location and those in the studio. Thus, from 1956 onwards, bounce lighting became an integral part of my working method. It enabled me to create convincing effects that I could not have got otherwise – such as bringing out the difference between direct sunlight and ambient diffused light in an interior day scene, or lighting up an interior in the studio to create the effect of fading daylight when cut with scenes shot in location exteriors at dusk. Apart from its capacity to simulate natural light, bounce lighting has a delicate artistic quality. For me, shooting with nothing but direct light inside the studio is like photographing the exteriors using only sunlight, sacrificing all the subtle tints of a rainy day or overcast sky or a dawn or a dusk. It is like refusing to shoot in the mist, or remaining indifferent to the poetry inherent in a rainy day. It needs to be mentioned here that bounce lighting does not merely imply bouncing off lights from walls and ceilings in a mindless, haphazard way to produce monotonous effects, as sometimes practised. On the contrary, it should be practised simulating the source of light and maintaining tonal richness. In my case, light always came through doors and windows, and not from the ceiling.

Alongside the advantages of bounce lighting, I was also aware of its limitations. At times, it required larger shooting space, restricting camera movement. For **Charulata**, Ray expressed his desire to move the camera a lot and asked me to sacrifice bounce lighting. My worries about hard multiple shadows even in interior day scenes were brushed aside by his remark: "What you're trying to avoid is seen all the time in films shot

(top) After shooting **Pather Panchali** with a Mitchell camera, Mitra (behind camera with Ray, photographed by Marc Riboud) shot **Aparajito** with a blimped Arriflex IIA – a more mobile, lightweight camera. In so doing he introduced the Arriflex-Nagra synchronised sound combination – which has since become standard – to the Indian film industry. But the most important aesthetic innovation of the film was the introduction of bounce lighting, seen in the two stills *(left)*. The first shows art director Chandragupta's set of a Benares courtyard. The problems of lighting this studio set realistically were solved by using bounced light. *(below)* Another set for **Apur Sansar**, the third film in the **Apu** trilogy, is lit by directional bounce lighting through doors and windows (not from the ceiling) to maintain source. Mitra imposed limitations on his lighting to maintain continuity with material shot on location.

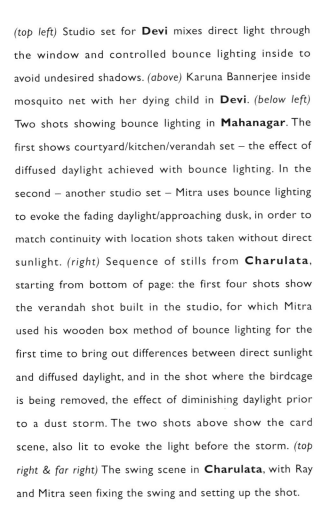

(top left) Studio set for **Devi** mixes direct light through the window and controlled bounce lighting inside to avoid undesired shadows. *(above)* Karuna Bannerjee inside mosquito net with her dying child in **Devi**. *(below left)* Two shots showing bounce lighting in **Mahanagar**. The first shows courtyard/kitchen/verandah set – the effect of diffused daylight achieved with bounce lighting. In the second – another studio set – Mitra uses bounce lighting to evoke the fading daylight/approaching dusk, in order to match continuity with location shots taken without direct sunlight. *(right)* Sequence of stills from **Charulata**, starting from bottom of page: the first four shots show the verandah shot built in the studio, for which Mitra used his wooden box method of bounce lighting for the first time to bring out differences between direct sunlight and diffused daylight, and in the shot where the birdcage is being removed, the effect of diminishing daylight prior to a dust storm. The two shots above show the card scene, also lit to evoke the light before the storm. *(top right & far right)* The swing scene in **Charulata**, with Ray and Mitra seen fixing the swing and setting up the shot.

by the best Hollywood cameramen." I felt let down that he settled for freedom of camera movement at the cost of lighting, but I was not prepared to compromise. I was also not trained to work in the manner other cameramen worked, and I knew I could not do what they did. So I had to devise some other effective way to achieve the same effect without actually bouncing the lights. I made a number of wooden boxes, each containing thirty-two 100-watt household lamps in four rows, with tissue paper covering the open side of the box. The boxes also had silver paper pasted inside on all five sides, and many holes top and bottom for ventilation. The boxes could be no smaller than three by two feet; the shadowlessness of light depends on the area of the source of light. The example is the small size of the sun compared to a wide overcast sky, where light comes from every point of the sky to create shadowlessness. It was fascinating to watch the quality of 'fake' bounced light from these crude boxes. A few years after my improvisation, a sophisticated version of these lights with quartz-iodine lamps was marketed in the U.S. But these 'softlites' were only good enough as fill-in lights, whereas my wooden boxes could serve as the main keylight. I've continued to work with them, replacing the 100-watt lamps with photoflood lamps when shooting in colour – to get the right colour temperature.

During a workshop, I urged students not to use their light meters blindly, but to use them creatively. There's no such thing as a 'correct exposure'. Correct exposure is that which gives us our desired effects and tones. Lighting obviously means intentional under- and overexposure. A black-and-white photograph looks tonally rich if there's rich black, pure white and at least three middle greys in between – although one can imagine innumerable shades of grey between the black and the white. Most reflected light meters indicate an exposure which would always produce a particular mid-grey, whether reading white snow or dark black cloud. So by under- or overexposure of the meter reading one can get darker or lighter shades of grey. We made a seven-step greyscale with five specific greys in between, with their individual tones/ reflectances relating to the difference of one f-stop to the next one. We wanted to be specific about the greys, so we named them: **sa** (black); **re – ga – ma** (mid-grey); **pa – dha – ni** (white) – which are the do-re-mi-fa… in the Indian musical system. A new 'musical' language was evolved for the students to communicate among themselves and create tonal symphonies. They could predetermine the different tones to be obtained by under- or overexposing with confidence, and could get rid of the tendency of playing safe. Incidentally, we do not always strive for all the tones – black is not required in a misty scene, or white in a scene depicting darkness. I always think in greys – even working in colour, I strive for tonal separation and don't depend on colour separation alone.

I once came across a statement by Jean Renoir where he complained that cameramen often create lighting that does not exist in the world. He insisted that cinematographers should study how nature illuminates everything. Ever since then, this became the principle guiding force in my work. I find that most of the time I am justifying the lighting of a scene, by simulating the source of light. But this practice does not make me a "slave of light", as Ray once called me in irritation. My

subrata mitra

main emphasis has always been to create mood and atmosphere. However, following the source of light faithfully does not inhibit me. There are so many other elements to play with. For example, the lighting ratios, i.e. the relationship between the highlights and the shadows, whether on an actor or on the set; or the degree of visibility in the shadow areas, ranging from full detail to complete darkness. One can vary the proportion of the volume of dark and light area in the frame. Style is not and should not be viewed as a strait-jacket. Take, for instance, the notion of beauty, glamour and sensuality. The powdered, well made-up leading lady of Hollywood is a glamorous icon. But a dishevelled sweating young woman can also embody glamour and sensuality. The so-called 'horror' lighting from below can also make a woman look glamorous. Watching **Bitter Rice**, I was amazed how casually Silvana Mangano's underarm hair was shown – a different idiom of sensuality, in complete contrast to Hollywood's glamour.

Style, for me, is a matter of one's taste and conviction, something implicit in the things that you use and you do not use. But my style has been determined by the material limitations of the circumstances in which I had to work. Photographing almost all of Merchant Ivory Productions' first film, **The Householder**, with six photoflood lamps naturally laid down limitations about what I could and couldn't do. However, in **Pather Panchali** a poverty of resources definitely contributed to the distinctive look of a film dealing with poverty. I cannot imagine photographing the film with a Panavision or Arriflex 535 camera, Cooke Varotal lenses and in colour. In fact, a slicker quality achieved with better equipment might

not have been in tune with a subject so strongly rooted in poverty and reality. But I have often chosen to impose limitations on myself – even when shooting in the studio, I restricted myself to the conditions and facilities I would have had if I had shot on location, for the sake of continuity and to match the studio shots with those on location. An actor can overact and underact – so can a cameraman. I am aware of my tendency to underact with my lighting – like a fear of appearing overdressed for an occasion. But when I saw the finished film with music, I often felt I could have done a little more.

Looking back on my career today, I find disruptive forces eroding my belief in the religion of cinema that the Renoirs initiated me into. I cannot find a single print of any of my films which would project me even as a mediocre cameraman. As cinematographers, we have no control over our work once the film is completed. Good films by well-known film-makers and also classics are being mercilessly and systematically massacred by poor projection and bad telecast, totally ignoring the international standards. Bad prints circulate in the market like counterfeit coins, and distorted, residual versions of great classics are preserved in archives with great care. Are future generations going to evaluate the great masters by these prints, with no clue as to how the original really looked? While the deterioration and neglect of the image assails my love for the cinema, I live in the hope that I am not the only madman searching for a beautiful frame on the screen; that others share my beliefs, my passion, and my anger at the state of affairs where our work is subjected to mindless assaults in labs, cinemas, archives and on television.

From 1962 to 1970, Mitra collaborated with director James Ivory and producer Ishmael Merchant on four films: **The Householder** (centre, left), **Shakespeare Wallah** (above, right), **The Guru** (top left) – the first Indian film shot entirely with halogen lamps – and **Bombay Talkie** (bottom, left).

biography

After serving in the French army in Asia (1945–53), Coutard stayed in Vietnam to work as a photojournalist. Returning to France, he was employed by a company which produced 'photo-romances' (love stories told in a sequence of captioned photos), before being approached to shoot **La Passe du Diable** (1956). "If I'd had any idea what it meant to be a D.P., I probably wouldn't have said yes – I'd have been much

raoul coutard

too intimidated." As a D.P. his photojournalist sensibility chimed perfectly with the ideas of the iconoclastic gang of polemical film critics who were about to burst out of the hot-house of 'Cahiers du Cinéma' to spearhead the *nouvelle vague*. Introduced to this group by two of their producers, Georges de Beauregard and Pierre Braunberger, Coutard proved an able collaborator. He liberated the camera, making it more mobile than it had been at any time since the silent cinema. His photography adapted naturally to the needs of different subjects, from the gritty monochrome of **A Bout de Souffle** (1959) to the lyrical grace of **Jules et Jim** (1962). Apart from his collaborations with Jean-Luc Godard and François Truffaut, he also shot films for Jacques Demy, Claude de Givray, Jacques Rivette, Bertrand Tavernier, Raoul Levy, Eduardo Molinaro, Nagisa Oshima and Costa Gavras, and has worked as a director himself. In 1996, his body of work – some 80 films – was awarded the American Society of Cinematographers' International Achievement Award.

interview

The key to setting the tone for a film's photography is the relationship I have with the director. Together, we have to decide how the film is going to look. Usually, a director has ideas for two or three key scenes, more often only two or three shots. In the final film, there may be anything between three and eight hundred (usually shot completely out of sequence), all of which have to link up to create a dramatic and visual whole. So you have to pin the director down – more difficult than it sounds, because how do you define lighting in words? I've directed myself, and on one occasion I began to explain what I wanted to my cameraman, thinking to myself, right, this won't be a problem, because I know how to explain this sort of stuff – seeing as how I'm something of an expert myself... But then I saw what he was doing, I thought, I don't believe it, I might as well have been talking to the guy in Czech! This isn't remotely like what I'm after. I had another experience where I agreed to photograph a film for a well-known director who was crazy about the look of **A Bout de Souffle**. While we were preparing the film, he never stopped talking about it – how did you do this, how did you achieve that? So I assumed he wanted the same look. Second day of filming, he says to me, "Listen, this is no good, you'd think it was **A Bout de Souffle**, the way you're shooting it..." I replied, "hold on, you never stopped talking about **A Bout de Souffle** in our meetings, of course that's what I thought you wanted." It turned out that he was after the kind of stylised cinematography that I hate: gimmicky shots of light through shutters, and so on. A very upsetting experience.

Arriving at a consensus with the director, then, is the most important – and most difficult – part of the job. It's a good idea to have references. Are we going to do this like an American musical? Or a Hitchcock thriller? Ultimately, however, it's only when you start shooting that you really set the tone for the whole film and discover if you're actually in agreement with each other. As you become more experienced, there's another kind of communication problem you can have, particularly with less experienced directors. They'll come up and ask, "if you were me, how would you do this shot?" But if they become reliant on such technical advice, you're in danger of making a hybrid film with no real individuality. In my opinion it's much better for a film to be clumsy, but sincere, than technically slick, but empty. So I chuckle whenever I'm asked that question, and reply, "I'm not going to tell you how, because if I really was you, I wouldn't know what I know." I prefer not to participate in the direction, just stand back and watch. As the cameraman, you're the film's first spectator. So if I see something that jars, I'll quietly point it out to the

director – for example, if one actor isn't on the same wavelength as another, or if I suddenly see something in a shot that would make a better cut for the editor. But this will be said discreetly, in confidence – never undermine the director.

There are other relationships you have to work at as the D.P.. Actors, for example: often very highly-strung people. They are very vulnerable when they go into character. You have to give them confidence – go to talk to them from time to time, explain what you're doing. They need to be reassured and feel that they are the centre of attention when it comes to the photography. If they're not happy, it's bad for the film. Some actors go to rushes – not to see the film, but to see themselves. Next day, it's a safe bet they'll want to alter some aspect of their appearance. You have to persuade them against this, because once it's established, you can't deviate from the film's look. Then there's also the relationship with a film's production designer. There are always going to be problems with the choice of colours he gives you to photograph. And this can make life tricky, because the designer wants to express his vision of the film, and often, as far as he's concerned, the cameraman is a royal pain in the butt. He's not about to do you any big favours. Same with the costume department. It's not exactly a joy when you arrive on set for a night shoot to find an actor dressed in black with a white shirt – a nightmare to light. Meanwhile, if a make-up artist puts too much red on the actor's face, the lab is going to compensate by putting more green into the image to reduce the red – which will result in the background also looking green. These are specific photographic problems, but you

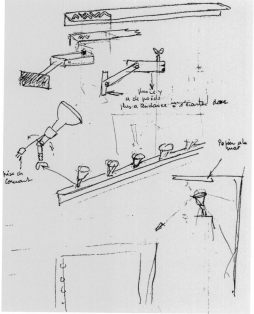

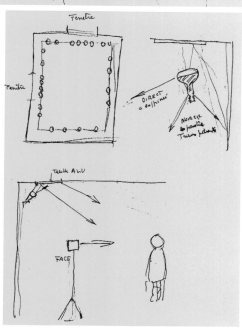

The two principle ingredients of Coutard's *nouvelle vague* cinematography: fluid, spontaneous camerawork, and bounce lighting. *(above, centre & right)* Coutard initially used the Eclair Cameflex, whose compact size, portability, adjustable eye-piece, revolving lens turret and easy-to-fit magazine meant the camera was truly mobile, facilitating the *caméra-stylo* (camera-as-pen) reportage style of many of the movement's directors. *(left)* Camera mobility, directorial impulsiveness, low budgets, (i.e., little time) and low film sensitivity required an ambient lighting style that was simple, flexible and of sufficient intensity. 500-watt bulbs (halogen wasn't yet available) were attached to metal rails perforated to allow the lamps' positioning to be adjusted. The lamps were then aimed at aluminium foil taped to the ceiling. The resulting soft light allowed shots from almost any angle, liberating directors and also actors, who would only need one additional keylight. Altering the number of lamps on the rail enabled Coutard to give an impression of the type of light source – daylight from windows, for example.

also have to try to make everyone understand your needs.

Just because you're the D.P., doesn't mean you have to behave like, "Eh, have you seen the number of stripes on my sleeves? See that, I'm the boss." No. You have to learn humility. In the days when France had guilds, the master craftsman would always wear an overall, which the apprentice would button up every morning. It served as a reminder that you rely on others to do your job. You have to include your own camera and lighting crew in the film-making process, be prepared to give them a certain amount of freedom. If a grip can't do a tracking shot the way a director wants, but has another idea, I accept that and then it's up to me to convince the director. As I almost always operate the camera, I have to be able to delegate because I can't check everything. I've got to feel confident that someone's keeping an eye on the type of film stock that's being loaded, for example. It is essential to keep a convivial atmosphere among one's crew, to avoid any divisions between the grips, electricians, camera assistants and sound technicians. There's nothing worse than someone harbouring a resentment during a shoot. Making a film is a team sport. You're all on the same side, everybody has to play together. In my experience, if there's a great working atmosphere on the set, it'll often make for a good film. **Jules et Jim**, shot in Alsace and the Vosges, was a wonderful film to make. So was **Le Crabe Tambour**, for which we were stuck on a boat for two months with 30 below outside and really rough seas, and then went off to roast ourselves in Djibouti where we lived in very insalubrious digs – but for all that, there was great solidarity. A team sport, then, but making a film is also a little like a love story. You have to fall in love with the project, want to work with the director and the cast and the rest of the team. You're not going to go to bed for two months with someone you don't like, after all.

People talk about the *nouvelle vague*, but it's very difficult to define what that means. Essentially, it referred specifically to the group of new directors who emerged from the editorial offices of 'Cahiers du Cinéma'. At the beginning of several new wave films, 'Cahiers' always made a 'cameo appearance' – a street vendor sells it in **A Bout de Souffle**, a delivery van passes by in **Tirez sur le Pianiste**. Other directors who started their careers at the same time were not considered part of the *nouvelle vague*. But it wasn't really a movement as such, because its directors made such different films.

Take Godard and Truffaut. Jean-Luc was perhaps the only director who consistently took risks, never stopped trying to break new ground. François experimented when he was forced to do so, mainly on his earlier films where there wasn't much money. Jean-Luc never worked from a screenplay – which caused some problems, because you can only obtain the necessary permissions to shoot in France if you have a shooting script. Two months before we'd start, Jean-Luc would hire an assistant and tell him some story he had on his mind. A script would then be written and sent off – but nobody else ever saw this document; it was purely for bureaucratic purposes. François, by contrast, always put a lot of work into his screenplays. And on set with him, everything was very much as it was in the days of the old directors we had once slagged

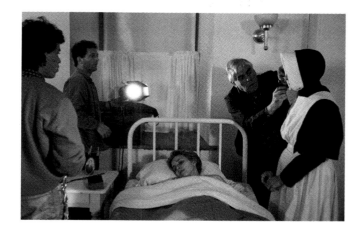

Coutard on set: "You build up an image by listening to what the director is saying to the actors." For Coutard, one of the joys of being a D.P. is the chance to do different kinds of work and constantly be faced with new challenges. *(lower left)* Shooting **Bethune** in 1988, a mini-series starring Donald Sutherland. *(top right)* Shooting a short film for Sabine Eckhard, a former assistant of Coutard – "Sometimes I've agreed to do a film with a friend if my name can help to get it made" – and at sea shooting Michel Piccoli in **La Diagonale du Fou** (1983, Richard Dembo). *(below, right)* Anouk Aimée as the cabaret singer in **Lola** (1960, Jacques Demy), a modern urban fairytale with elaborate tracking shots inspired by Max Ophüls' films.

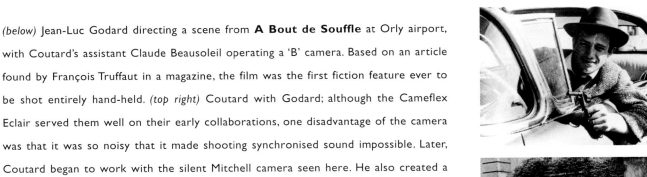

(below) Jean-Luc Godard directing a scene from **A Bout de Souffle** at Orly airport, with Coutard's assistant Claude Beausoleil operating a 'B' camera. Based on an article found by François Truffaut in a magazine, the film was the first fiction feature ever to be shot entirely hand-held. (top right) Coutard with Godard; although the Cameflex Eclair served them well on their early collaborations, one disadvantage of the camera was that it was so noisy that it made shooting synchronised sound impossible. Later, Coutard began to work with the silent Mitchell camera seen here. He also created a customised dolly with three wheels (which became known as the 'Western dolly'), permitting the mobile, spontaneous feeling of his early work to be retained.

Among the 17 films Coutard shot for Godard were: **Week-end** (1967) *(two stills, lower left)*, a savage satire on the age of the automobile (one 10-minute shot tracks through a traffic jam to the carnage of a terrible crash); **Pierrot Le Fou** (1965) *(two centre stills, left)*; **Alphaville** (1965) *(top three stills, left)*, whose eerie futuristic *noir* atmosphere was achieved by shooting on Ilford stock which, pushed in the labs, gave the film its grainy texture; **Une Femme est Une Femme** (1961) *(above)* was shot mainly in a Parisian apartment in colour Cinemascope in hommage to MGM musicals. *(top right)* Coutard shooting with Godard, who was, the D.P. insists, the only true revolutionary of the *nouvelle vague*.

off; François had his director's chair, and took plenty of time over the *mise-en-scène*: whereas Jean-Luc got his intentions over in a flash. On **A Bout de Souffle**, he'd ask the script-girl what kind of shot was required next to fulfil the requirements of traditional continuity. She'd tell him, and then he'd do the exact opposite. He almost always refused to use any lights – there would have to be a very compelling reason if you wanted them. François would frame with the characters in mind; Jean-Luc for the camera movement he wanted. Ultimately, Godard's films aren't films in a conventional sense; they don't tell stories. He was a true revolutionary. François made much more classical films with all the different elements – photography, acting, design, music – serving the story. What sets him apart was that he put so much of himself, his feelings, into the films. Godard once said to me, "I make cinema, not films. François makes films."

The other problem in trying to define the *nouvelle vague* is that so much of what we did in aesthetic terms was determined by lack of money rather than artistic intention. For example, from the start I wanted to make films in colour, in Cinemascope. But at that time, a colour film cost five times more to make than a film in black-and-white. For one thing, colour film was a lot less sensitive than the stock we have today; that meant hiring more lights, more crew. Also, because lab technicians worked with black-and-white film all the time, you were able to make optimum use of all the possibilities that exist in the medium. For instance, on **A Bout de Souffle**, we were able to shoot at night by using high-speed Ilford film (as used in stills cameras; we only had 15 seconds for each shot – that's how long a roll lasted). We then pushed the film in development. The lab also made available a device which enabled us to time the film in the developer ourselves. And they helped us to level out fluctuations in contrast (which might happen if a cloud passed across the sun while we were shooting an exterior scene).

Although I don't have a particular preference for black and white over colour, it's true to say it can be bloody beautiful if it's well done. And what's more it can really make you think about your compositions in a way that colour doesn't. Look at black-and-white newsreel footage from the 1939–45 war: it's amazing – even when shells are pounding down around him, you can tell that the cameraman has invariably got himself into the spot where the light was most interesting, so the images are really vivid. Now compare that with today's colour news cameramen. They don't give a damn, they never go to any effort to find an interesting angle, because you don't need to for an image to read in colour. Whereas with black-and-white, you have to find a good contrast between light and shadow – that's how you give strength and definition to a shot.

The *nouvelle vague* film-makers were also fêted because we shot many of our films entirely on location. At the time, all films – interiors and exteriors – were shot in the studios; but for us the costs were prohibitive. Grotesque greed obliged one to buy or hire all raw materials and equipment (such as timber or lights) from the studio at a 300 per cent mark-up. So we had no choice. We were forced to take to the streets.

Jules et Jim (1961): Jeanne Moreau, Oscar Werner, Henri Serre and Marie Dubois in Truffaut's portrait of a doomed love triangle. Coutard's cinematography, seamlessly integrating newsreel and stills, was attentive to every nuance in the story, effortlessly mirroring the spontaneity of the storytelling. When Moreau impulsively begins a sprint *(top left)*, Coutard picked the camera up and ran with her. "A good film is a whole package of stuff. In **Jules et Jim**, the actors are wonderful, the story is pretty amazing, the photography, well it's not too bad, and the music is absolutely superb, but the audience is so stunned by the film's overall impact that it's impossible to single out one element over another — which is the effect you want." *(above, right)* Truffaut and Coutard filming the boating scene in **Jules et Jim**.

(above, right & lower right) Coutard shot **Tirez sur le Pianiste** for Truffaut in 1960. Based on Dave Goodis' pulp fiction, the film, starring Charles Aznavour, combined a *film noir* feeling in its Paris locations with the energy and reportage style typical of the *nouvelle vague*. Another American pulp novel (by William Irish) was the basis for Truffaut's Hitchcockian **La Mariée Etait en Noir** (1967) *(below, left)*, with Jeanne Moreau. Truffaut (seen with Coutard, *far right*) would always specify to Coutard what he wanted in the frame, whereas Godard would tell him what he didn't want.

And that affected everything – how the actors performed, how the films were shot. (In **A Bout de Souffle**, we were filming Belmondo and Seberg in the Hotel Suède in a room two metres wide; there was just enough room to get the camera in and shoot as best we could.)

Shooting on location also created technical problems, due to the relatively low sensitivity of film stocks, and slower lenses (the widest stop available was f2). Film lighting at the time was also totally geared to studio production, so it was heavy and cumbersome. As well as these technical limitations, there were some additional human problems. A lot of directors wanted to emulate the example of **A Bout de Souffle** (although they ignored the fact that what defined the film was not merely its style, but Godard's genius – which couldn't be copied). They wanted to shoot their scripts in sequence, which meant the lighting had to be constantly changed. Moreover, they would frequently change their minds about what they wanted. The innovation with which my name became associated around this time – bounce lighting – therefore came about not because of any aesthetic principle, but because one had to adapt to these circumstances and the low budgets of the films. If you only have the money for a 2CV, you can't hope for the performance of a Jaguar. I had to devise a lighting approach that was quick, flexible, time- and cost-effective. I worked with lights used by amateur photographers, directed at the ceiling, which I partly covered with aluminium foil. The resulting 360 degree bounce lighting was of sufficient intensity for the film's sensitivity, and yet provided an overall soft light that could be adjusted to provide a sense of source – from windows, for example. It gave great freedom to the director for camera movement, and also alllowed the actors to be more spontaneous.

I find it a bit dodgy when you meet a director who doesn't give a damn about how the audience responds to the film; after all, it's an expensive medium. We all bitch about producers, but backing a film is a huge investment; the least a producer should expect is to make back his money, plus a little bit more. Otherwise he could put the money into a savings account and come back a day later for his two per cent without going to all the bloody trouble. All my *nouvelle vague* colleagues get terribly offended when I say to them that I think that cinema is for the audience. Sure, it's interesting to make intellectual films; but it's also great to sell plenty of tickets. I'd have loved to photograph a big American musical. A film should be made to be seen.

biography

A key figure in modern American cinema, Haskell Wexler's cinematography is continually nourished by his work as a documentary director, which includes films such as **Brazil – A Report on Torture** (1971), **Introduction to the Enemy** (made in 1974 with Jane Fonda to counter government propaganda during the Vietnam War), **Target Nicaragua: Inside a Secret War** (1983) and **The**

haskell wexler

Sixth Sun: Mayan Uprising in the Chiapas (1996), and his two Oscar-winning films, **The Living City** (1953) and **Interviews with My Lai Veterans** (1970). His documentary approach inspired the style and content of the two features he directed – **Medium Cool** (1969) and **Latino** (1985) – and many of the films he's shot as D.P. Citing Raoul Coutard's hand-held camera and use of bounce lighting as an influence, Wexler has won two Oscars, for **Who's Afraid of Virginia Woolf?** (1966, Mike Nichols) and **Bound For Glory** (1976, Hal Ashby) – the biopic of a former fellow merchant sailor from the war, Woody Guthrie. He has collaborated with some of America's leading post-war film-makers, including Elia Kazan (**America, America**, 1963), Norman Jewison (**The Thomas Crown Affair**, 1968), George Lucas (**American Graffiti**, 1973), Milos Forman (**One Flew Over the Cuckoo's Nest**, 1975), Terrence Mallick (additional photography for **Days of Heaven**, 1978) and John Sayles (**Matewan**, 1986 and **The Secret of Roan Inish**, 1993).

interview

Before I started shooting features, I had the opportunity to work for the legendary cinematographer (and former prize fighter), James Wong Howe. He'd taken me under his wing (we were both designated 'premature anti-Fascists' by the U.S. government in the '50s), and I shot second unit material for him on the 1956 picture, **Picnic**. I was assigned to the last scene of the film, which was to be a rare aerial shot. In those days, that meant standing out on the strut of a military helicopter, a rope around the waist, trying to control a camera in the gusting wind. The shot opened on Kim Novak in a house; pulling back to see a railroad train and then Bill Holden on board. As the train travelled away, the camera climbed up and up into the sky and the end credits rolled. It was as much as I could do to hang on for dear life while trying to steer the Cinemascope camera, so I didn't know what the hell the shot was going to look like. Next day I went into the theatre to see rushes with Jimmy Howe (who could be a mean S.O.B.) sitting next to me, and when my shot came up, he

cinematography

(above, left) **America, America**, Kazan's 1963 immigrant saga, was Wexler's first film as D.P.: "Never seeing the dailies made me brave, not conservative. I thrive on adventure, on danger." *(right)* **Who's Afraid of Virginia Woolf?** (1966): "An intense set; the picture was considered risqué, dangerous. There were pressures from the stars. Richard Burton didn't want to look pock-marked; Elizabeth Taylor didn't want to look dumpy. Mike Nichols had never directed film. He knew nothing; I knew two steps above nothing. I had ideas about the look, but my crew's experience was invaluable. All my lights were on dimmers; I had a terrific guy operating them, enabling us to adjust light levels as the actors moved across set."

nodded his head and said, "Aah, very good, very good." It was the best day of my life. Ever since then, whenever I've done a shot I'm happy with, I hear his Chinese-accented voice in my head, saying those words.

After serving as a merchant sailor in the Second World War, I was supposed to go into one of my father's businesses in Chicago, but instead I managed to piss away an entire trust fund in various marvellous ways. Dad said to me, "You know you shoulda been a chemist." "What do you mean?" I asked. "Well," he replied, "you're the only person I know who can take good money and turn it into shit." I told him I wanted to make movies. (In childhood, I travelled a lot with my parents, always feeling an outsider when we moved somewhere new. I shot home movies on my father's 16mm Bell & Howell, which made me feel simultaneously involved and yet distanced from my experience, like a voyeur.) Hoping this was the answer to the question of what I was going to do with my life, my long-suffering father agreed to finance the rental of studio space, purchase of a new camera and some lights, and the employment of a cute secretary. I was ready to go into business.

Of course nobody was ready to go into business with me. Finally, Dad found me a client – a friend who owned the Opalika Textile Mills in Alabama and wanted a film to celebrate its 50th anniversary. So off I went to Opalika, where I hung out with all the employees of the mill, and began to make a documentary about their lives – every aspect of which was totally controlled by the company they worked for, living in this town that had grown out of the business. Then I went to

the mill itself and shot some footage showing how the raw cotton was transformed into cloth, before editing and delivering the film to my dad's friend. "What is this crap?" he shouted, "kids in school, guys playing dominoes, the company store... I have 50 carding machines and they cost $4,800 apiece and I want to SEE those machines, not all this other human-interest crap." And so I got my first big dose of commercialism and the bottom line.

By the time I'd re-shot and re-cut the film, I realised I didn't know a goddam thing about film-making, so I went to work as an assistant cameraman on newsreels and the occasional feature film shot in the Chicago area, while continuing to shoot documentaries on my own for civil rights organisations and unions, which I guess made me look like an anti-establishment figure in the pernicious era of McCarthy. I was, however, employed by Encyclopaedia Britannica to shoot educational films, one of which, **The Living City** won the Academy Award for Best Documentary, and led to an offer to travel to England to make a series of Shakespeare films. But at this point my passport was confiscated, and I was informed that the only way I could get it back would be to name my friends, who attended such and such meeting at the Farm Co-op or the Joint Anti-Fascist Refugee Committee or Russian War Relief – organisations deemed subversive by the Attorney General. Of course I wasn't about to name names, so the U.K. and Shakespeare was out. But I didn't need a passport to get to the West Coast, where I cut a deal with Roger Corman to make a low-budget feature which we subsequently sold to Warner Bros. and which brought me to

One Flew Over the Cuckoo's Nest (1975): "I used fluorescents to give the lighting an institutional flavour. This was before the advent of Kinoflos (designed for film, with a precise colour temperature); I had to run a lot of tests to find a commercial brand which wouldn't photograph green as fluorescents normally did." Soft lighting with overhead fluorescents freed up space on the set, enabling multi-camera shooting in the therapy sessions. This gave actors more freedom to interact and overlap dialogue.

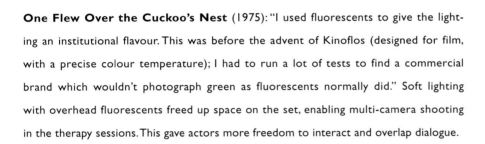

the attention of Elia Kazan as he was preparing to shoot **America, America**.

It took courage for him to hire me – not only was I inexperienced, but he knew I was hostile to his political views (he was a stool pigeon of the first order and had ruined the lives of some friends of mine). However, I liked what the film had to say about America as a place of refuge for immigrants who wanted a better life. It also features what I believe to be some of my best photography. I guess you could say I didn't know what I didn't know. I had no one and nothing to answer to except my imagination, and my sense of freedom was increased by not seeing any rushes while we were shooting. I had learned to be daring from the example of Jimmy Howe (who would often shoot a scene with just one light – rare in the days of catwalks and multiple light sources), and from my documentary work.

When you shoot a documentary, you're in a position where you're constantly struggling to get a good shot of the important thing and put it in the right part of the frame – but you never can get it exactly perfect. And that makes for a compelling sense of reality, which I've translated into the way I shoot drama. I deliberately withhold information so that the audience has to work to get the whole picture. I'll put things in the foreground of the shot that partly obscure the action, for example. The idea is to involve an audience – to lead them to discover things in the frame, get them to notice without feeling that they are being told to look at this, look at that. Then they will feel as if they have participated in the realisation of

the importance of something, like participants in the drama. Documentary aesthetics also affect the way I light. In documentary, you're mostly working with the light you find. Because you have to work fast, you have limited opportunity to control the exposure. So although you might make the right stop for part of someone's face, bright sunlight might mean that other parts of their face or body will be overexposed. Again this can be applied to give cinematography in feature films a more heightened sense of reality: on **Coming Home**, for example, I used arc-lights to simulate sunlight slashing through the windows, and if I was shooting someone against a window, I'd let them go partly overexposed.

My documentary work has also helped me to avoid cliché and be open to the unexpected. I once shot a film about an emergency ward in New York, and a kid who had been knocked off his bike was brought in, accompanied by his mother. Now had this been a regular dramatic film, the mom would be distraught, crying, "Oh, my son, is he going to live?" But in reality, this particular mother was walking around the kid lying on the gurney, yelling at him: "How many times have I told you not to ride that bicycle in the street? I've told you a hundred times..." Seeing things like this helps you learn from reality (unfortunately, most people's frame of reference in this business is another film).

When we were preparing to shoot the heist sequence in **The Thomas Crown Affair**, I wanted to avoid the phoney background action found in Hollywood movies. I said to director Norman Jewison, "Let's shoot the robbery for real with hidden

cinematography

Following Raoul Coutard's example, Wexler was one of the first American D.P.s to work with bounced light. Apart from bouncing off silks stretched over the top of sets, Wexler pioneered the use in films of still photographers' umbrella lights. This caused much mirth among his crew, but the superbolic umbrella shape meant soft light could be obtained from a small unit. **In The Heat Of The Night** (1967, *above right*) used these techniques to create a desaturated colour look. **The Thomas Crown Affair** (1968, *above*) required something different – vivid full colour to evoke the hip '60s atmosphere. **American Graffiti** (1973, *below right*): credited as visual consultant, Wexler helped George Lucas achieve a 'guerilla film-making' style in a wide-screen format, using French Cameflex cameras (*see* Raoul Coutard's chapter).

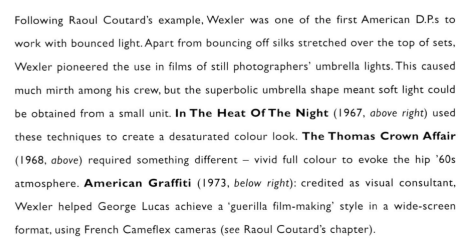

cameras." He liked the idea, so I had one camera across the street, another in a van, a third shooting from above, as our characters performed the robbery. And real people were walking past the bank as this apparently real heist took place – and they just kept walking, pretending not to notice what was going on, not wanting to get involved. Finally someone actually did call the cops, whereupon Norman shouted "cut". I also used multiple cameras in **One Flew Over the Cuckoo's Nest** for the group therapy sessions, where having several cameras likewise created the feeling of a live event and allowed the actors to overlap and interact.

It's important to differentiate between documentary and drama. I came in to shoot about 50 minutes' worth of material for **Days of Heaven** after D.P. Nestor Almendros had to leave to start on another picture. Nestor was telling me how he wanted to use natural light. And yes, it looked natural – but in reality there was an arc-light out the window, four inky-dink lights, eye-lights, and so on. (Once, when asked by a director to shoot something using only available light, D.P. Owen Roizman replied, "Sure, I'll use whatever's available on the truck...") And even if you are going for an 'unlit' look, there are always certain expectations the D.P. has to satisfy. Photographing Paul Newman on **Blaze**, there were a couple of times when I didn't make his baby-blue eyes 'pop' and a producer said, "guess you missed the eye-light in that scene..." I explained that I didn't want it on that scene, and the reply was, "well, Paul's gotta look good..."

Making movies is an unnatural act. It is an entirely inter-pretative, artificial medium. We are making theatre, we are making drama. It's never just a question of filming whatever happens in front of the camera. There's a wrong-headed assumption that the *laissez-faire* style of cinema is somehow more creative, but in my book that's an excuse for laziness. There are directors today who will allow the actors to wander wherever they feel like – which is to ignore the fact that where an actor is in the frame is an important tool in the craft of cinematic story-telling. Henry Fonda, with whom I worked on **The Best Man**, was a consummate screen actor who respected the cinematographer's work and knew that it was important for his performance and the film that he stuck to the moves planned in rehearsal. Good film-making means control. Making a 'cuttable' feature film involves a body of specific knowledge and professionalism.

I'm not as smart as Vittorio Storaro, who works on an intellectual level with the psychological meanings of colours. My own approach to a film's look often comes out of the collaborative process and the practical decisions that you make when you prepare to shoot. On a recent location scout, I visited a number of schools with the movie's director, designer and costumier. As we articulated our thoughts about which might be best for the film ("well, I liked that one, the dark wood seems to fit with the religious nature of the school in the script"), so we were beginning to express what feeling we wanted the film to have. If we're shooting in the studio, the designer may ask me if I want to have ceilings on the sets. This makes me think about whether I may want to shoot from low angles, in which case I'll ask for a roll ceiling. Or I'll think about how much distance I'll need to set the lights from a window, because depending on how far or close they are, you'll either get the same exposure throughout the interior, or a difference of up to five stops across the set. These decisions influence the look of a film more than any other form of preparation.

I'm also dependent on the collaborative aspect of film-making. The pastel quality of the cinematography on **Bound For Glory** was not only achieved solely by what I achieved in flashing the negative; production designer Mike Haller was also involved, studiously avoiding strong, saturated colours in the film's design. If there was a bright red billboard in shot, a stand-by painter would go to work on it without my having to say anything. Mike also helped me achieve the film's dusty look with bags of Fuller's Earth, tumbleweed and garbage which we blew into shot with fans.

Bound For Glory illustrates another point about my profession. When I first considered flashing the film, I talked to Vilmos Zsigmond, who had done extensive testing with the technique on Robert Altman's **McCabe and Mrs Miller**. His generosity in helping me is typical of the camaraderie that exists between cinematographers. When one of us finds something that works, we're always prepared to share it – rare in a business which is characterised by a dog-eat-dog mentality.

For the most part, this is a sad time for film-making. There are few directors in America who have enough power to make films with integrity. Shooting a bar scene recently, I noticed a huge Coca-Cola sign in the background. "Get it out", I said, "it doesn't belong in the shot." The producer came up to me, saying, "that sign has contributed $200,000 to our budget." Commercial considerations have always loomed large in the industry, but now more than ever money is the bottom line. Most people don't care what a movie is about so much as whether they can get it out by December 14th to get the Christmas market. Directors are driven to direct a scene by fear of the people upstairs rather than any ideals of good film-making. Focus groups dictate what we see. After I'd shot **Rich Man's Wife**, the test screening concluded that the bad guy at the end didn't die badly enough. As it was, Halle Berry shot the guy, bang, he died. When we redid the scene, she shot him, kicked him in the nuts, struck him with a hatchet so he fell back, shattering a car windscreen before hitting the ground, where she stabbed him with her highheel... As a cinematographer, you're only considered to be good if your last picture made money. Nevertheless, I'd still say to anyone trying to break into the business: don't just be interested in movies. Be interested in life. Be a person. Be in touch. Want to do something with your art besides getting a job.

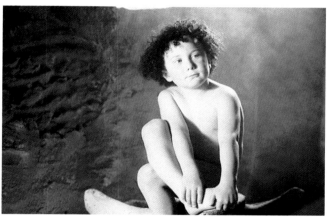

Apart from its striking desaturated look, the cinematography of **Bound For Glory** (1976, *right*) used Steadicam for the first time on a feature film to pull the audience into the heart of big crowd scenes. **Matewan** (1986, *top right*) had no budget for 'toys' like Steadicam. For tracking shots, Wexler customised the dolly to run on abandoned rail track. In the mining scenes, glitter was sprinkled on the walls and reflective aluminium cards bounced light from flame lamps on the miners' hats. Wexler worked again with director John Sayles ("an honest, terrific film-maker") on **The Secret of Roan Inish** (1993, *above*), where he capitalised on the extended 'magic hour' light available in Ireland to enhance the mythical story. *(far left)* Wexler on board the helicopter for the aerial shot in **Picnic** (1955) described at the beginning of the chapter.

biography

In Godard's **A Bout de Souffle**, Belmondo's anti-hero uses the alias 'Laszlo Kovacs'. His namesake laughs this off: "In Hungary, my name is like John Smith!" But as coincidences go, this one was prophetic, for Kovacs was one of a group of new wave-inspired film-makers in '60s California who would bring a new sensibility to American cinema as the golden era of the Hollywood studios faded. After shooting the landmark

laszlo kovacs

interview

Easy Rider (1969, Dennis Hopper) Kovacs went on to work with other modern mavericks; Robert Altman (**That Cold Day in the Park**, 1969); Bob Rafelson (**Five Easy Pieces**, 1970, and **The King of Marvin Gardens**, 1972); Hal Ashby (**Shampoo**, 1975); Martin Scorsese (**New York, New York**, 1977); as well as forming a partnership with Peter Bogdanovich (**Targets**, 1968; **What's Up Doc?**, 1972; **Paper Moon**, 1973; **At Long Last Love**, 1975; **Nickelodeon**, 1976 and **Mask**, 1985). Mainstream Hollywood credits include **Ghostbusters**, (1984, Ivan Reitman), **Shattered** (1991, Wolfgang Peterson), **Copycat** (1996, Jon Amiel) and **My Best Friend's Wedding** (1997, P. J. Hogan). Kovacs also teaches: "Now it's time for me to pass on all my experience and knowledge to a new generation. This is wonderful – as long as my students realise that if we're ever in competition for the same job, I'm gonna put up a helluva fight!"

Just outside the peasant village where I grew up in Hungary, there was a railroad track which had an incredible effect on me as a boy. I'd watch trains pass through and disappear off into the horizon, and I'd wonder, what's at the end of these rails? In the village itself, my mother's best friend ran film shows on the weekends. The cinema was a schoolroom, the screen a white sheet pinned on the wall, and the projection booth was a couple of chairs placed side-to-side, on which the 16mm projector was mounted. My first job was to distribute leaflets advertising the next programme through the village and hammer them on telephone poles. My salary was that I got to see the films for nothing. I'd sit in the front row, staring in awe at the images flickering on that sheet, which to me was like a window through which I could glimpse magical worlds that existed at the end of the railroad.

My parents wanted me to take after my first cousin and become a doctor, but as I got older my obsession with films grew. In Budapest, where I was at boarding school, I learned by heart the programmes of each cinema in the city, and I'd skip classes, sometimes seeing four movies a day. One day I discovered to my astonishment and delight that there was a film school in Budapest. The following January I applied, and somehow was selected. Illes Gyorgy, head of the school, then became my spiritual father, as he continues to be for Hungarian cinematographers all over the world. His credo was that he couldn't teach you talent – but if you had talent, he could help you to discover it.

Practical film-making was only one part of the course. Because film was regarded as a blend of many different arts, we had to study architecture, the history of art, world literature, music, theatre. The idea was that students should open their minds and build up a rich mental library which would serve us in our careers. I continue to supplement this library today; it contains all the visual memories of my life up to now – events I've witnessed, emotions I've felt. In particular, it contains all the feelings that different kinds of light provoke in me. Having this library means that whatever project I work on – whether it's comedy or drama, period or contemporary (as cinematographers, we should be able to do all kinds of stories) – I can always find a reference, a memory, a feeling from which to work.

My story is also the story of a friendship. At film school, I met Vilmos Zsigmond. He was in the year above me and I worked as an assistant on his diploma film. So I knew him a little when our respective fates suddenly got thrown together one autumn day in 1956 as the Hungarian revolution broke out. Standing outside the school building together, we watched the Russian tanks roll through the streets, firing indiscriminately. We looked at each other. Vilmos said, "Let's go to the camera department..." We picked up an old Arriflex camera with a three-lens turret, attached a battery, loaded two 400-feet magazines of film – and put everything in a shopping bag, so we wouldn't stand out in the streets where everyone had packed their belongings into shopping bags. We walked all over the city, pulling out the camera to shoot whenever we heard gunfire. It was an intense, exciting experience – but also terribly emotional; the freedom of our country was at stake. By November, when the Russians finally crushed the uprising, we had a complete record of everything that had happened. The secret police had begun to investigate the film school, trying to identify anyone who had been involved with the uprising. Vilmos and I decided to smuggle our precious rushes – and ourselves – out of Hungary. We hid the film, some 30,000 feet, in three big potato sacks, and then we headed for the Austrian border.

Images from my 'library': hundreds of people hanging out of trains, on the roofs of the carriages (like you see in India). Near the border: dark, misty, an endless, frozen landscape dotted with little black figures – of men, women, children – all heading in the same direction... Interned in a prison camp: Vilmos giving me the watch his father had given him for his graduation from film school – in case I needed to bribe my way out... Escaping from Hungary: the single faint light bulb in a church whose cemetery was right on the border... There is

(left) The Hungarian Uprising: "Vilmos Zsigmond and I walked all over Budapest and started shooting the scenes we came across. It was crazy. People were being killed. The city was being reduced to ruins. We shot for four or five days before the Russians finally crushed the revolution." *(right)* Kovacs shooting 'motorbike movies' in 1960s' California, and *(lower right)*, with Boris Karloff on the set of **Targets** (1968).

"Before shooting **Easy Rider** (1969), I hadn't travelled much in America. So the film became like a journey of discovery for me. We went to places I never dreamed existed. I wanted to find a way to make Hopper and Fonda's characters a part of these magical landscapes, and I discovered that if I had them in shot at a certain angle, back-lit by the sun, rainbow-coloured rays of light would appear in the lens, and I was able to direct the rays so they were just overlapping the two characters. After the film's release, I was accused by some big name D.P.s of being an amateur, because I couldn't keep the lens 'clean'. But it was a deliberate effect."

Kovacs choreographed the bikes from the roof of the camera car: "I would yell and gesture to Fonda and Hopper so that the bikes would alternately move forward or drop back. I wanted it to look like a ballet on the highway." *(above)* 'Story conference' between Kovacs and Hopper. **Easy Rider**'s success ushered in a new era of film-making on location rather than in studios, and brought a new spontaneity and naturalism to American cinema.

no colour in these memories; everything, even the grass, seems to be black or grey.

Once in Austria, we tried to peddle the film, convinced of its significance. But by now, the revolution was old news. We grew disillusioned; eventually, however, we managed to sell the footage to a Hungarian producer from Munich who we met in Salzburg. We got enough money to cover the lab costs and the price of our room in the fleabag hotel where we were staying; but he also threw in a second-hand Arriflex camera, which we hoped would soon be useful. Exiled from our country, there was only one place for us to go...

In the Hollywood of the 1960s, everyone started on the same level: ground zero. Didn't matter if you were a graduate from N.Y.U. or a refugee from Hungary. It was the end of the big studio era; fly-by-night independent producers were everywhere, eagerly supplying the drive-in cinemas' demand for cheap 'product'. A new generation of film-makers (including Coppola, Scorsese, Sayles and Bogdanovich) cut their teeth on exploitation films; and alongside them, a new generation of cinematographers. After shooting newsreel and medical films on 16mm (where Vilmos and I were often each other's only crew), we became part of the gang working for Roger Corman. His 'factory' was both sweatshop and film school. Corman exploited us, sure, but – and he knew this as well as any of us – we were getting the greater benefit. We usually had around eight days to complete a 70–90 minute picture. And although they were mostly formulaic schlock, the more talented directors and writers always tried to sneak something interesting into the story, or experiment visually. There was something of the pioneer spirit about that time in our lives. We were all in film-making heaven. We worked around the clock, grabbing a few hours' sleep in a sleeping bag on the set or the location.

In time, I developed a reputation for photographing biker movies; at the point when I was crying out, "no more!", I got approached by Dennis Hopper to shoot **Easy Rider**. He entered our meeting dressed like Billy the Kid, said, "here's the script", and wildly threw it up in the air. As the pages floated down all over the office, he said, "but we don't need it, because I'm gonna tell you the story..." By the time he'd finished, I'd forgotten my objections to doing another biker picture. "When do we start?" I asked.

I'm a very emotional person, and my job is about using light to manipulate emotion; so when I read a screenplay for the first time, I always try to see what images it provokes in me, and what feelings lie behind them. I'm very intuitive, and I will often rely on these first impressions. I do a lot of silent preparation before I start a film; I don't write notes or sketch; I just immerse myself in the script so that I feel like I'm living it. Of course, planning is vital; you have to anticipate all the technical problems that might arise, all the disasters waiting to happen. I love going on recces; because apart from seeing locations for the first time and assessing their photographic viability, the actual experience of everyone being cooped up in a van together – director, production designer, myself, the gaffer and grip – is invaluable. On **Easy Rider**, our recce

Paper Moon (1973): "The script was a gem, and it was an incredible opportunity to shoot a movie in black and white. To make the skies look dramatic, I used red filters (at Orson Welles' suggestion). However, that meant losing three stops on my exposure. Peter Bogdanovich wanted to have a real deep focus feeling, so I had to use big arc-lights placed three feet from the actors in the foreground in order to achieve a stop where everything would be in focus. For Tatum O' Neal, who was only eight, and her father Ryan, it was like being exposed to the burning intensity of the sun. But that kind of hard light is what the great Hollywood D.P.s used to achieve those classic close-ups."

89

laszlo kovacs

"For me, each film, each director has a unique chemistry and emotional magic. Once I am involved with a new project, I live it." *(left)* **New York, New York** (1977, Martin Scorsese); *(above, centre)* **Shampoo** (1975, Hal Ashby); *(above, right)* **Five Easy Pieces** (1970, Bob Rafelson).

90

cinematography

traced the route of the films' characters from Los Angeles to New Orleans. For me it was a revelation; it was the first time I'd really travelled in America, and I began to get a sense of this incredible, vast country with such amazing visual contrasts. There was a constant dialogue between all of us on the trip; and even if the discussion didn't appear to be specifically about the film, somehow the undercurrent of what was said always seemed to be related. By the end of the trip, I had a very clear idea of what I wanted to go for, what I wanted to emphasise in the cinematography.

Film is a director's medium, not a cinematographer's. I see what I do as helping the director to achieve his vision, his dream, his ideas. Each relationship with a director has its own unique chemistry, and I must try to understand what is in his mind and his heart so that I can tailor my photography to his ideas. If he says "red", I have to be sure exactly what kind of red he is talking about. Similarly, every film has its own identity, and the cinematographer must be able to create visual images that serve each particular story. Like actors, we can get typecast, which is very frustrating. After **Easy Rider** became successful, I was put up for a film which was mostly interiors. My agent had to persuade the producers that just because I had shot a location picture, didn't mean I couldn't light! So then I did a string of films that were mostly interiors; and when the possibility of shooting a western came along – "Kovacs does interior pictures; can he do this?"

One of the movies of which I'm most proud is Peter Bogdanovich's **Paper Moon**. We wanted to evoke the classic

black-and-white Hollywood tradition pioneered by cinematographers like Arthur Miller, John Alton and Gregg Toland. **Citizen Kane** was our biggest influence; I had seen it for the first time in Budapest in 1948 and it had made an indelible impression. Orson Welles and Peter were very close friends, and I got to meet my 'god' while we were preparing our film. I'd been testing black-and-white film with various filters but still hadn't found the right look; Orson said, "Use red filters, my boy". And I did, because although the filters reduced the film speed and meant I had to use big arc-lights to achieve the deep-focus look Peter wanted, the red filters created incredibly beautiful, dramatic skies and gave us exactly the expressionistic look we were after.

However much preparation you do, a film never truly comes alive until you show up on the first morning of the shoot, and all the elements combine for the very first time. As far as it's possible, you have to keep an open mind about how you're going to shoot something until you begin to see what the actors are doing. That's why I've never done floor plans, because a scene may not happen the way you anticipate. I always aim to support the actors' performances, down to the smallest detail. For example, if I notice an actor wearing a cap, I'll ask why. It may well be because he's trying to prevent another character seeing into his eyes; in which case I'll design the lighting so that if there comes a moment in the scene where he feels he does want to catch the other person's eye, all he has to do is incline his head slightly. This is why I only feel ready to light a scene appropriately after watching the rehearsal.

cinematography

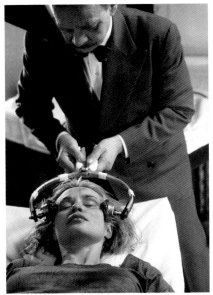

(top left) **Copycat** (1995, Jon Amiel). *(left, above)* **My Best Friend's Wedding** (1997, P. J. Hogan): "For me, the challenge was trying to do a comedy in a wide-screen format." *(centre, above)* **Heartbeat** (1980, John Byrum): "We were very influenced by Edward Hopper in our approach to the framing – but not so an audience would say, 'Oh, they're doing a Hopper number here'. We emulated the way he stylised and simplified his compositions, and depicted frames within frames; we used people looking out of windows, slashes of light falling on the foreground or on a wall." *(right)* **Frances** (1982, Graeme Clifford): Jessica Lange as doomed 1930s Hollywood star Frances Farmer; Kovacs is seen preparing a Steadicam shot for a scene in the mental asylum. *(far right)* Shooting **Targets** in 1968 *(above)* and **Copycat** in 1998 *(below)*: "In one person's career, there's no formula, no recipe, especially as between the '60s when I started, and the '90s, the industry has totally changed."

When I'm lighting, I like to feel that every light has a dramatic logic and function in the composition. It really is like painting; each piece of light is a brush-stroke, giving different emotional values, defining and texturing each part of the shot from foreground to background, highlighting what's important for the audience to see. This is the aesthetic heart of my work and it gives me the most joy and pleasure. But it can also be the point of most responsibility and pressure, because the tempo of the shoot, and the morale of the unit, depends on how quickly you work. The cinematographer has to be a strong leader. I have my own repertory company of lighting and camera crew who I've worked with over decades, which gives us a kind of mutual respect and trust. We have a shorthand after all this time and that enables us to work together like a well-oiled machine.

The moment when the camera rolls is always intensely exciting. Not only are you capturing the electricity, the drama between the actors as it happens, but it's also the moment where you crystallise everyone's efforts over weeks, months, years – the screenwriter, the director, the designer, wardrobe, hair, make-up – in the final composition. This is what makes my job so exciting that I forget whether I'm hungry, or sleepy – I just stand there and think how lucky I am to be a humble soldier of this wonderful art of film-making.

biography

The son of a cameraman whose career dated back to the beginnings of film production in England, Billy Williams naturally gravitated to a career in cinematography. Aged 24, he photographed his first short film, before working in documentaries and commercials. He shot some low-budget feature films, including Tony Richardson's **Red and Blue**, but his big break as a cinematographer came when Ken Russell (for

billy williams

whom Williams had shot commercials) asked him to photograph **Billion Dollar Brain** (1967), an experience which Williams described as "diving in at the deep end". However, the rich visual tapestry which he wove for the film, and then for Russell's **Women In Love** (for which he was Oscar-nominated in 1969), established Williams as one of the pre-eminent cinematographers of his generation. His subsequent work – some 40 features – included the atmospheric intimacy of films such as **Sunday, Bloody Sunday** (1971, John Schlesinger) and **On Golden Pond** (1981, Mark Rydell, which brought Williams his second Academy Award nomination) to expansive epics such as **The Wind and The Lion** (1975, John Milius), **Eagle's Wing** (1979, Anthony Harvey – a western for which Williams won the British Society of Cinematographers' Award) and **Gandhi** (1982, Richard Attenborough), for which Williams won an Oscar. He has taught in workshops and masterclasses in the U.K. and U.S.A., and in Munich, Berlin and Budapest.

interview

Since 1979, I have been conducting student workshops at the National Film and Television School near London. In my role as cinematographer, I have, as a result, looked at the nature of my craft. The Greek word *kine* means movement. I am therefore a photographer of movement.

My father Billie was a cinematographer. He started in 1910, in the days when the studios had glass walls. A cameraman in the Navy during the First World War, he then travelled across Africa, photographing expeditions. By the '30s, he was working in features. In those days, there were no film schools; you learned on the job – and so very often you'd find father/son relationships in the camera department. When I left school at the tender age of 14, it was completely natural for me to serve my apprenticeship with him as an assistant. After completing national service, I began to photograph documentaries, and with basic lighting skills, I got the feel for making the best of a location with limited resources.

cinematography

(above & left) **Women In Love** (1969): "Probably my best work – there was so much opportunity in the subject matter: day/night interiors and exteriors; day for night; the firelit wrestling set-piece; an extensive magic hour sequence (shot over three evenings); scenes lit by oil-lamp; and the climactic sequence shot in the snow in Switzerland. The film has tremendous range in terms of light, which I really tried to explore and exploit. I worked with filters and later in grading to ensure that the colours really evoked the time of day in the story – the deep blue of the sky after the sun has gone down, for example, or the golden quality of candlelight or firelight."

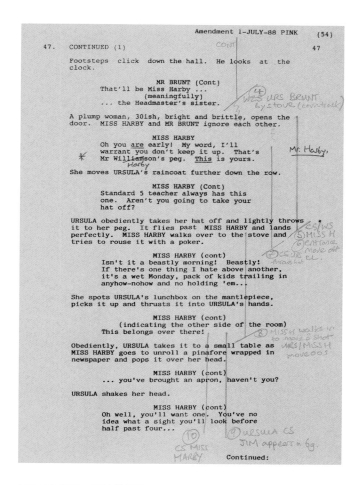

47.   CONTINUED (1)   47

Footsteps click down the hall. He looks at the
clock.

MR BRUNT (Cont)
That'll be Miss Harby ...
(meaningfully)
... the Headmaster's sister.

A plump woman, 30ish, bright and brittle, opens the
door. MISS HARBY and MR BRUNT ignore each other.

MISS HARBY
Oh you are early! My word, I'll
warrant you don't keep it up. That's
Mr Williamson's peg. This is yours.
She moves URSULA's raincoat further down the row.

MISS HARBY (Cont)
Standard 5 teacher always has this
one. Aren't you going to take your
hat off?

URSULA obediently takes her hat off and lightly throws
it to her peg. It flies past MISS HARBY and lands
perfectly. MISS HARBY walks over to the stove and
tries to rouse it with a poker.

MISS HARBY (cont)
Isn't it a beastly morning! Beastly!
If there's one thing I hate above another,
it's a wet Monday, pack of kids trailing in
anyhow-nohow and no holding 'em...

She spots URSULA's lunchbox on the mantlepiece,
picks it up and thrusts it into URSULA's hands.

MISS HARBY (cont)
(indicating the other side of the room)
This belongs over there!

Obediently, URSULA takes it to a small table as
MISS HARBY goes to unroll a pinafore wrapped in
newspaper and pops it over her head.

MISS HARBY (cont)
... you've brought an apron, haven't you?

URSULA shakes her head.

MISS HARBY (cont)
Oh well, you'll want one. You've no
idea what a sight you'll look before
half past four...

Continued:

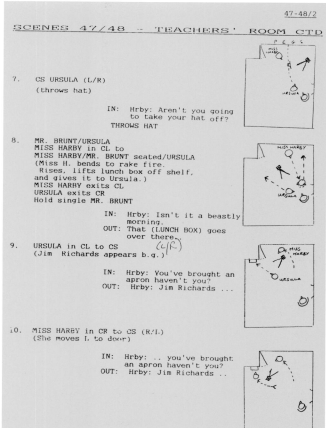

47-48/2

SCENES 47/48 - TEACHERS' ROOM CTD

7.   CS URSULA (L/R)
(throws hat)

IN: Hrby: Aren't you going
to take your hat off?
THROWS HAT

8.   MR. BRUNT/URSULA
MISS HARBY in CL to
MISS HARBY/MR. BRUNT seated/URSULA
(Miss H. bends to rake fire.
Rises, lifts lunch box off shelf,
and gives it to Ursula.)
MISS HARBY exits CL
URSULA exits CR
Hold single MR. BRUNT

IN: Hrby: Isn't it a beastly
morning.
OUT: That (LUNCH BOX) goes
over there.

9.   URSULA in CL to CS
(Jim Richards appears b.g.)

IN: Hrby: You've brought an
apron haven't you?
OUT: Hrby: Jim Richards ...

10. MISS HARBY in CR to CS (R/L)
(She moves L to door)

IN: Hrby: .. you've brought
an apron haven't you?
OUT: Hrby: Jim Richards ..

Twenty years after **Women In Love**, Williams was reunited with director Ken Russell to shoot the 'prequel' to Lawrence's novel. However, the film was made on a tighter schedule and budget which necessitated creative compromises and **The Rainbow** (above) fell far short of its predecessor's accomplishments. Williams emphasises the importance of coverage – knowing exactly how many shots will be required to cover a scene; critical when shooting a low-budget film. (above, left) The script page shows how an interior school scene was covered, with descriptions of each of the shots based on technical rehearsals (lower left).

These beginnings gave me a sense of discipline. As cinematographers, we have to know our technique, to develop a thorough understanding of all the elements and the chemistry of photography. We need to know what different lenses and filters can do, and to know our emulsions and our lights. Just like a painter with different colours and brushes, we have to know how to mix the various elements. Today, such knowledge is even more essential as the palette available to the cinematographer becomes increasingly sophisticated. Lenses are sharper and faster (great for action or science fiction, but sometimes too hard-edged for more romantic subjects; it's necessary to know how to use nets and diffusion to soften the image). And whereas the cinematographer in the '70s had only one type of film stock (100ASA); today you've got a much greater diversity in terms of speed, contrast and grain characteristic. This choice also means you can use different film stocks for different sequences in a film – useful if you want to create a visual contrast between different narrative or stylistic elements. In addition, digital film effects in post-production offer enormous opportunities to alter the look of the original material. Cinematographers need to stay closely involved at this crucial stage.

In the 1950s, feature films were regarded as the premier league; my lower-division background in documentaries was not highly esteemed. So I went into commercials, which were really just starting up, and which enabled me to work in studios with more sophisticated equipment. Many cinematographers past and present have found themselves taking this route, and there's a lot to be said for it. Again, it gives one the opportunity to learn one's tools, to play around and experiment and take chances to gain a particular effect. You can't afford to do this on a feature film because if it doesn't work out, you could find yourself on the next plane home. Commercials have also been influential in other respects; because of them, audiences have become increasingly receptive to startling imagery in feature films. But for me at that time, the big advantage of working in the fledgling commercials industry was meeting directors such as Ken Russell, John Schlesinger and Ted Kotcheff, all of whom I would later work with on feature films.

On becoming more experienced, I came to appreciate that there was a lot more to cinematography than just getting the exposure right. So much could be done with light, composition and movement to create the right atmosphere for a scene. As I travelled more, I built up a library of visual images of how light behaves in particular places, at different times of day, according to weather, or the kind of lighting. A room lit by fluorescents is going to generate a different atmosphere to a room lit by candles or a table-lamp. An appreciation of this is so important if you are to avoid falling into a pattern where everything is lit the same way. The cinematographer always bears in mind that the film is ultimately for an audience; so it's really important that you conjure an atmosphere for them with your lighting and your composition.

Learn from stills photography and painting. Study the masters, and see how compositions are put together, how light and shade are used to create depth and perspective. I try to

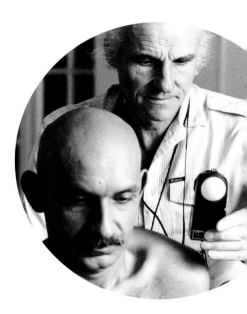

Gandhi (1982): "After discussing the film with director Richard Attenborough, it was clear that we wanted to be as truthful as possible to the man, who was played with such remarkable commitment by Ben Kingsley. A realistic style of photography seemed appropriate. No diffusion was used (apart from the dust of India). The tight schedule meant we had to shoot the film very economically, with no frills. India itself provided the colour with an infinite variety of light, and designer Stuart Craig found locations possessing tremendous natural richness."

99

(above & right) **Sunday, Bloody Sunday** (1971): "When I first met John Schlesinger to discuss the film, he told me he wanted it to be much more understated than my previous work on **Women In Love**, he didn't want the audience to be so conscious of colour and light." In keeping with the director's brief, the photography may not be as eye-catching in the finished film, but Williams always sought to make it three-dimensional through his control of composition and light and shadow. "I always think tonally, even in colour I'm conscious of building light colours on dark colours. Look at an old master, like 'St Jerome in his Study' by Antonello da Messina (below): there's always tonal separation; if you look at it in black and white, it's still a good picture – it's not flat."

(left) **Eleni** (1985, Peter Yates): A story set around the Greek civil war. "I wanted to shoot the film in black and white, which I felt would be perfect for the subject, but the financiers wouldn't hear of it. A pity; I feel the film would have had much more impact." (above) **The Wind and The Lion** (1975, John Milius): "When we started shooting, we were based in Madrid, and I was living in a hotel opposite the Prado. I was inspired by the Goyas in the museum, and I tried to bring a Goya quality into the film's photography. It was a boy's own adventure (Milius is a great action director), so it had to be colourful, but the visual look was helped by the desert, which gives a very simple, plain background, and by the contrast between the black robes worn by Sean Connery's bandit and the off-white wardrobe of Candice Bergman, his American kidnap victim."

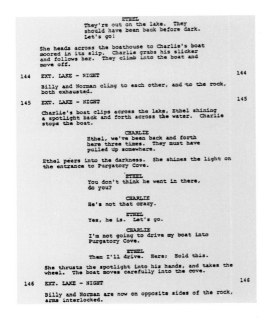

```
                        ETHEL
            They're out on the lake.  They
            should have been back before dark.
            Let's go!

      She heads across the boathouse to Charlie's boat
      moored in its slip.  Charlie grabs his slicker
      and follows her.  They climb into the boat and
      move off.

144   EXT. LAKE - NIGHT                              144

      Billy and Norman cling to each other, and to the rock,
      both exhausted.

145   EXT. LAKE - NIGHT                              145

      Charlie's boat clips across the lake, Ethel shining
      a spotlight back and forth across the water.  Charlie
      stops the boat.

                        CHARLIE
            Ethel, we've been back and forth
            here three times.  They must have
            pulled up somewhere.

      Ethel peers into the darkness.  She shines the light on
      the entrance to Purgatory Cove.

                        ETHEL
            You don't think he went in there,
            do you?

                        CHARLIE
            He's not that crazy.

                        ETHEL
            Yes, he is.  Let's go.

                        CHARLIE
            I'm not going to drive my boat into
            Purgatory Cove.

                        ETHEL
            Then I'll drive.  Here; Hold this.

      She thrusts the spotlight into his hands, and takes the
      wheel.  The boat moves carefully into the cove.

146   EXT. LAKE - NIGHT                              146

      Billy and Norman are now on opposite sides of the rock,
      arms interlocked.
```

```
146   CONTINUED:                                    146
                        BILLY
            Maybe I should try swimming to
            shore.

      Norman shakes his head, too tired to answer.  Billy
      grips him tighter.

147   EXT. LAKE - NIGHT                              147

      Ethel steers the boat past the rocks, while Charlie
      tries to find them with his light.

                        CHARLIE
            Left, Ethel.  Now right!  Oh, my
            God.

      He can barely watch, but the boat winds along.  Suddenly
      they hit something.

                        CHARLIE
                        (continuing)
            Uh, oh.

      He shines the line on the water.

                        CHARLIE
            Holy Mackinoly.

      WE SEE a section of the Thayer-four floating in the water.
      Ethel sees it too.  She shouts.

                        ETHEL
            Norman Thayer!  Where the hell are
            you?

      Ethel maneuvers forward, and Charlie slowly passes the
      light across the path.  A dark mass looms ahead of them.
      Ethel brings the boat closer and WE SEE Norman and Billy
      just barely hanging onto the rock.

                        ETHEL
            There they are.  Take the wheel, Charlie.

      She suddenly jumps into the water, and swims to the rock.

                        NORMAN
                        (weakly)
            Ethel.  You shouldn't be out here
            in this sort of weather.
```

On Golden Pond (1981): In the original script, the rescue scene on the lake had Katherine Hepburn's boat draw up by the rock where Henry Fonda and the young boy were stranded after their fishing boat crashed. "We had a script conference at which Miss Hepburn suggested; 'Wouldn't it be wonderful and much more exciting if I see them with the flashlight, take my coat off, jump in and swim over to them?' *(as per revised script, above)*. It was probably the most difficult shot I've ever done. It needed to be almost dark. We wanted to shoot at 'magic hour' – in reality only a few minutes. Everyone was anxious about putting Henry Fonda into the water – he was very sick at the time, although game for anything. I had a few moments to set the scene up, and only one take to capture it on film. Afterwards, I kept worrying, have I got it right? I'd had to underexpose to get the pinpoints of light from the flashlights, and I'd put in only enough fill-light to read the faces. There was no latitude for error. Luckily, it was perfect and the scene never failed to win applause in cinemas."

get my students to think in black-and-white – even though they'll be working in colour most of the time – in order to work tonally, building light on dark, dark on light, and so on. This is how to create depth, the illusion of a third dimension. Look at a reproduction of an old master in black-and-white, it still holds up as a good painting – it's not flat (it distresses me when I see the same tone applied to both face and background). Watch and learn from other films.

My own heroes were Gregg Toland for his black-and-white cinematography, and Jack Cardiff for his work in colour. Cardiff swam against the mainstream, pointing the way to the future. He always seemed to be experimenting, pushing the bounds of what was deemed acceptable. His achievements are all the more astonishing when you consider that he was working without the lights we have now, and with very slow film stock. He was a true visionary. Whenever I'm with students, I say, you must have vision, be able to picture a scene in your mind before you start applying light. One of the great advantages of going to film school, of course, is that it gives the student an environment in which to really study the aesthetic aspect of cinema, to be able to look at old movies and analyse them. Studying with the masters – whether they're directors, cinematographers or editors – presents one with the opportunity to talk about how certain things are done. On this level, it can really help to develop one's awareness. However, ultimately, to be able to put all that appreciation – of art and composition, and things achieved in the past – into practical effect, can only really be learned by hard experience. A large part of the job is to do with solving problems, and knowing how to turn them into opportunities.

I sometimes liken a feature film to an ocean liner at sea. The director is the captain, responsible for everything that happens on this ship. The cinematographer is the chief engineer – the one who decides how the ship is going to run and the best course to reach the destination. With today's tight schedules, the director/cinematographer relationship is critical – not just in terms of getting the visual look right, but also in terms of staying on budget and on time. As cinematographer, one is at the sharp end of the film-making process – the shoot is the point where most of the money is being spent, with highly-paid actors and the full team standing by. The camera is the crucible for everyone's efforts, so the cinematographer has got to be able to communicate, not just with the director, but with all the other creative departments and personnel.

The way I like to work with directors is to be present at rehearsals in which scenes are blocked with the artists. Seeing how the scene is to be played gives one ideas about where to place the camera – how close or wide I'm going to be, whether I'm going to have a track, how I'm going to capture the feeling of the location – and how many shots are required to cover the scene (tailor your coverage to the amount of time allowed by the schedule to complete the scene; unnecessary over-coverage can waste precious time). During a rehearsal, I might also pick up some small detail that will really capture the essence of the scene. An example: working on **Eleni** with Peter Yates, a film set during the

(below) Lighting plan drawn up by George Cole, Williams' gaffer, for the 90-second opening scene of **Dreamchild** (1985). Williams: "Darkness. The camera with a 10–30mm zoom lens on a remote head and crane is buried in green silk. Wind machines create a wave effect. Sequins, initially out of focus, sharpen like sparkling water as the light slowly increases. At 30 frames per second, the camera lifts to reveal the horizon in the cold light of dawn. It passes a breakwater, skims across a stony beach and an old boat. The light, 6,000 amps on dimmers, is coming up, touches of gold mix with the blue. In the distance are two rocks silhouetted against the brightening sky. The camera moves towards them to reveal an old lady in between. Dramatically the dimmers come right up, the rocks become the Gryphon and the Mock Turtle (see still, right). The lady is Mrs Hargreaves, who 70 years before had been the model for Lewis Carroll's 'Alice In Wonderland'."

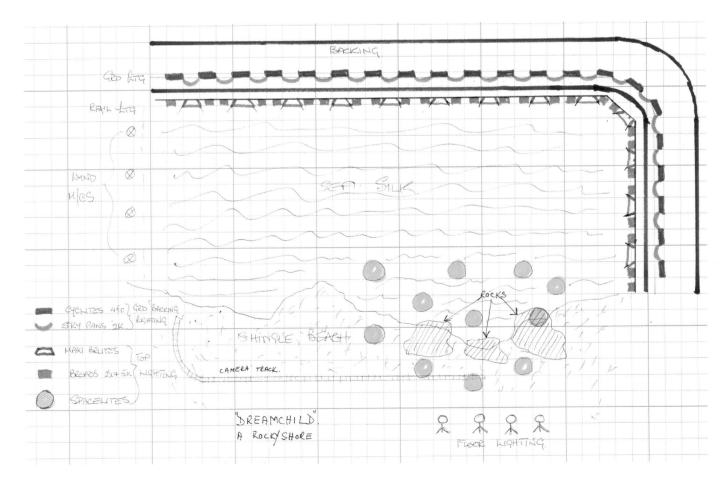

Greek civil war, we had a scene in which Kate Nelligan was explaining to her children that they were about to be sent to America, knowing that she wouldn't see them again. During the rehearsal, Kate took the hand of the youngest child (who as an adult becomes the story's central protagonist, returning 30 years later to find out what happened to his mother). This gesture wasn't in the script, but I thought it was critical, and so I said to Peter, "why don't we start on that moment of her taking the boy's hand and then pull back while she's talking?" Had I not been at rehearsals, I would never have picked up on it. That's why it's important to be there and watch for those things. The director, remember, has many other concerns and responsibilities, so part of the cinematographer's job is to be his eyes, to see everything: make-up – variations in skin tone; hair-styling, costume and set design – how different colours interrelate. If one detail is out of place, then the illusion will be broken for the audience.

The good cinematographer also develops an understanding of the way actors work. One must learn how to make them feel secure, without making concessions to them which might threaten to interfere with the look one's trying to achieve. In **On Golden Pond**, we wanted a muted look. Our palette was made up of blues and greens and earth colours. The interiors were timber, and we avoided any strong colours. Katherine Hepburn kept coming up to me with this scarlet cardigan and saying, "Billy, this is a wonderful colour…" The more I demurred, the more insistent she became. "Why don't you like this colour?" "Well, it's such a strong colour…" "So? Haven't you ever seen any of the French Impressionist

paintings? They always have a little stroke of red in them…" "Yes," I said, "and your eye goes straight to it." To which she replied: "That's exactly what I want!" She knew. She knew if she wore red she'd stand out. She knew *exactly* what the camera would see, and how to upstage everyone else! Miss Hepburn is a survivor of the Hollywood studio system, where part of the actor's craft is knowing what the camera sees, and what size you'd be in the shot at any given distance on any given lens. This led to a remarkable technical understanding (Elizabeth Taylor, for example, needs only one rehearsal to be perfect on her first take). These days, actors don't always have that sort of training. Some have a natural aptitude for precisely hitting a difficult mark (like moving bang on cue into a position where a specific part of their face or body is in hard shadow); others lack the ability to do so. Find out, and adapt lighting effects accordingly – give actors with less aptitude more freedom.

Thorough knowledge of the equipment and technique of film-making; aesthetic understanding of how to control light and use composition; ability to communicate and collaborate with colleagues – apart from these essentials, the cinematographer also requires real stamina for today's crazy schedules, where you're expected to work at speed and the hours are often punishing. I feel I've been very fortunate to have spent my working life in the film industry. I've had some wonderful experiences, met some marvellous people, been to some very exciting and beautiful places. There aren't many jobs that offer such a wealth of opportunity.

biography

After film school in Holland, Robby Müller worked in a film laboratory. In Germany, he assisted D.P. Gerard Vandenburg, who instilled in him an approach Müller calls "creative laziness – doing no more than is necessary – but always enough". Müller then shot a TV film and met "a long-haired assistant director named Wim Wenders". The Wenders-Müller collaboration spearheaded the renaissance of German

robby müller

cinema in the '70s with a trilogy of road movies (**Alice in the Cities**, **Wrong Move**, **Kings of the Road**), and produced a haunting vision of contemporary America in **Paris, Texas** (1984). Among other films Müller shot for Wenders: **Goalkeeper's Fear of the Penalty Kick** (1971), **The American Friend** (1977) and **Until the End of the World** (1991). Müller credits the trust which Wenders put in him as a key motivating factor in his career, and it's a trust that has been repaid handsomely to all the directors he has worked with. He shot **Repo Man** (1984, Alex Cox), **Barfly** (1987, Barbet Schroeder), **To Live and Die in L.A.** (1985, William Friedkin) and **Mad Dog and Glory** (1993, John McNaughton). For Jim Jarmusch, he shot **Down By Law** (1986), **Mystery Train** (1989) and **Dead Man** (1996). For Peter Bogdanovich, **Saint Jack** (1979) and **They All Laughed** (1981), and for Andrzej Wajda, **Korczak** (1990). For Lars von Trier, **Breaking the Waves** (1996); for Sally Potter, **The Tango Lesson** (1997).

interview

I was born in 1940 in Curaçao in the Caribbean. My father worked in oil fields for Shell and B.P., so for the first 13 years of my life, I travelled with my family through the U.S. and around the world, before living in Indonesia for seven years. We were always on the move, and I was constantly changing schools. I had to develop an ability to recognise who my friends could be and develop friendships very rapidly, because I knew we wouldn't be staying for long in any one place. This experience later helped me greatly when I began to work on road movies with Wim Wenders and Jim Jarmusch, who would often involve me at an early stage of a film's development. I could be useful to them because I knew what it was to travel long distances, to be on the road for weeks at an end, to arrive in new, unfamiliar surroundings – a complete stranger. I knew all the feelings associated with that way of life, and how it makes you look at the world around you.

While growing up, I developed an interest in photography. I

sometimes wonder if I wouldn't have preferred to be a photographer for an agency like Magnum rather than a D.P., because with stills, you can have a real contact with the subject. Film-making, by comparison, is an artificial pursuit. You're in a world which is totally fake – and it's very rare that something with real emotional truth happens for the camera. However, the experience of seeing Fellini's **8½** when I was a student in Holland in the 1960s electrified me and, for the first time, I dreamed of being a cinematographer. To make a bridge between that dream and reality, I went to film school and worked as a camera assistant before beginning to shoot films in 1968. Even so, it took almost ten years, until I saw the dailies from **Kings of The Road**, for me to feel I had mastered the technique of cinematography. Then, for the first time, I realised I could 'speak' – I could express myself through images like a musician with his instrument.

When I began working with Wim, we made low-budget, independent films – so we felt no pressure to please an audience. We felt that films were art. However, it was difficult to develop visual concepts for the films, because even when we had an idea for a particular style, we didn't have the money to follow it through. We couldn't afford to paint a background to conform to my colour scheme, for example, or hire a particular crane we might have wanted for the camera. I tried instead to respond simply to what actually occurred in front of me, to the point where now I'm not afraid of going totally unprepared on to a set. However many plans you make, something will always happen during a shoot that will be different to what you anticipated.

In certain situations, of course, you do have to be prepared on a technical level. The car chase on the freeways in **To Live and Die in L.A.** (Billy Friedkin wanted to outdo the one in **The French Connection**!) was thought out to the smallest detail, with all the incredible expertise and professionalism of the Hollywood machine at our disposal. At present, I'm talking to Wim about his next film which will entail a lot of preparation because it's set in a futuristic hotel filled with interactive television screens. We'll be making two parallel films, one which you see unfolding on the TV, and one in the hotel itself.

When I choose to work on a film, the most important thing to me is that it is about human feelings. I try to work with directors who want their films to touch the audience, and make people discuss what the film was about long after they've left the cinema. I'm interested in films that take their time to go under the skin, films which take risks to express the real things that go on between people and explore emotions which I can connect with. (When we made **Kings of the Road**, I had the strange feeling that I was shooting my own life: I was going through the same shit as the character phoning long distance to try to make contact with his ex-wife. It was a film about my generation, about our relationships with our fathers, about lost love.) For these reasons, I choose to work with – and am chosen by – particular directors, like Wim Wenders and Jim Jarmusch.

Just as it's important for a D.P. to find the right directors to work with, the director must also choose a D.P. who is on the

Müller's collaboration with Wim Wenders began in 1970. Their shared sensibility means they rarely need to talk about how a shot should look. "For some reason, I can't explain it, I always feel exactly what he seems to need." *(top right)* **Alice in the Cities** (1974) and **Paris, Texas** (1984) *(below)*: "I came from Europe to the middle of Texas; the light contrasts, the big skies, the colours were all so new to me. I was afraid that it would look as if we were showing off, but Wim just said, 'Let's go for it, let's show America as it really is'." There was no pre-planned visual approach to the film – "it all came out of the moment, straight from the belly". Rather than impose lighting on locations, Müller prefers to respect the natural lighting conditions. Among other films Müller has shot for Wenders: **Kings of the Road** (1976) *(above, centre, b&w)*, **Until the End of the World** (1991) *(above, centre, colour)* and **The American Friend** (1977) *(above, left)*.

cinematography

For Müller, cinematography is more about observing and thinking than technique and equipment. He takes time to think about the feeling behind a shot, and tries to understand the state of mind of a character before making a decision about how to reveal a scene. He strives not to point things out with the camera, preferring the audience to discover for themselves what is important in the frame. *(above, left)* For **To Live and Die in L.A.** (1985), Müller had the entire Hollywood machine at his disposal: "Whatever you ask for is possible. You mumble a request, and it's already built. The expertise is incredible." But the D.P. has tended to work outside the mainstream, finding more freedom in having less resources: "Some cameramen can't have enough lights, but I find that having too much choice distracts me." *(right)* Sally Potter's **The Tango Lesson** (1997).

same wavelength as him, who doesn't have a hidden agenda – for example, making the film to prove his own worth, and destroying the story with beautiful images. I once said in an interview that it would be great if an audience saw a film without being aware of the photography. A few years ago, I was setting up a big, difficult scene with a lot of lights. Finally my gaffer turned to me and said, "that's really beautiful." I realised he was right, and I replied, "yes, but now we're going to destroy it." I felt that the kind of perfection we'd achieved was wrong for the story. But my gaffer was in shock; film crews always take pride in their work, and their natural instinct is that something should look beautiful. When I shot **Breaking the Waves** for Lars von Trier, he wanted the colours to be subdued, and the actors to be right in the middle of the frame so that the natural beauty of Scotland would be glimpsed only on the edges of the shot. He wanted the whole film to be hand-held, with the camera free to look wherever it 'felt' like looking, depending on what the actors were doing. This meant, of course, that I couldn't use any film lights (the camera might see them). The only important thing to Lars was the performances; there were no second takes – he was afraid the actors would start 'acting'. So if there was a technical problem (for example, if we lost focus, or if there was a scratch on the film), Lars would just say, "Sorry, I got it." So – no safety net. I'm very proud of our work, but I know other D.P.s who took the film almost as an affront to the profession, who thought I had set out deliberately to attack the craft of cinematography. Of course I didn't. But as the D.P., I believe that my role is to reflect the story and work with the director to achieve his vision of it, not to try to impose my own. Lars wanted to make a film that would hit people in the belly and take them on an emotional rollercoaster ride; and this required something different from the conventional, honourable cinematography you see in so many films.

Recently, I felt as though I was 100 years old when a young guy in a lab asked me how I did the black and white in **Down By Law**. I told him I'd shot on black-and-white negative, and he said, "Wow, I never would have thought of that." Mainly because of commercial factors, black-and-white cinematography is now almost a thing of the past. Yet nobody questions stills photographers who continue to choose to photograph in black-and-white, or pauses to wonder why Rembrandt chose to work sometimes in colour, sometimes in black-and-white (in his etchings). Every time I begin to work on a film, there's a little exercise I do: to imagine with the director whether the film would be best photographed in colour or in black-and-white. Some films do not need to be in colour, and even though I have been lucky enough to shoot in black-and-white, it saddens me that there is an attitude which believes that if it isn't in colour, it won't sell. **Down By Law** could not have been shot in colour – it would have destroyed the film. Colour would have distracted attention from the characters and the fragility of the story. Likewise, **Alice in the Cities**. The plan was to shoot the film in the U.S. in colour on 16mm with a shoestring budget (we had so little money, the entire crew slept in one hotel room, and all our production meetings were held in the local McDonald's). However, when we were preparing to shoot in New York, I became very worried that the riot of colours which assaults your eye in that city would

Breaking the Waves (1996): "The look of the film was the result of the way the director wanted to tell the story. I was asked to be innocent, to look with the camera wherever I wanted to look, at any given time – to be curious." Lars von Trier intended the film's chapter shots *(above)* to be "God's view". The only vivid colour images in the film, they were the fruits of a collaboration between director, cinematographer and Danish artist Per Kirkeby. Before shooting on the film began, Müller and von Trier toured Scotland to shoot background plates. In post-production, elements of landscape like mountains or climatic effects (which would gradually appear or disappear in shot) were added digitally. *(below, left & far right)* The shooting of the film photographed by Rolf Konow.

overwhelm Alice, the young girl who is going through a big upheaval in her life after losing her mother. Wim agreed, so we shot the film in black-and-white.

I encountered a slightly different problem shooting **Saint Jack** for Peter Bogdanovich in Singapore. In this case, I chose to shoot with Fuji negative, because Fuji reproduced the colours in a way that appeared to me culturally closer to Asia, whereas I was worried that Kodak might have 'colonialised' the city with full American-style colour. For **Breaking the Waves**, we evolved a colour palette that was somewhere between colour and black-and-white, because Lars was not making a film about the beauty of Scotland. Muting colours in film processing has always been a problem; if you diminish one colour, you get more from another; whereas we wanted to subtract colour across the whole spectrum – an effect we ultimately achieved by transferring the exposed negative to high-resolution digital tape, and then playing with the colour until it was exactly as we wanted it.

I consider that lighting and operating the camera are both part of my job as a cinematographer and, as a result, I almost always operate the camera myself. Just lighting the set and then handing the operating over to someone else is, to me, like making a big painting and then allowing another person to cut their own piece out of the canvas. Also, I find that doing both enables me to work more quickly and efficiently – for example, as I think about how to move the camera, it helps me to realise where I can skip lighting altogether, because the camera won't see there. When I'm setting a shot up, there are certain questions I always ask myself. Should the lighting reflect the drama of the scene? Or should it counterpoint it? A scary scene doesn't require *film noir* lighting to be effective, nor should a love scene always need obviously romantic lighting. By counterpointing the mood of a scene, you can sometimes give it added emotional realism. I'm also very aware of how I'm using film language. I don't want to mindlessly repeat the same kinds of shot. If you shoot too many close-ups, for example, it becomes like repeating the same word again and again: it starts to lose any meaning (to me, medium shots can be more interesting than close-ups, because you see not only the detail of the face, but also the actor's body language. Another principle which is in my blood is that I always avoid anticipating the action with the framing. I prefer the audience to discover something for themselves, as if by accident, rather than have their eyes slammed into it.

When I started to work in cinema, I was forced to find my own way of shooting films – not because I wanted to be original, but because I was overwhelmed by all the influences, all the choices, the techniques, the new ideas. If Wim Wenders suggested that I go and watch **Taxi Driver**, for example, I'd feel very uncomfortable; I'd worry that he wanted that kind of photography. So I didn't go to the cinema, because I felt that the only way I could approach a film was through my own response to the script, without outside influences. When I went to live in L.A., I also felt overwhelmed – by the way life revolves around film, the way your position in society is related to how much success you have, by the speed with which people steal each other's ideas. L.A. is to film what

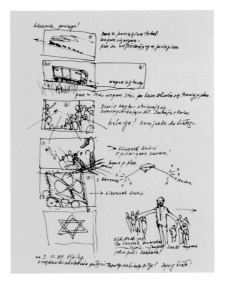

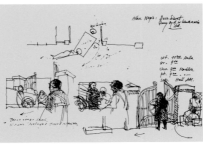

cinematography

(left, third & fourth stills from top) **Down By Law** (1986): "Jim told me, 'It's very simple, it's a fairytale', and from that moment I knew how to handle the film." Jarmusch and Müller worked together again on (top left) **Mystery Train** (1989) and (lower left) **Dead Man** (1996). (above, centre & right) **Korczak** (1990): Wajda's preliminary sketches for the film, alongside stills. "During the shoot, it was a strange experience seeing the old suitcases of the Jews being put on the train: I had the eerie feeling they were being used for the second time in the same place." Müller studied Nazi newsreels and even found some of the lenses used to shoot them, which he had adapted to modern cameras. (far right) Müller on the set of **Korczak** during filming.

Detroit is to cars. It's an industry town, where everything is based on marketing and consuming products. When I watch mainstream films, it strikes me that, photographically, they are all of an incredibly high quality – but they all look the same. New technology seems to cover up a lack of original thinking. It makes me sad as a human being, just as travelling today does. Take me from any airport to the city centre in any big city – North America, Holland, France, Italy – and the journey is exactly the same. Cars all look the same. Signs, buildings, shops all look the same. Everything is levelled out. However, I've learned that although you can't fight the mainstream, you can choose to branch off from it and be involved with films which are closer to life, closer to human emotions. That is where my heart is.

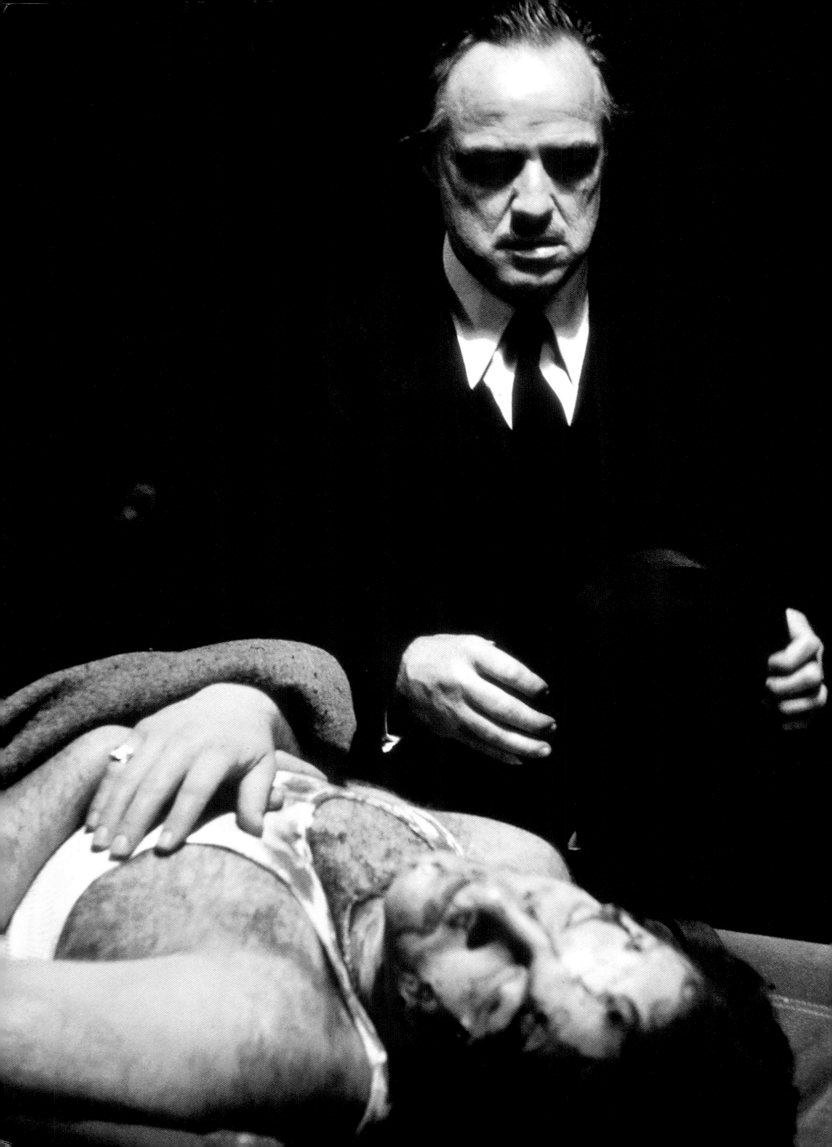

Gordon Willis' interest in film was fuelled from an early age; his father was a make-up artist for Warner Bros. After being cast in several kids' roles, he turned to other aspects of stage-craft and stills photography. Following the Korean War (where he made documentaries for the U.S. Air Force), he worked in the camera department for 12 years before photographing his first feature, **End of the Road** (1969). Since, he has built

gordon willis

up a body of work (some 32 films) which has made him one of the most highly respected cinematographers working today. In one sense a traditionalist – passionately committed to the tenets of classical narrative cinema, he's also a truly modern thinker whose startlingly original work has inspired a new generation of film-makers. His work with Woody Allen – including **Annie Hall** (1977), **Interiors** (1978), **Manhattan** (1979), **Stardust Memories** (1980), **Broadway Danny Rose** (1983), **Zelig** (1984) and **The Purple Rose of Cairo** (1985) – is rich and diverse in style, in itself a heritage to be cherished. **The Godfather** trilogy (1972–90, Francis Coppola) is an unique partnership not only with a director, but with a subject. If it helped to redefine the gangster movie for modern cinema, then Willis' collaboration with Alan Pakula – including **Klute** (1971), **The Parallax View** (1974) and **All the President's Men** (1975) – reinvented the thriller. He received the American Society of Cinemato-graphers' Lifetime Achievement award in 1995.

I spent a lot of time in movie theatres while I was growing up in New York during the '40s and '50s, so I was greatly influenced by the body of work that was coming out of the Hollywood studios at that time. Each studio had its own genre, its own set of emotions it would tap into, its own photo-graphic style – even its own musical sound. I could walk into a theatre lobby and tell which studio made the movie just by listening to the orchestration. There were a lot of remarkable directors of photography who specialised in different genres according to the studio to which they were contracted, and although they didn't ultimately influence my visual aesthetics, they certainly influenced the way I think about shot structure. The cumulative effect of watching all these movies was that I was enchanted by the medium, and I became smitten by the idea of making movies.

Like many people, when I first started shooting film, I emulated other cinematographers' work – because that's all I had to relate to. I didn't do it very well – but it's a learning process, and it enables you to develop your craft. No one can teach you talent, or creative judgement, but craft in cinematography can and must be learned. If somebody said to me, "I've got a great idea for a painting", I'd ask, "can you paint?" If the reply was "no", I'd think, "well, your idea isn't worth much". For the cinematographer, the camera is a tool. The film stock is a tool. The light you choose to work with is a tool. The laboratory is a tool. A thorough knowledge of these tools must become second nature.

As I went from shot to shot, from film to film, the accumulation of experience enabled me to become more and more selective; once I began to understand, for example, what the focal length of a particular lens would look like on the screen, I started to make conscious choices about when to use it based on whether it was the best lens to realise the drama of a particular shot or scene, or the best choice to photograph a particular actress, or how well it would cut with another shot using a lens of different focal length. I realised that you could use lenses for counterpoint or to punctuate the narrative. In becoming more selective in this way, I began to develop my own, personal way of seeing things – so rather than walking into a room with a script and wondering, "how should I photograph this?", I'd be thinking instead, "how do I want the photography in this scene to affect the audience who will ultimately watch it?" My aim was to apply the cinematographer's tools to tell the story in the most effective way.

This selective approach also makes you eliminate anything that might be superfluous or distracting. What you choose *not* to do is just as important as what you choose to do. Subtractive thinking helps one to distil an idea so that it is totally accessible to the audience – visually, emotionally, narratively. Simplicity, to me, is always the most beautiful and effective means of expression. The tortuous film-making process – especially the politics of decision-making – can often confuse the issue. Likewise, the film labs and equipment manufacturers, who try to drown you in a *bouillabaisse* of film: "Oh, have you tried this latest super-duper lens/filter/camera/gizmo?" "Have you tried leaving out the bleach and adding the dye?" When I get into this kind of a conversation, my response is usually, "No, I haven't done any of that; I haven't found the need." I'm a very contemporary thinker, but I won't jump on to a bandwagon just because something is new. If one day I find that one of those things might help me to express better a particular emotion on the screen, I'll experiment with it and test it to make sure it really is the most appropriate choice. I'll take a Steadicam out on to the street for a day and find out if it really is the most effective tool for doing this particular chase in this particular script.

People often say to me about my work, "it's so real." But it's not. It's entirely interpretative. My daughter coined a phrase to describe what I do. She calls it "romantic reality" – and I think she's probably right. I've never photographed anything by pulling it out of somebody else's head, whether it's art or another movie. If I want a soulful lesson in beautiful light, yes, I'll walk around the Metropolitan Museum of Art and look at Vermeer, but I'm certainly not going to try to

(left) The way Willis arrived at the look of **The Godfather** (1972) proves that necessity is the mother of invention: "Brando had to be lit in a fashion which made his make-up look real. The answer was overhead lighting, which had of course been around for years, but not really as a means of keylighting. That's the system I used to light Brando's office at the beginning of the movie, and it worked so I extended it into the rest of the picture." Willis also manipulated the light so that at times Brando's eyes were in darkness, making it difficult to tell what he was thinking. The sinister atmosphere of the office interior was juxtaposed with a bright, 'Kodachromey' look for exterior scenes of the wedding (which were intentionally overexposed), giving the film its bright/dark visual relativity (above, top left & below).

(above) For **The Godfather, Part II**, Willis extended the overhead lighting approach applied to Brando in the first film to Al Pacino, going even darker (by underexposing) to evoke the quality of Greek tragedy in the story. He also characterised the film's past and present time-frames, using "dirty, brassy, yellow" filtration for the turn-of-the-century scenes featuring Robert De Niro. "Often with period movies, everybody gets dressed up in period costume with period props and then it's photographed and looks like it was shot yesterday. When you're watching a period movie you shouldn't feel like you were just sent in from the parking lot a few minutes ago."

(above & right) **The Godfather, Part III** was, unlike the first two parts of the trilogy, a contemporary film – but it nevertheless needed to feel of a piece with them. Rather than seeking to reproduce exactly the same look, Willis used the modern lenses and film stocks available today, while maintaining the same colour/lighting structure and overall tableau quality as the earlier films. The result was that while the film didn't have an obviously modern look, it felt more up-to-date, while remaining in the genre. *(above, top right)* Willis on set with Francis Ford Coppola.

Willis and Woody Allen, *(from top left)*: **Manhattan** (1979): "We both visualised New York as this great Gershwinesque place, and the visual style of the film grew out of that. Woody suggested black and white and I felt the city would look great in anamorphic." **The Purple Rose of Cairo**'s (1985) look grew out of the downbeat Depression era scenes against the magic of the movies in which the heroine loses herself. *(lower left)* **A Midsummer Night's Sex Comedy** (1982). *(top right)* **Zelig** (1984) – a huge technical challenge: Willis had to intercut and match his cinematography with archive footage as seamlessly as Allen's human chameleon moved between different social and historical contexts. *(centre right)* **Broadway Danny Rose** (1983): a personal favourite of Willis'. *(lower right)* **Annie Hall** (1977): the first film Willis worked on with Allen, shot in a 'romantic reality' style that helped to change received Hollywood wisdom that comedy had to be shot differently to drama.

reproduce it in a film. When I agree to do a movie, it's never because I'm thinking, "gee, this could look beautiful on film." I'm interested only in how the script affects me emotionally.

The best movies, like life itself, have a sense of relativity, for example between good and evil, bright and dark, big and small. I try to structure my photographic approach around this relativity. For example, in **The Paper Chase** (James Bridges' film about the relationship between John Houseman's domineering professor and Timothy Bottoms' freshman student) relativity of size became the hook I hung my hat on. At the beginning of the movie, the compositions always favoured the domineering professor, so that he appeared huge in relation to the little figure of the student. As the story progressed and the student began to get even with the professor, so their visual presentation reflected the change – the student appearing physically more equal in the compositions. Finally, as he got one up on the professor, he began to dominate the frame, with Houseman's figure becoming smaller. In **All The President's Men**, the two worlds of the story gave me an automatic relativity between light and dark on which I could build the visual structure of the movie. You went from the bright, fluorescent, poster-colour feeling of 'The Washington Post' newsroom to the gloomy garage where Bob Woodward (Robert Redford) meets his source, 'Deep Throat'. With **The Godfather**, the relativity came out of the dark, brooding atmosphere of the interior scenes, juxtaposed with bright, 'Kodachromey' exteriors, like the wedding sequence at the beginning of the film. This creates two visual layers, cutting back and forth – dark and bright, good and evil.

After **The Godfather**, I became jokingly known as "the prince of darkness", because of a handful of scenes in which you couldn't see Brando's eyes. It got blown out of proportion, but it is true to say that because I constantly think in terms of the visual relativity between light and dark, I don't feel compelled always to light an actor so you can see every single hair on his head. I prefer to have characters moving between light and dark. To me, it's very powerful when you have people talking in a darkened corner, or a character dying in long shot – what you don't see sometimes can be just as effective as what you do see. The important thing is that the light you have in a scene – bright or dark – functions emotionally. I used to be very literal about lighting from a visible source. I still like the light to feel as if it's coming from a source, but I no longer feel the need to be so rigorous. If I need two sources in a room, and there's only one obvious source, I'll 'cheat' a second one. As long as I know in my mind that it's going to function on screen, I'll do it.

I also like using 'negative space' in my compositions. I love anamorphic lenses because you can put a close-up way over on the right side of the screen, leaving the rest of the frame empty; but it's not really empty, it's filled with design. In order to get good compositions that will serve the film and look effective on screen, you need the actors to be co-operative. When a scene is being blocked, I try not to ask them to do anything that isn't comfortable – that's foolish. You block for the actor, then you light what you block (meaning where the actor is in relation to the camera). The best screen actors will always understand that, if they miss the marks you give them

(above) **All the President's Men** (1975) contrasted the fluorescent-lit atmosphere of the newsroom with the dark car park where Redford meets informer 'Deep Throat'. *(lower right)* **Klute** (1971) contrasted Jane Fonda's nocturnal, subterranean existence with the villain living high up in a glass tower "these may seem simplistic ideas – but they're not if applied properly". *(above, right)* **Pennies From Heaven** (1981): Willis used the contrast between MGM-style dance numbers and the grim reality of the Depression, for which he drew on his childhood memories of the '30s. He was also asked to use three Edward Hopper paintings, including 'Nighthawks' *(top left)*: "I had to fudge it, because painters often work in two or three different perspectives, whereas a lens gives you just one."

in the blocking, the visual structure of the set-up – in terms of lighting and composition – will break down, and the shot won't work. This can be a frustration for some people who think they can get better results by doing whatever they 'feel' is right in the moment, and expect everyone else to work around that. To my mind, when that happens, you're no longer making a movie. You're doing theatre in the round, or radio. I've been fortunate to have worked with wonderful actors. Marlon Brando might be 'Mr Method', but he understands the craft of screen acting perfectly. The bottom line is that there's a lot more expression and freedom in containment than in turning everything loose, doing whatever you feel like and hoping for a happy accident.

To be able to apply one's craft successfully, the cinematographer is dependent not only on a good script, but also on the director one is working with. There are two kinds of director. One is those who take an overview of the material, with whom you can design the shot structure for each scene. This approach – which is again built on a foundation of craft – formulates a definitive point of view for the film and gives you great strength when you're shooting (everyone knows exactly what they're supposed to be doing). The other kind of director is what I call the 'dump truck' type, whose approach is to shoot a scene from every possible angle and size, and then hand the rushes over to the editor who makes the movie in the cutting-room. This can work – but there's no point of view. I've been blessed to have been involved in some wonderful collaborations. Shooting for Woody Allen was a joy. He'd specify what he wanted to achieve, but then give me great freedom to shape and structure the images. While I was preparing a shot, he might go off and play chess, then he'd come back and say, "that's fine, let's do it", or, "let's try it this way, right, that's better." So it was an editorial process. Alan Pakula also gave me a lot of freedom to do what I thought was appropriate visually, and so did Francis Ford Coppola. The process of preparing and shooting a film is made easier if you've worked with a director before; it's easier to explain oneself, you know what to expect from one another.

I'm often asked, "how did you get such and such an effect?" I wish I could say, "well, it's number 23", but it's never that simple. After **The Godfather**, I got a lot of phone calls from people wanting to know what I did to get the brassy, slightly yellow feeling to the photography. They thought that they could emulate the look of the film simply by reproducing that one element. There was a rash of bad movies printed with yellow! But the truth is, that colour effect wouldn't have worked without the lighting structure of that film, and the lighting wouldn't have worked without Dean Tavoularis' wonderful set designs and Anne Hill Johnstone's costumes. All these visual elements are interconnected with how the director sees the film, how individual scenes are played, how an actor speaks his lines. Film-making is an organic process; it's never one thing that makes a movie work. Assuming you know your craft, why you do something is more important than how.

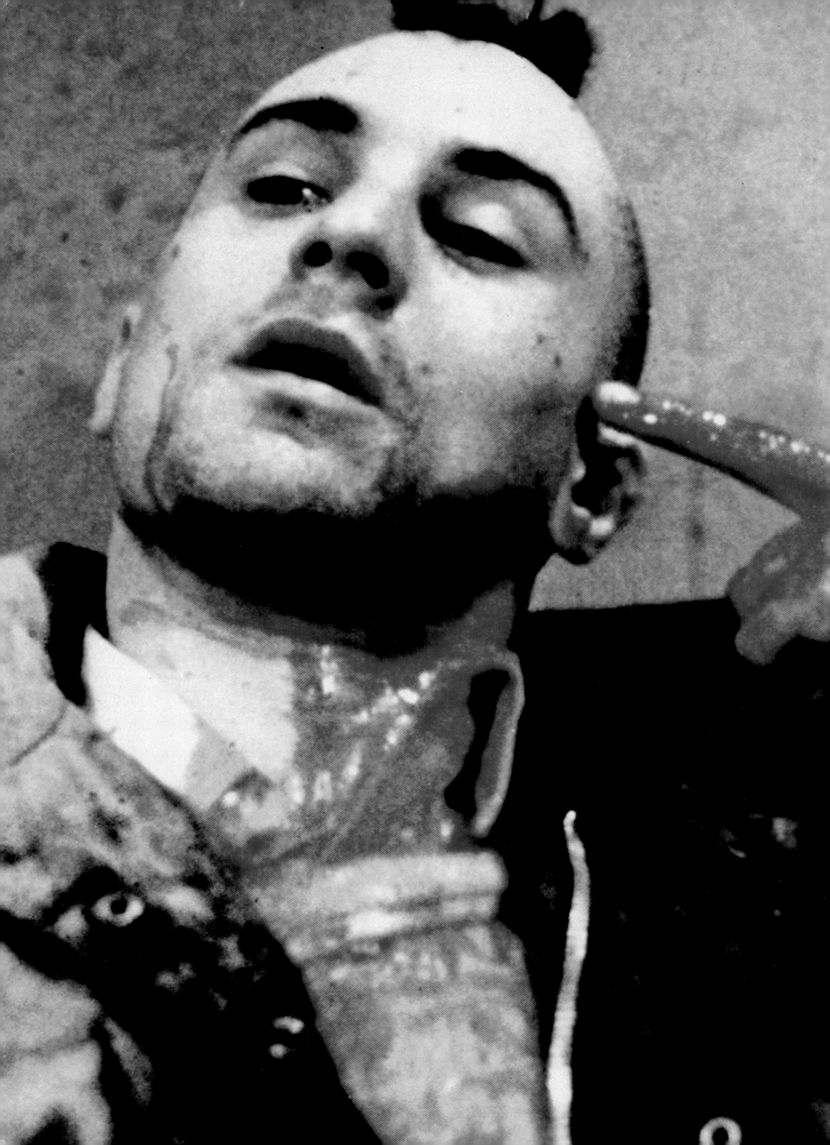

Growing up, Michael Chapman had no idea how movies were made – "I assumed they were made by some sort of mythical people out in California." Having graduated from college and hung about on the fringes of the New York avant-garde art scene in the '60s, Chapman began an apprenticeship working as a camera assistant in commercials, before becoming Gordon Willis' camera operator on features such as **Klute**

Michael Chapman

and **The Godfather**. Since photographing **The Last Detail** (1973, Hal Ashby), Chapman has built up a diverse body of work; but he is perhaps most celebrated for his collaboration with Martin Scorsese on **Taxi Driver** (1976) and **Raging Bull** (1980) – visceral, haunting, cinematically daring visions of New York subjects. Based in New York, Chapman also shot **The Front** (1976, Martin Ritt) and **The Wanderers** (1979, Philip Kaufman). His collaboration with Kaufman over 20 years also includes **The White Dawn** (1974), a gleeful remake of **Invasion of the Bodysnatchers** (1978) and **Rising Sun** (1993). Since moving to Los Angeles in the early '80s, Chapman has shot mainstream studio films such as **Dead Men Don't Wear Plaid** (1982, Carl Reiner), **The Lost Boys** (1987, Joel Schumacher), **The Fugitive** (1995, Andrew Davis), and **Six Days Seven Nights** (1998, Ivan Reitman). In 1983, Chapman directed **All The Right Moves** starring Tom Cruise. **Raging Bull** and **The Fugitive** were both nominated for Academy Awards.

interview

Making movies is an industrial process. You want to do the industry as well as you can, and occasionally – just occasionally – something like art slips between the cracks. But what you really should be thinking about is how to do a scene as efficiently as possible, as quickly as possible and as intelligently as possible. Much of what people think of as art is actually just the intelligent solution of technical problems. It's true of painting too, and poetry – you try to think of a good rhyme, or how to make the meter work – and in dealing with those questions sometimes something more unconscious comes out. But I know that you mustn't think about it. People call me up – sometimes in the middle of the night – to ask me how to become a cameraman. If one is practical about it, you have to say, people breaking into the industry are coming from film school, so that's the safest bet. But if I could arrange for things to be done differently – if I were king – I'd ban film schools and turn them into something useful like shelters for the homeless. I'd make all aspiring film-makers go to

cinematography

SCREENWRITER'S NOTE: The screenplay has been moving at a reasonably realistic level until this prolonged slaughter. The slaughter itself is a gory extension of violence, more surreal than real.

The slaughter is the moment Travis has been heading for all his life, and where this screenplay has been heading for over 100 pages. It is the release of all that cumulative pressure; it is a reality unto itself. It is the psychopath's Second Coming.

                                        FADE TO:

Police SIRENS are heard in b.g.

With great effort, Travis turns over, pinning the old man to the floor. The bloody knife blade sticks through his up-turned hand.

Travis reaches over with his right hand and picks up the revolver of the now dead Private Cop.

Travis hoists himself up and sticks the revolver into the old man's mouth.

The old man's voice is full of pain and ghastly fright:

                    OLD MAN
          Don't kill me! Don't kill me!

Iris screams in b.g. Travis looks up:

                    IRIS
          Don't kill him, Travis! Don't
          kill him!

Travis fires the revolver, blowing the back of the old man's head off and silencing his protests.

The police sirens screech to a halt. Sound of police officers running up the stairs.

Travis struggles up and collapses on the red velvet sofa, his blood-soaked body blending with the velvet.

Iris retreats in fright against the far wall.

With great effort, Travis, slumped on the sofa, raises the revolver to his temples, about to kill himself.

First uniformed POLICE OFFICER rushes into the room, drawn gun in hand. Other policemen can be heard running up the stairs.

Police Officer, about 4 feet away from the velvet sofa, looks immediately at Travis: he sees Travis about to put a bullet in his brain.

Police Officer fires instinctively, hitting Travis' wrist and knocking the revolver over the back of the sofa. It THUDS against the orange shag carpet.

Travis looks helplessly up at the officer. He forms his bloody hand into a pistol, raises it to his forehead and, his voice croaking in pain, makes the sound of a pistol discharging.

                    TRAVIS
          Pgghew! Pgghew!

Out of breath fellow officers join the first policeman. They survey the room.

Travis' head slumps against the sofa.

Iris is huddled in the corner, shaking.

LIVE SOUND CEASES.

OVERHEAD SLOW MOTION TRACKING SHOT surveys the damage:

--from Iris shaking against the blood-spattered wall

--to Travis blood-soaked body lying on the sofa

--to the old man with half a head, a bloody stump for one hand and a knife sticking out the other

--to police officers staring in amazement

--to the Private Cop's bullet-ridden face trapped near the doorway

--to puddles of blood and a lonely .44 Magnum lying on the hallway carpet.

--down the blood-speckled stairs on which lies a nickle-plated .38 Smith and Wesson Special

--to the foot of the stairs where Sport's body is hunched over a pool of blood and a small .32 lies near his hand

--to crowds huddled around the doorway, held back by police officers

--past red flashing lights, running policemen and parked police cars

--to the ongoing nightlife of the Lower East Side, curious but basically unconcerned, looking then heading its own way

"The **Taxi Driver** script was drenched in images. Above is a perfect example of: (a) what a great script it was, because it inspired us to respond to what Paul had written, and (b) the improvisational flair of a good crew. To do the overhead shot, I chalked a line on the ceiling of our location (a derelict building), and the guys cut through it with their chainsaws, bracing up the building so it wouldn't fall apart. Then we hung the operator through the hole on a kind of scooter and we pulled him along above the action."

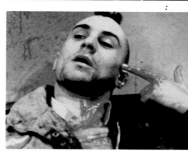

"To me, real storyboards are the death of movies. You might as well just publish them as a comic book and forget the movie. *(left)* Scorsese drew his storyboards for **Taxi Driver** as a rough thing for the two of us to work from, and they're a good example of what storyboards should accomplish — act as suggestions, give you the minimum you need to shoot the scene. But you should be able to go from there where the scene leads you; if an actor makes some gesture or some move, you should be able to go with it — not be trapped by the storyboard. That's why it's good if the storyboard is very sketchy."

cinematography

"Growing up, all the fights on TV were in black and white, so the decision to shoot **Raging Bull** in black and white seemed natural." The film's look was influenced by Weegee's 1940s photojournalism *(above, right)*; Chapman evoked a gritty, realistic period atmosphere by shooting on grainy, contrasty Eastman Double X stock. The boxing sequences were precisely choreographed to thrust the audience into the action: for one shot, fires were lit under 600mm lenses. The heat waves rippled the image so the audience saw the fighter coming at them as if through the eyes of a punch-drunk opponent. *(above)* The home movie sequences were based on La Motta's own super-8 films. "When we staged them, Marty and I couldn't make them look bad enough, so we asked the teamsters to shoot them." *(far right)* Stills from **L'Atalante** and **On the Waterfront**.

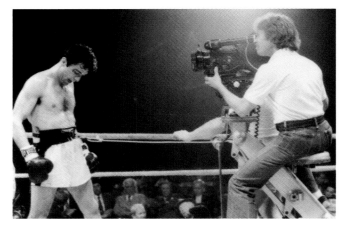

university and study history, literature, the classics. To para-phrase Auden, art must be attendant – never independent. In film school, you get taught to think that whatever you do is art. And that's nonsense.

When I began my career, there were no film schools. You had to serve an apprenticeship. You learned how to thread a camera and load magazines, then how to pull focus, then how to use the operating wheels. And in the process, you got to watch a lot of D.P.s. I was lucky to witness two masters at work. I worked as an assistant to Boris Kaufman in his last years. No one talks much about him any more, but he was one of the true greats – he photographed **Zéro de Conduite** and **L'Atalante** for Jean Vigo, **On The Waterfront** and **Baby Doll** for Elia Kazan, **12 Angry Men** and **Long Day's Journey into the Night** for Sidney Lumet. As you stood on a set and watched him, you realised this man was literally 'painting with light'; you couldn't help but be awed by him. As a staff assistant cameraman in a big New York commercial house, I also worked for Gordon Willis – a wonderful accident of fate; Gordy gave me my break as a camera operator, and I subsequently operated for him as he embarked on a feature film career which was to change the face of American – and world – cinematography. He was probably the hugest, certainly the most immediate, influence on me, not that I light like him (nobody lights like Gordy), but he instilled in me certain work habits, a way of thinking about movies, and the realisation that cinematography was to be taken seriously.

If I hadn't been driven by greed and vanity to be a D.P., I could have stayed a camera operator forever. Operating is the most immediately satisfying job you can do on a movie. It has a visceral satisfaction like sport; it requires you both to be athletic and to make aesthetic choices. You have to achieve what the director wants and what the scene requires – but there's always the opportunity to take chances, and ultimately the final decisions about the minutiae of framing a shot are literally in your hands. I am truly, vulgarly proud of my operating. **Jaws** is as good as it gets. Once the story became ocean-bound, it had to be shot almost entirely hand-held (Steadicam wasn't around in 1974); the joke among the crew was that it was the most expensive hand-held movie ever made. When I became a D.P., I was lucky enough to operate a number of the early movies I shot. I'd do it today except I've lost a step or two; I don't have the reflexes I once did.

Operating is to cinematography what drawing is to painting. Just as line in drawing gives structure to the image, so operating defines the composition. Cinematography gives it colour and depth. As a D.P., I don't think I've ever really had an aesthetic in the sense that, say, Gordon Willis does. None of my movies look alike – intentionally so. However, the experience of shooting my first film gave me an invaluable insight in terms of how to approach the job – it was **The Last Detail**, directed by Hal Ashby and starring Jack Nicholson. When I started on it, I was terrified. I felt I was a fraud. I genuinely thought I didn't have the chops to do it, so I just decided to trust what I saw. For example, I'd go into a railroad station and I'd know that there was nothing I could do to the light in that location that was going to be anywhere near as interesting as the light itself – so the best thing I could do was to try to transfer that light onto film as it was, perhaps supplementing it with a little fill-light for the actors' faces. In so doing, I began to realise that the basis for cinematography is the reality you see. If you trust what you see, you have a guide of how things look – not how they should look, but how they *do* look – and that gives you a basis to work from. Later you can learn how to impose your will on what you see, although personally, I've always been driven by and responded to reality.

I've done a lot of movies for less than noble reasons. There's obviously an economic determinant (you have wives and ex-wives and kids and colleges to think about), but I guess I always wanted to do movies in each genre. I've done thrillers, comedy, action adventure, westerns, romantic comedy, horror, a pretty good boxing movie and a rock movie (**The Last Waltz**). I've done low-budget and high-concept. Sometimes, by happy accident, a project will connect with a particular personal interest. For example, **The White Dawn**, was set above the Arctic Circle, and was about Eskimos. I was desperate for money when the film was offered to me, so I had no hesitation about taking the job – but it so happened that I'd always had a fascination for the Arctic. I'd read a lot about it and had lived in Greenland for a year. (Incidentally, **The White Dawn** was my western – it was like the American West of the 19th century, only a lot colder.)

Taxi Driver was another example of happy coincidence – a group of people who came together at a particular moment in time, who had some emotions about New York that they wanted to unload. Myself, I had lived there a long while; 'vision' sounds too pompous, but you can't help but be inspired by the place and have strong feelings about it. Furthermore, when Marty Scorsese and I first met, we also found that we both had a common interest in European cinema. Godard and his cameraman Raoul Coutard were big influences on us. But **Taxi Driver** is ultimately Paul Schrader's movie. His script remains the best I have ever read – not only in terms of its wrenching emotional content, but also because the pages dripped visual imagery. Marty did an incredible job with it (he has an instinctive understanding of the emotional content of a camera set-up, like nobody else); Bobby De Niro was fantastic; but it's quite depressing to think that the greatest thing I've ever done was 25 years ago – and, unless I'm very lucky, I'll probably never get to do anything that powerful again.

Preparation is desperately important. It gives you a sense of method and structure, which you can always fall back on when things get tough on the shoot. It'll get you through the headaches, hangovers, late actors, broken hearts and broken perfs. When you begin shooting, a movie always takes on a life of its own – new ideas which you never anticipated are constantly presenting themselves. You have to be well-prepared, but also open to what happens around you when you're shooting. On **Raging Bull**, we had elaborate plans for each of the fight sequences to differentiate them visually and emotionally. We planned to do one fight with a long lens, another hand-held, a third on dollies, a fourth in a false-

(above) **The Last Detail** (1973): Chapman's first movie as D.P.: "I covered up for the fact that I was terrified by saying, 'I want this to look like the 11 o'clock news'. I thought my work was extraordinarily primitive, but I saw the film again recently, and it works." *(lower, right)* **White Dawn** (1974): "Almost an anthropological film, recording a disappearing way of life." *(above, right)* Chapman returned to operating for **Jaws** (1976; D.P., Bill Butler): the scenes at sea were all hand-held. Apart from the technical feat of maintaining the position of the horizon in the shot on pitching boats, the way Chapman kept the camera close to the water was a major factor in the film's evocation of terror below the surface.

cinematography

(above, left) **Invasion of the Bodysnatchers** (1978): Preparing the remake of the classic B-movie, Chapman and director Philip Kaufman were influenced by old horror movies like **The Island of Lost Souls**. *(lower, left)* "I had a miserable time shooting **The Fugitive** (1995), every day I'd wish, 'please fire me' – and yet in retrospect there is marvellous stuff in the movie". *(above, right)* "When I shot **Dead Men Don't Wear Plaid** (1982), the crew included some great veterans of Hollywood's golden age. Watching them and learning their tricks of the trade made one really appreciate just how much all those old movies that we think of as masterpieces were in fact products of an industrial process, like building cars. It made me wish I could have been a staff cameraman at Universal in the 1930s; this week a western, next week a horror movie – imagine what that must have been like."

perspective ring. Although we had decided to shoot the fights at 24 fps (frames per second), while filming we experimented with changing the camera speed before and after the fights. For example, after Jake has punched his opponent out, he walks over to a neutral corner and we cranked the camera to 72 fps (frames per second) (slowing the action right down); then as the fight resumes, we came back to 24 fps (the f-stop diaphragm on the lens had to be adjusted manually as the camera sped up or slowed down). Another shot – where Jake's in the corner after taking a bad beating and water's being poured over him – was also overcranked to 120 fps, a decision made on the floor, and the resulting stillness made the shot even more like Mantegna's 'The Deposition of Christ' than had been envisaged. It's a perfect example of what can happen when you're well prepared and incredibly focused – you begin to 'feel' the scene rather than think about it. It's at such times that the industrial aspect of film-making can be transcended, and you start to use the mechanical process to make unconscious material visible.

Anyone who wants to be a cinematographer had better learn how to run a crew. A lot of the energy of a movie comes from the crew – more than most producers or directors would care to admit. I like to have people around me who have drive and emotional commitment. They can save you time and money. They can get things done and make the experience enjoyable. But the onus is on you to make them a crew which gives every ounce of its energy and talent to the film, rather than one which harbours resentments and does things out of fear (Scorsese is a brilliant seducer of crews). For them to respect you, you have to respect them. An experienced grip or gaffer will have been exposed to hundreds of different ways of doing things, so their suggestions about how to approach a particular technical challenge are always invaluable. They may not always be formally educated, but they're smart and they know what works and what doesn't. And good crew people also have a wonderful ability to improvise a solution which will answer a creative problem.

Of all the arts, I think movies most closely resemble opera. Opera in the 19th century was the amalgamation of all the arts of the time; movies have taken on that mantle today. Both are popular entertainment with a certain healthy vulgarity. The day after 'Rigoletto' opened, so I've read, the urchins in the streets of Naples were whistling 'La Donna è Mobile' – it was a hit the way a movie is a hit. And if you want to find out what making a movie is really like, read Verdi's letters – impresarios and producers screaming at him, a diva who doesn't want to sing this aria – here is the man who is thought of as one of the great geniuses of his century, and he sounds like some poor harried hack director trying to do an episode of 'NYPD Blue'... Think of movies as popular entertainment. Think of them as industry. And remember, if they're an art, they're only an art by the back door, by virtue of the fact that, every now and then, some person (like Boris Kaufman or Gordon Willis) or some script (like **Taxi Driver**), or some situation comes along and allows us to do something that transcends the norm.

biography

Born and bred in Sydney, John Seale worked as a camera operator with top Australian cinematographers such as Russell Boyd, Don McAlpine and Peter James on several key films of the 1970s Australian 'new wave' – "very good men", Seale reflects, "who taught me a lot about loyalty to the director and to the film." Operating on **Picnic at Hanging Rock** (1975) and **Gallipoli** (1981), Seale met director

john seale

Peter Weir, for whom he was later to photograph **Witness** (1985), winning his first Academy Award nomination. He went on to shoot **The Mosquito Coast** and **Dead Poet's Society** for Weir. He has always sought out projects with bold, dramatic stories and his unique ability to interpret them has made him much sought after by some of the finest directors working today. His filmography includes: **Children of a Lesser God** (1985, Randa Haines); **Stakeout** (1987, John Badham); **Gorillas in the Mist** (1987, Michael Apted); **Rain Man** (1988, Barry Levinson), for which Seale was again nominated for an Academy Award; **Lorenzo's Oil** (1992, George Miller); **The Firm** (1993, Sydney Pollack); **The Paper** (1993, Ron Howard); **The American President** (1995) and **Ghosts of Mississippi** (1996), both for Rob Reiner; **The English Patient** (1997, Anthony Minghella), for which Seale won the 1997 Academy Award and BAFTA; and **City of Angels** (1998, Brad Silberling).

interview

After leaving high school, my life seemed to be going nowhere until I discovered that I had an uncle I'd never met who owned a big sheep station up in Queensland. I hitchhiked to the 30,000-acre property, where my uncle offered me a job as a jackaroo. It was a hard life, up before dawn, to bed with the sun, mustering sheep, mending fences – but I loved it. I had with me a cheap little 8mm camera, so that I could film life on the station and send it home to my parents. As time went on, I knew I didn't want to be a jackeroo forever; but I looked at the little camera that had been recording this world I enjoyed so much, and the thought dawned – wouldn't it be great to go round the world recording places and people and things that other people might never get to see themselves, but could experience through film...? A couple of years later, I returned to the sheep station; this time as a cameraman working on a documentary about jackeroos for ABC (Australian Broadcasting Commission).

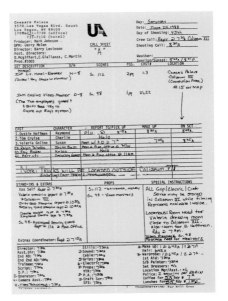

cinematography

(lower right) Seale operating on a television series: "In Australia, unlike the U.S., the camera operator is regarded as a key creative individual. I loved the job. Working on episodic television, I was able to experiment like crazy – each director always wanted their episode to look different." (right, fourth & fifth stills from top) Operating **Nickel Queen**, a 1971 feature film; (right, third still from top) operating on a rig built by Seale and his grip for an underwater tracking shot; (above, centre & right, second still from top) shooting **The American President** for Rob Reiner, 1995; (above, top right & left) location shooting on **The Firm** and discussing a set-up with director Sydney Pollack. (above, centre left) Call sheet from **Rain Man** referring to the scene set in Caesar's Palace.

At the time, ABC was one of the best training grounds a cameraman could wish for. I travelled the length and breadth of Australia, working on news programmes and documentaries. But the real revelation for me was when ABC moved into drama; I fell in love with the idea of placing fictitious stories in authentic backgrounds. When I finally left ABC after seven years, it coincided with the emergence of the Australian new wave – including directors like Peter Weir, George Miller, Bruce Beresford and Gillian Armstrong; their feature films created an industry for freelance technicians. Initially I worked as a focus-puller, before becoming a camera operator. I loved operating. Even now, as a director of photography, I still try to operate the camera whenever I can. 17 years in the job taught me that you can find the whole film in a single frame – like a movie poster. When you're rehearsing the shot, you've got the camera in your hand, you can spray it around, zoom into this or out of that, play with the size of the image, search the actors' faces to find a window into what they're feeling. It's not the same watching the video assist, surrounded by circuit city and the crew looking over your shoulder, talking away – it just doesn't work for me. I've got to feel the blackness of the viewfinder – like the darkness of a movie theatre – where all you're looking at is the film that'll be up there on the big screen.

When I'm operating, I feel close to the film, and I can pick up on things, unplanned moments that no storyboard could ever anticipate. An example; On **Rain Man** – a film which, for union reasons, I didn't operate, there's a scene near the end of the film where the psychiatrist is interviewing Dustin

Hoffmann and Tom Cruise. When we saw the dailies, I noticed something: not quite in frame, the psychiatrist's hand was tapping a pencil impatiently against his thumb. "God, that's the bloody movie!", I thought. Had that tap-tap-tap been in shot, you would've seen the psychiatrist's brain working away – "these two guys are losers, gonna have to send Raymond back to the institution, open and shut case, I'm off to play golf." Because of the way I search for the film in the frame when I operate, I may have picked up on that gesture (probably unconscious on the actor's part).

Operating taught me that each shot has got to explain the film, keep it moving forward. (Anything that doesn't is going to wind up on the cutting-room floor, so why waste the time and money?) I dislike gratuitous camera movement. When the director tries to use the camera to create the energy in a scene, it's normally a sign that something is wrong with the script or the performances. The operator's job is to second-guess what the audience might want to see, and then try to capture it unobtrusively. I spent years learning how to hide zooms, cranes or tracking shots in the movement of whoever or whatever was in front of the camera. As operator, you've also got to be aware of basic continuity so that everything you shoot will cut together – or you'll drive the poor editors crazy. You can break the rules, sure, but you've got to know them first. An editor once paid me a great compliment: "When I saw your name come up as the operator", he said, "I knew I'd get good cuts, because you always kept the camera rolling long enough for me to find the very best frame to cut out of." I enjoyed operating so much that I wasn't in a hurry to move up

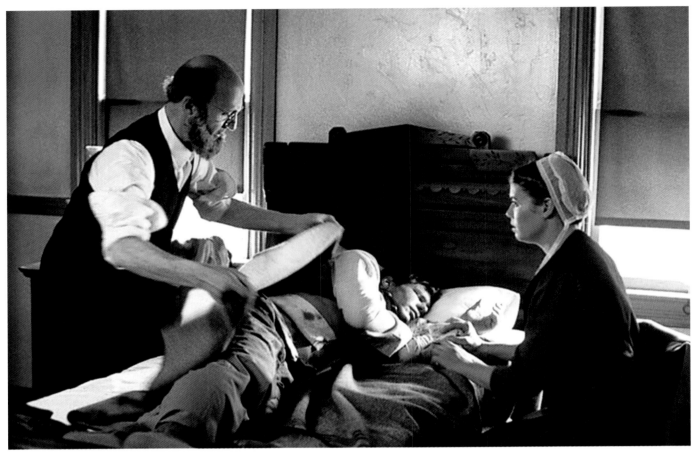

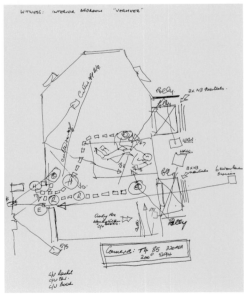

"We picked out Vermeer as a reference for **Witness** (1985). He seemed to have hit on a style: using the light from the window as the complete, absolute source of light, and allowing it to fall away into the dark corners of the room. We decided to shoot the sequence where Harrison recovers from his gunshot wound using that principle. Additionally, Peter Weir gave me a wonderful little lighting challenge: at first, when he's at his sickest, the blinds were to be almost completely drawn, so the room was really in darkness. As he recovers, we raised the blinds up and up until he's well again, when it's really quite bright. (above) Vermeer's 'Woman Weighing Gold', and Seale's plan to realise the Vermeer lighting for the sequence.

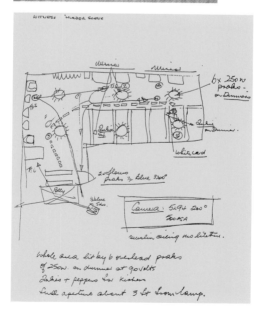

(above, left & right) Samuel, the boy, in the Philadelphia station, and lighting plan for the station toilet where he witnesses the murder. *(above, top left)* Lighting plan for the Happy Valley bar where the detective finds his prime suspect, only for the Amish boy (waiting in the car outside with his mother) to tell him it's not the murderer he witnessed. *(top right)* "We used softer lights and wider lenses for the Amish scenes, whereas the city scenes were defined by harder light and a more contrasty, sharper sort of image with less fill-light."

john seale

to director of photography. I was offered one film to shoot, took it, and got the fright of my life: What's this bloody light meter doing? Damn needle won't stay still, how am I supposed to know what stop to put on the lens? HELP! The experience was so horrific it drove me back to operating. But then I really knuckled down and studied what the cinematographer did, so when I got my next opportunity, I was ready.

I'm not a showy kind of cinematographer. I've been fortunate to work with some very good directors who've taught me that the film is more important than the picture. At first, I think I probably tried – like many others – to make my images perfect; but I've come to learn that you can crush the film by doing that. I reached the peak of my own perfectionist tendency with a film called **Goodbye Paradise** in 1982. Although I didn't ruin the film, I started to think, "OK, let's throw away the photography and go for the film." Primarily, I think I light for reality. Perhaps this is born out of my background in documentaries and low-budget Australian films. I always look for the window to key off, or the practical light. I'll also talk to the director to find out how he sees the film. He is ultimately responsible for creating the emotional arena with the actors, and the cinematography has to support it. But my realist approach makes me wary of shooting a whole movie in one style where every scene looks the same. No two places ever look quite the same in reality; nor should they on film.

Some of the best directors I've worked with have taught me to work against cliché – using certain types of light to create certain moods. Just because a character is bereaved, doesn't mean it should be raining outside. It could be a lot more interesting to put her in a sunny, beautiful situation. I tried to make the desert in **The Hitcher** the most beautiful, peaceful place in the world (using pola filters to darken the blue in the skies so the clouds popped out, for example) – a counterpoint to the horror wrought by Rutger Hauer's character. And for **The Mosquito Coast**, we didn't want the Central American jungle to look like paradise, we wanted it to look dirty (Peter Weir used the word "slimy") – so we shot tests on the three stocks, and chose Fuji, the emulsion of which reacted against the greens and gave us exactly the right feel (whereas Agfa, which loved the greens, made them look very pretty).

Whenever I'm asked what my favourite film is, I'll say, "the next one". I'm very conscious that my decision to shoot a film is often determined by wanting to do something different to the last movie. I'll follow a small, interiors-based film like **Children of a Lesser God** with a jungle adventure like **The Mosquito Coast**; after doing **The Hitcher** and **Stakeout** – a fairly violent thriller – I was ready for **Gorillas in the Mist**, where the story was about saving something rather than killing. This kind of variety stops you getting typecast. I also like working with different directors. It's quite easy to get locked into one style or energy if you always work with the same director. You may get stale. Working with someone new can jog you into different ways of looking at things. This carries a risk; you might find yourself working with a director who's very pedantic and dogmatic about what he wants. I feel the cameraman has an important creative contribution to make to a film – not just a technical one – so I'd

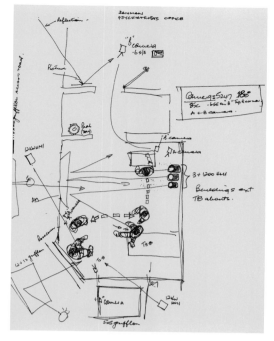

(far left) "I recorded my lighting on **Rain Man** (1988) as we shot, so that if three months later we needed to do a pick-up, we wouldn't be thinking, "how the heck did we do that scene...?" *(left)* A scene from **Dead Poet's Society** (1989) and references for the film's look: "I can't even remember where I got them. Probably cut them out of a magazine. I liked the light, the blueness." *(below, right)* **Lorenzo's Oil** (1992): "George Miller was great to work with. He put his fingerprint on that film, he wouldn't let up with the emotion, he wanted the audience to go through what the parents went through." *(below, centre)* **Children of a Lesser God** (1985): "I decided to shoot the movie when I heard William Hurt was doing it – he was perfect for the role."

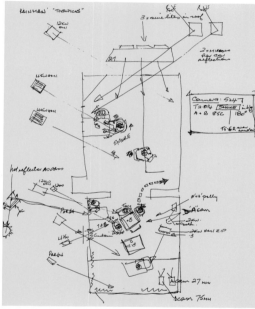

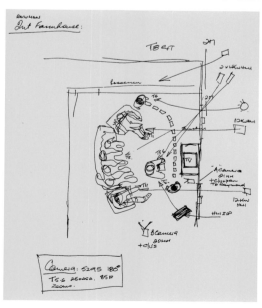

cinematography

Two jungles, two films, two visual approaches: *(above, left)* **Gorillas in the Mist** (1987), shot on Agfa film stock, which brought out the colours and beauty of Diane Fosse's environment. *(above, right)* **The Mosquito Coast** (1986), shot on Fuji, which made the greens of the jungle more olive, dirtier in quality, more appropriate for director Peter Weir's vision of the central American jungle. *(top right)* Peter Weir, here with John Seale on location for the filming of **The Mosquito Coast**.

rather work with directors who value that contribution.

When I begin to work on a film, I'm like a sponge. I soak up information which is bombarded at me. I study the script, analyse the design sketches; I confer with the production designer (who's been on the picture for months before I turn up) to make sure I've got good sources for the lighting on sets which are being built. Sometimes I arrive and I'm handed a telephone book of storyboards and I think, "Oh dear, no contribution expected from me on this one"; but I've found that you can quietly work them over, especially if they're just the director's first thoughts. I'll do my own little sketches to see how I can improve the flow of the action or increase the dramatic tension. I'll also look at the thousands of snaps taken on location recces; although they're shot on automatic cameras, very often I'll see something I love in the natural ambient lighting – a shaft of light that falls in a particular way, for example – and I'll keep the photo as a reference, something to go for when I come to light it with my gaffer.

I'll discuss other references with the director – photographs, paintings, films – we all steal bits of other people's movies (although I deplore the idea of lifting somebody's style for a whole film). We'll also discuss the format for the film, which can have big implications on the overall style. For example, on **The English Patient**, Anthony Minghella and I discussed shooting with anamorphic lenses – wide screen is perfect for drawing the eye to the beauty of the flat desert horizon; but ultimately we opted for 1.85:1, because the film was about people in the desert, not the desert with people.

My reality-lighting approach and my low-budget background enables me to shoot fast. If the cinematographer can work fast, I really believe there's an excitement, an energy, which transmits itself to all the other departments. There's no hanging around for the lighting. Actors don't lose their impetus. On **Rain Man**, Hoffman used to say, "I don't believe it, you go too fast for me even to go off and make a phone call." "Good, good", I'd say, "Keep you on the set, keep you in character." He loved it. Being the operator also helps me achieve this speed – I can work with greater precision – only lighting what I know the camera is going to see. The ability to work fast helps you to think fast on your feet. For example, if we have to shoot cold on a location I haven't been able to prep, I'll just use the available light, maybe whack a bit of fill in, and that's it, let's go. Sometimes the energy of winging it creates a style that no amount of preparation would be capable of capturing.

Sadly, in my mind, the days of classic film-making are numbered. Audiences are reared on the 'MTV style' and movies are under pressure to move faster, bombarding the viewer with imagery. (**The English Patient** was very much against the grain in this respect; perhaps that's why it did so well.) It follows that the cinematographer's craft is an endangered species; you see directors now compose the shots on video monitors. Video is everywhere. One day, it'll all be video, including my job – or at least digital. But it's no good trying to hold on to the past. When I lecture in Sydney, I always ask, "who's shooting on tape?" 60–70 per cent of the hands go up. Then I say, "Keep your hands up, those of you who are using

(above) The complex structure of **The English Patient** (1997) made it imperative to differentiate the scenes in Tuscany from the desert flashbacks. "Everyone on the film was working towards a common goal so that if Anthony Minghella chose to cut to even a close up of a woman's hand playing a piano, the colour scheme and the light, the design and set dressing would immediately tell you that you were back in Italy." Seale took his cue from the visual qualities inherent in the locations: the ochre warmth and brightness of Tunisia, which he enhanced by using coral filters, compared with the cooler, more sombre quality of Italy. *(far right)* Seale with his gaffer, Mo Flamm – "A wonderful man who loves making movies, and whose lighting expertise allows me to continue operating the camera" – on the newsroom set of **The Paper** (1993). *(below, far right)* Lighting plan of the newsroom set.

film filters, pola screens, colour grads, grad filters on your video cameras." No hands. "Well, why not? Why aren't you creating a craft with your video cameras, using our film filters to enhance the image?" A student who worked in news television rang me up a couple of weeks after one of these lectures, and said, "I put a grad in, like you said, to control the contrast, and everyone's asking me, how did you get these amazing images?" Whatever the future holds, you've got to keep your blinkers on and learn your craft.

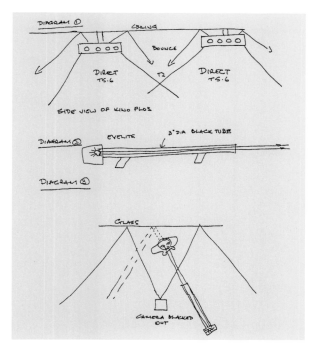

stuart dryburgh

biography

The story of how Stuart Dryburgh was drawn towards a career in cinematography emphasises the importance of having a visual background (he studied architecture), but also provides a fascinating insight into what it was like to be present at the birth of a new film industry in New Zealand. Once accepted as a D.P., he shot pop videos and commercials before photographing an acclaimed short film for director Alison McLean which led to **An Angel at My Table**, 1990, the first film he shot for Jane Campion. Their collaboration has flourished and matured with **The Piano**, 1993, (for which he was nominated for an Academy Award) and **Portrait of a Lady**, 1997. "Collaborating with Jane", Dryburgh reflects, "is a unique privilege for a cinematographer, because she's a film-maker who thinks very clearly about the visual language of film". Director and D.P. share a similar visual sensibility and also a fervent belief in the importance of the photographic image in film, and this has allowed them to work together to achieve the wholly original textures of the three films to date. In this work – and in his other features (**Once Were Warriors**, 1993, Lee Tamahori; **The Perez Family**, 1994, Mira Nair; and **Lone Star**, 1996, John Sayles) – Dryburgh has developed an approach to colour which – despite his claim that it is almost embarrassing in its simplicity – has given each film a powerful cinematic identity entirely appropriate to the dramatic content, and made him one of the most visionary of contemporary cinematographers.

interview

Growing up in Wellington, New Zealand, I felt drawn to the world my father worked in. He was an architect, and he exposed me to some of the tools of his trade – drawing and photography. Learning to draw at an early age gives you an instinctive understanding of visual language and enables you to begin to think and communicate visually. I went on to study architecture at university, and I was lucky because the curriculum reflected the liberal climate of the 1970s. So apart from straight building design, I was also able to embrace a wide range of interests including sociology and media studies. We used video to do research for projects and although the gear was fairly primitive, we also used it to shoot experimental shorts. Around this time, I began going to movies a lot. The '70s was a fertile time for the cinema – the U.S. industry didn't know how to fight back against television; and my assumption is that a lot of great, independent-minded mavericks were able to take advantage of this situation to get their films made – Altman, Rafelson, Pakula, Casavettes,

In **The Piano** (1993), Dryburgh and director Jane Campion worked to achieve a colour palette that would help to characterise different exteriors and interiors with specific emotional values: "The beach was played with yellow, pink and mauve tones – a magical place. The forest was depicted as a submarine environment, oppressive, claustrophobic. We achieved this with blue filters, cold light, a lot of dark shadows. Meanwhile, the home to which Sam Neil brings Holly Hunter is a stark, destructive, anti-environment which we made almost brutally brown. Keitel's house starts out being identified with the forest, washed in blue – but as the love story develops we subtracted the blue and introduced warm, sensual candlelight. Even when it's shut up at the end, we see sparks of light creeping through the walls."

Bogdanovich, Coppola, Scorsese. I hadn't yet really identified the possibility of a career in cinema, but the excitement engendered by seeing these films, the sense of life and emotion in them, were a very definite influence on me.

Meanwhile, the Australian film industry was up and running, establishing a wonderful sense of national identity for Australia. A number of my friends, inspired by that example, got involved in a fledgling film industry in New Zealand. In my final year at university, I made my own 12-minute 16mm film, camera in one hand, 'how to' manual in the other. By the time I'd finished it, I was much more interested in being a film-maker than an architect. Eventually I got a job as dogsbody on a low-budget film being shot in Auckland. The crew was mostly made up of the first wave of New Zealand film-makers – including performance artists who'd used film, technicians who'd come out of television, professionals who'd worked overseas. So I was in the right place at the right time, and I loved being part of a crew. Over the next ten years, I slowly gravitated towards cinematography, freelancing as an electrician and grip on films, commercials and documetaries. There were very few people with any technical training, so if the cameraman wanted you to do something, first he'd have to teach you how to do it. As a result, I got a tremendous hands-on education from some of the great New Zealand and Australian cinematographers. I became a proficient lighting gaffer and built up an equipment company. I also met future directors who, like me, were serving an 'apprenticeship' – Alison McLean did props on a couple of films; Jane Campion was a trainee assistant director.

The great advantage of beginning to work as cinematographer in a relatively young industry was that although there was an older generation of established technicians (including those who were expensively flown in from Australia), there was really no one of my age (in their early 30s) breaking through. So once I became a D.P., I was able to get fairly regular work. There's no real single thread that runs through the choices I make about what work I do. Sometimes it will be the script that excites me. Or it may be the cast. Another time it's the location. Going somewhere unfamiliar and receiving a whole new set of visual stimuli is a unique moment for any photographer. But probably the most important element that affects my decision is the director. If my agent rings me up and says, "Bob Rafelson" or "John Sayles" – I just say "YES". These are people one dreams of working with.

I'm sure that if you looked hard enough, it would be possible to discern stylistic threads in the way I light or frame; but I'm not conscious of them. The key to my approach is that I try to build up a visual language which is appropriate and evocative for each film I shoot. Invariably this starts with the source material and the director's vision. Someone like John Sayles, a writer/director, is very clear about what each scene, every beat of character development, contributes to the gross of the story. If you listen to him you'll know exactly what part of the story is being told in each shot – so then my job becomes a matter of bringing the elements of composition, choice of lens, camera movement and lighting to support his interpretation. His specific visual ideas will be less evolved than Jane Campion, who thinks about a film primarily in

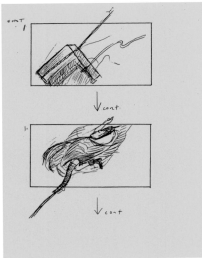

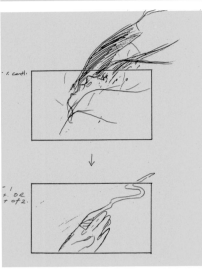

BAINES
(anxiously) What?

FLORA
She says, throw it overboard. She doesn't want it. She says it's spoiled.

BAINES
I have the key here, look, I'll have it mended ...

ADA mimes directly to BAINES, "PUSH IT OVER". Her determination is increasing.

MAORI OARSMAN
Ae! Peia. Turakina! Bushit! Peia te kawheha kite moana.
(Yeah she's right push it over, push the coffin in the water.) SUBTITLED

BAINES
(softly, urgently) Please, Ada, you will regret it. It's your piano, I want you to have it. —

But ADA does not listen, she is adamant and begins to untie the ropes.

FLORA
(panicking)
She doesn't want IT!

The canoe is unbalancing as ADA struggles with the ropes.

BAINES
All right, sit down, sit down.

ADA sits, pleased. Her eyes glow and her face is now alive.

Sc 145 Continued:

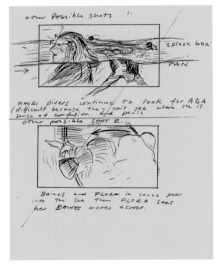

BAINES speaks to the MAORIS who stop paddling and together they loosen the ropes securing the piano to the canoe.

As they manoeuvre the piano to the edge ADA looks into the water. She puts her hand into the sea and moves it back and forth.

The piano is carefully lowered and with a heave topples over. As the piano splashes into the sea, the loose ropes speed their way after it. ADA watches them snake past her feet and then out of a fatal curiosity, odd and undisciplined, she steps into a loop.

The rope tightens and grips her foot so that she is snatched into the sea, and pulled by the piano down through the cold water.

Sc 146   INT   SEA NEAR BEACH   DAY   Sc 146
Bubbles tumble from her mouth. Down she falls, on and on, her eyes are open, her clothes twisting about her. The MAORIS diving after her cannot reach her in these depths. ADA begins to struggle. She kicks at the rope, but it holds tight around her boot. She kicks hard again and then with her other foot, levers herself free from her shoe. The piano and her shoe continue their fall while ADA floats above, suspended in the deep water, then suddenly her body awakes and fights, struggling upwards to the surface.

Sc 147   AT SEA BEACH   DAY   Sc 147
As ADA breaks the surface her VOICE OVER begins:

ADA
(VOICE OVER)
What a death!
What a chance!
What a surprise!
My will has chosen life!?
Still it has had me spooked and
many others besides!

Sc 147 Continued:

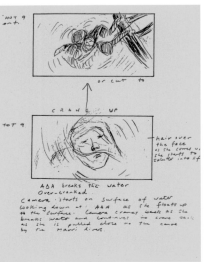

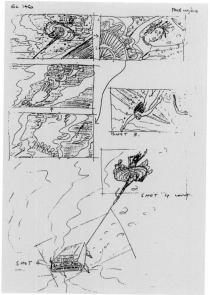

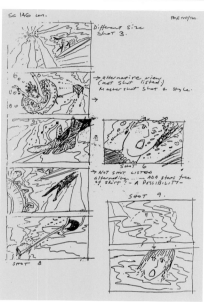

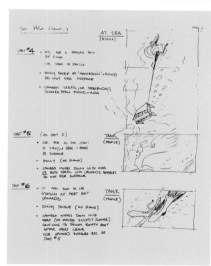

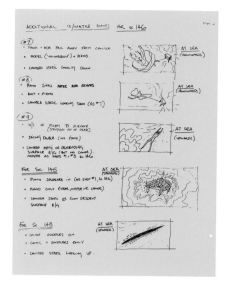

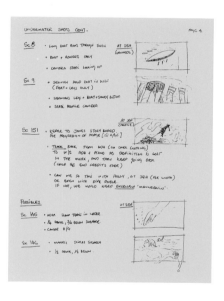

At the end of **The Piano**, Ada demands that her beloved piano is thrown overboard from the canoe in which she travels with her lover Baines and daughter Flora (see script, *facing, centre*). Ada then allows herself to be pulled over with it. The working materials included here trace the evolution and realisation of the scene, from Jane Campion's screenplay and her own conceptual drawings intended as a starting point for her preparation with Dryburgh *(facing, right)*, to the more detailed storyboard which Dryburgh drew up based on the shot-list he and Campion jointly developed *(this page, top & middle left)*, and finally, Dryburgh's breakdown of underwater shots *(lower left & above)* prepared for the underwater specialist riggers and camera crew. *(above, right)* Frames from the completed sequence.

cinematography

Whereas colour was used to give emotional definition to space in **The Piano**, it was used to characterise time in **Portrait of a Lady** (1997). "The opening of the movie depicts a lush, English summer; green and yellow tones dominate. This is a time when Isabel is most idealistic and impressionable, her life before her. A hint of sombreness is introduced when Sir John is dying, but then we're in Tuscany, the mood is romantic, we move into oranges and sepias and corals, rich warm tones. The following act takes place three years later, when Isabel is trapped in her soulless marriage with Osmond in Rome; it's a gloomier world, it's winter – we introduce colder, blue tones, the feeling now is almost monochromatic. Lastly, we return to the English countryside, also in winter, the black trees standing out against the snow, a sense of loss expressed by a slightly softer blue wash." *(above & top, far right)* Photographs taken by Lulu Zezza during the shoot of the film.

visual terms. Many of the strongest and most expressive compositions in **The Piano** are rooted in the storyboards she did herself before shooting began. So she'll always provide a visual framework which you can add to, discuss, modify.

Evolving the visual language of a film is a very stimulating process. Different directors bring with them different kinds of references – pages torn from magazines, paintings in art galleries, photographs. The production designer builds on this foundation, producing a great store of images, including his or her own drawings. As the cinematographer, I'll start to focus in on specific moments and bring my own visual ideas to the table. Out of this pool, and with a lot of discussion, you begin to define and refine the film's visual identity. Quite often I'll then go off with a stills camera to the locations where we're going to shoot (or an environment where the light is similar), and I'll experiment with whatever photographic elements are being discussed (for example, film stock or colour filters). I'll then give a slide show for everyone. So the visual language evolves very organically. It's one of those foolish truisms that a lot of what is perceived as great cinematography actually is really good production design or really good location choice. Often it's that easy – it's so damn good, just photograph it...

My lighting is naturalistic. If it's a day interior scene, I like to feel that my keylight is coming from a window; if it's a night scene, I try to light from real practical sources. But for me, the colour of the light is as significant as its placement, its modelling, or its contrast. With Jane Campion, I have evolved a way of thinking about colour that I've carried on through all my work. The idea is to find the right colour temperature for different emotional values, different places and different time-frames in the story. We first applied it to **An Angel At My Table**. The protagonist Janet Frame's childhood on the South Island was depicted in golden tones; her subsequent life in the city was played colder and flatter. For a scene like the one in which Janet discovers her older sister has drowned, the colour was cranked right down into a sort of sombre blue twilight. In **The Piano**, we further developed this approach to identify place. In **Portrait of a Lady**, we used it to define time. I don't think there's anything particularly mysterious or sophisticated about this approach in theory or practice, it's outrageously simple – but it seems to work.

With the director, I also consider how composition will contribute to the visual language of a movie. For example, in **Portrait of a Lady** we used long lenses for close-ups, which have the effect of throwing the background out of focus, thus isolating the character in the environment. This had two important benefits: firstly, most period movies use a lot of wide shots; Jane felt that Isabel's character was a very contemporary woman and that although we had to observe the period detail, we should also strive to maintain a quality of modernity. Secondly, she was interested in expressing Isabel's internal feelings without always making recourse to dreams or flashbacks. So, by staying very close to her face, we were able to pick up every nuance of her thought processes. Jane and Nicole Kidman gave the character a restless quality (particularly when she's trying to disentangle herself from her marriage); she'd move at times like a startled animal, and

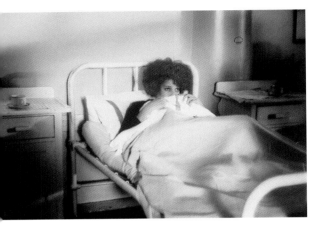

(left) **An Angel at My Table** (1990): Dryburgh's first collaboration with Campion. He has continued to explore the emotional values of colour with other directors. *(top right)* **Once Were Warriors** (1993): "Despite the brutal and harsh story, director Lee Tamahori wanted the film to celebrate the essential beauty of the Maori protagonist; partly achieved by pumping up the reds and oranges and ensuring the skin tones were always a rich brown." *(above)* **The Perez Family** (1994), directed by Mira Nair: "By applying an overall tonality, we subordinated the riot of colour in downtown Miami to the film's emotional message." *(below)* **Lone Star** (1996) enabled Dryburgh to work with one of his idols, John Sayles.

we'd just follow her with the lens, almost as though we were shooting a wildlife film. If **Portrait of a Lady** was about isolating the characters, then **Lone Star** was about rooting them in their environment. We used a much wider-angled approach to accommodate the multi-layered nature of the storytelling, so even if you have a medium close up of an actor, you still see an enormous amount of detail behind and around him, telling you where he is and what's going on.

Once you know the visual language of your film, you develop an instinctive understanding of what belongs in the movie and what doesn't. Sometimes you'll hit upon a great composition, but you realise that it's the wrong movie for it. At other times, you'll discover something by accident which seems to express what the film is about. When we were shooting a scene in **Portrait of a Lady**, we discovered that a Victorian mirrored screen in the background of a shot had bevelled edges which produced a prismatic effect. And as we stepped back to do a long shot, the prism, now out of focus in the foreground, created a double image in the lens. Applied to a character, this effect evoked a sense of alienation and dislocation. Jane responded to it immediately, and thereafter we looked out for other opportunities to use it. Later, while shooting a café scene, we came across a bevelled glass cake cabinet which produced the same effect. We purchased the cabinet from the café and then carried it around with us for

the rest of the shoot. And wherever the abstraction of the double-image was appropriate, we'd shoot through the bevelled glass.

I've continued to work in advertising throughout my feature film career. One of the great things about shooting commercials is that your job is basically to go out and create great pictures, which is fun and stimulating, especially as a counterpoint to drama where the images must always work within the specific visual context and continuity of each film. In advertising, you'll often just go out and get 20 or 30 stunning images – and that's the commercial. You also get to play with toys. There's often the budget to work with a new camera system or a crane, or a new remote technology, or post-production technique. As a result, when it comes to doing a feature film (where you are often working with a more limited budget) you'll have 'tested' a lot of these tools. You'll know how effective they are, and if it really is worthwhile asking the producer to overspend on his equipment budget in order to hire a particular piece of equipment for the film. But almost the most important reason for doing commercials is that they give me the freedom to pick and choose what film work I do. I am very selective. It's such a commitment to do a feature film, you put so much of your life and your art into it; so I think it's really important to choose to do work that you believe in and care about.

biography

After graduating from Bath Academy of Art, where he studied painting and photography, and the newly-founded National Film and Television School in the U.K., Roger Deakins directed and photographed documentaries – anthropological films, war reportage, current affairs and arts films. Shooting a film about Van Morrison, he met director Michael Radford, who asked him to shoot his first feature, **Another Time,**

roger deakins

159

Another Place (1983). He subsequently shot **1984** and **White Mischief** (1988) for Radford, and other British features: **Defence of the Realm** (1985, David Drury), **Sid & Nancy** (1986, Alex Cox), **The Kitchen Toto** (1987, Harry Hook), **Personal Services** (1987, Terry Jones) and **Stormy Monday** (1988, Mike Figgis). His naturalistic soft lighting style, although very new to British cinema, was rooted in his own documentary work, and also influenced by French films and American D.P.s like Gordon Willis and Conrad Hall. In 1990, he shot **Mountains of the Moon** for Bob Rafelson, and has since been based in the U.S.A. Apart from his collaboration with the Coen brothers (**Barton Fink**, 1991; **The Hudsucker Proxy**, 1994; **Fargo**, 1996; and **The Big Lebowski**, 1998), he has shot **Homicide** (1991, David Mamet), **Passion Fish** (1992, John Sayles), **The Secret Garden** (1993, Agnieszka Holland), **The Shawshank Redemption** (1994, Frank Darabont), **Dead Man Walking** (1995, Tim Robbins) and **Kundun** (1998, Martin Scorsese).

interview

When I was a kid I remember seeing **Doctor Strangelove** in Torquay, and then wandering home just in awe of this feature film. It was like a different world. At the time I hadn't really been out of Devon much – I was a real country boy. What's so great about the film industry is that people come from such diverse backgrounds, and each person's way in is so totally different. My own background was in photography and documentary. I'd characterise myself as an observer. I'm quite shy and I've always been happy to stand back and watch the world around me. That's perhaps why I was initially drawn to fly-on-the-wall documentation through stills and film; but ultimately I began to feel that it was too voyeuristic. I went to countries like Eritrea and Rhodesia where there was a lot of strife, a lot of poverty; I saw some harrowing things. I found it increasingly difficult to distance myself from what I witnessed. Making a documentary in a mental hospital, there came a point when I actually couldn't film something; it was just too uncomfortable for me. I knew then that I couldn't go

"I rarely look at specific painters or photographers, or even other films, when I'm preparing a movie, but this jumble of images includes some of the paintings, films and photographs I've grown up with which have influenced my way of seeing things." *(left from above)*: El Greco, 'The Trinity', c.1577/79; Henry Fuseli, 'The Nightmare'; Vincent van Gogh, 'The Potato Eaters', 1885; Giorgio de Chirico, 'The Silent Statue' (Ariadne), 1913; Edward Hopper, 'From Williamsburg Bridge', 1928; *(above, centre)*: William Blake, 'The First Book of Urizen: Man Floating Upside Down', 1794; *(below, centre)*: J.W.M. Turner, 'Whalers'; Winslow Homer, 'Summer Night', 1890; *(below, right)*: Edvard Munch, 'The Storm', 1893.

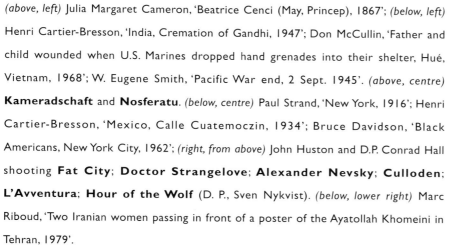

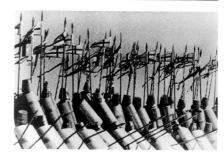

(above, left) Julia Margaret Cameron, 'Beatrice Cenci (May, Princep), 1867'; (below, left)
Henri Cartier-Bresson, 'India, Cremation of Gandhi, 1947'; Don McCullin, 'Father and
child wounded when U.S. Marines dropped hand grenades into their shelter, Hué,
Vietnam, 1968'; W. Eugene Smith, 'Pacific War end, 2 Sept. 1945'. (above, centre)
Kameradschaft and **Nosferatu**. (below, centre) Paul Strand, 'New York, 1916'; Henri
Cartier-Bresson, 'Mexico, Calle Cuatemoczin, 1934'; Bruce Davidson, 'Black
Americans, New York City, 1962'; (right, from above) John Huston and D.P. Conrad Hall
shooting **Fat City**; **Doctor Strangelove**; **Alexander Nevsky**; **Culloden**;
L'Avventura; **Hour of the Wolf** (D. P., Sven Nykvist). (below, lower right) Marc
Riboud, 'Two Iranian women passing in front of a poster of the Ayatollah Khomeini in
Tehran, 1979'.

roger deakins

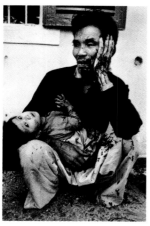

on making documentaries. However, something of the motivation that initially drew me to that medium has stayed with me. I've always wanted to understand the world around me, and communicate my experience of it to other people. For that reason, I've tried only to do films that touch me personally and that I feel are worth doing. My benchmark is John Huston's **Fat City**. It was the first Hollywood feature I saw that used a real situation, migrant workers in Stockton in a boxing scenario. It brought a whole world to life in a very truthful and accessible way. And Conrad Hall's cinematography was inspirational – it wasn't just about technique; there was so much humanity in it.

I've never consciously set out to do anything radical or different or new. I just try to picture things the way I see them, which means working without preconceptions about how things should be done. There's this whole school of thinking which says you must have keylight, back-light, fill-light, a kicker. Well, how many Rembrandt paintings have got anything except for one soft source light? Basically they're lit by north light coming through one big studio window. That's it. No kickers. No back-light. I'm not saying you should throw the manual out, but I do believe that every situation demands a different look. If you think naturalistically – as I do – there's an infinite number of ways to light the face, depending on the circumstances. Working on documentaries definitely helped me appreciate this; it also made me realise how little light you can get away with. Often I'll light a big sequence and I won't have a single conventional film light on the set. **Kundun**, the film I shot for Martin Scorsese, was lit mainly

with oil lamps, and with little kit bulbs on dimmers to give the effect of candlelight.

Some people have said of **Dead Man Walking**: "Oh, there's not much to shout about in the photography, is there?" And there isn't. When I first met Tim Robbins to discuss it, he said he wanted it to look anonymous. As a cinematographer, you might think, "well, what's in it for me?" But that's not really what it's about. It's about the script and the story. The best photography, I'm afraid, is the photography which doesn't get any mention (the best films are the ones where you don't single out any one element, you just say, "what a great movie"). I used to do a lot of rock videos and if the band was no good, you'd move the camera a lot and do flashy lighting. But if it was someone like Eric Clapton or Muddy Waters, you really didn't want to do much. You'd light it simply and just let the camera watch them. It's a similar thing with movies. I tend to gravitate to more intimate films, and you don't want technique to interfere with the storytelling. I try to make everything appear seamless; if you change the focal length of the lens or the style of the lighting without justification, the audience will be jolted out of the flow of the film, even if only subconsciously. Sometimes I'm in awe of stylish, eye-catching cinematography, but mostly it's done purely for effect; style with no content. I always start with the script. What's the scene about? What's going on in the characters' minds? How can I reflect that in the lighting or the composition? How will the different shots that make up a scene juxtapose with each other? How will all the scenes that combine to make the whole movie interrelate?

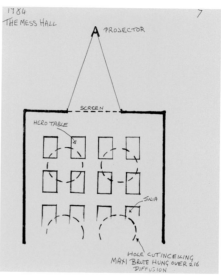

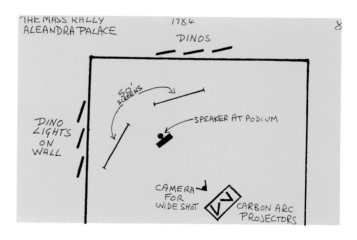

1984's desaturated look was obtained by bleach by-pass printing. "The process's only disadvantage is that you can't vary colour levels. As we wanted some idealised shots of rolling, golden countryside to have a heightened beauty *(top right)*, I had to rely on heavy orange filtration to enhance the colour." *(centre, left & right)* "The mess hall set was built on location. A hole cut in the wall facilitated the depth required for back projection of the telescreen image. Holes were cut in the ceiling to accommodate pools of light with little spill (so as not to pollute the projection)." *(above, left & right)* "Shooting the mass rally, our main concern was to make the telescreens part of the scene, so actors and extras could react to the images on them, which were projected as in a cinema (the screens were coated with a paint usually used for front projection, which gives a bolder picture and more reflected light)."

(above, right) **Mountains of the Moon** (1990): "I didn't want David Lean epic-style photography, but to draw the audience into the story with a quieter, elegant style. Primarily the story is about two men and their relationship." *(left)* For Martin Scorsese, the way Deakins applied colour in the film "like a painter" and used naturalistic light made the D.P. a natural choice to shoot **Kundun** (1998). On the film, "more a poem than a traditional narrative", Deakins worked from the meticulous shot structure which Scorsese had planned in advance, and which included complex set-ups like a dream which begins tight on Kundun's eyes and lifts away to reveal him standing in a field of dead monks. "We combined a 18–100mm zoom lens with an Akela crane move which took us up to 75 feet, and then added the last part of the move digitally and composited more corpses into the edges of the shot."

It's important to have an overall concept of a film's look which will enhance the story. When I shot **1984** for Michael Radford, we wanted to reflect the fact that George Orwell was not writing science fiction, but an allegory about post-war Europe (I've got a copy of his original manuscript, which was entitled '1948'). Michael eschewed the temptation of a high-tech look and went for design in which everything was made from Bakelite. We talked about shooting in black and white – but the financiers wouldn't hear of it. So I began to explore ways of desaturating the colours with the lab, and we came up with a process that had never been used before on a feature – the bleach by-pass. Usually, in printing a film, the bleach bath removes the silver crystals after they have catalysed the colour couplers. By skipping the bleach, the image retains the silver, which acts as a black-and-white emulsion layer. This gives you a really striking desaturated colour image that's partly black-and-white. The bleach by-pass worked for **1984** because it was organic to the film's content. For **The Shawshank Redemption**, I thought of using ENR, which is similar to the bleach by-pass but gives you more colour control. I'd always loved the ENR look, and initially I felt it would suit the subject; I'd light the film softly, naturalistically – but ENR would put some guts into it. Ultimately, I decided against it because I was worried it would be too 'in your face'. I wanted to give the film a very simple and consistent look. So I settled on a contrasty naturalism, with a cool grey look for the day scenes (obtained by pulling out the colour-correction filter) and a sickly, yellow, nicotine-stained kind of look for the night scenes. However, to achieve the photographic style of a film, you are dependent on the relationship you have with the production designer. In order to get the cool grey atmosphere we were after on **The Shawshank Redemption**, designer Terry Marsh and I had to discuss exactly what shade he painted the prison walls. And on **1984**, because the bleach by-pass process desaturated the colours, Allan Cameron, the designer, had to paint his walls bright yellow in order for them to come out the creamy colour he wanted (similarly, the colours in costume and make-up had to be exaggerated). As cinematographer, you're also reliant on the designer to build into the set the sources you require for lighting. Sometimes, as with Terry and Allan, you work together in total synchronicity and the solutions to problems come out of the relationship. Other times, it can be a struggle. You'll say, "this set's great, but we've got one day scene which the director and I want to play in a wide shot and I'd like to have a soft side-light effect – so I could really do with a window here." Some designers react as if your trying to violate their work. When this happens, it's sad and frustrating for the D.P.

Although I'll always have a visual concept for a film, I like to work from instinct when we shoot. To some extent, this is imposed on you by circumstance. A lot of the films I work on tend to be shot on location, which can be very unpredictable and difficult to control. You may want a particular shot at 10am because the light will be ideal, for example, but it's not going to happen because the actors aren't out of the trailer. Or the weather may not be what you hoped for. So you have to compromise and to some degree, make your lighting up as you go along. I enjoy working like this – spontaneity can be beneficial, both to the actors and look of the finished film.

On set, I'm very energetic and hands-on. I like to be totally involved in the whole process. I also insist on operating the camera myself. There's a lot of antagonism towards camera-men who operate – it's a job-protection thing, which I can understand – but I can't work that way. Cinematography to me is so much about the composition and the way the camera moves, and that is very instinctive to me. Working with Joel and Ethan Coen (or Martin Scorsese), for whom the camera is often like a character, you can sense when there's something slightly wrong with the mechanics of a shot, and adjust the camera movement and framing so it exactly expresses what is required of the scene. It's all to do with subtle differences – how quickly something comes into focus, for example; and you can't gauge that by watching on a video monitor. There are other reasons for operating. On **Kundun**, we were working with Tibetans who'd never acted before. So we wanted them to feel comfortable and not overawed by the situation. Having a smaller group of people around the camera definitely helped and enabled me to have one-to-one contact with them. Also, Marty is famously specific about his camera movement; so if we did a first take and the actors didn't hit their marks, it wouldn't be a big deal, I could adjust the shot to accommodate them, and give them a bit more freedom. Even with professionals, I prefer this way of work-ing; I hate being in the actor's face. I work with an assistant who hardly ever uses tape measures; he gets his focus by eye. The camera department should be as unobtrusive as possible to give the actors the freedom they need to do their work.

I choose the films I work on very carefully, and I'm bitterly disappointed if they don't turn out as we hoped. I became very disillusioned with the business after **Air America** (we had **M.A.S.H.** in mind when we started; the studio ensured it ended up a lightweight buddy movie), and at that point I was honestly thinking of backing off, moving to the country and doing only low-budget British films. By a wonderful stroke of luck, I got the call from the Coen brothers to shoot **Barton Fink** and my enthusiasm was rekindled. They are wonderful to work with. Everything goes up on the screen, there's no waste. They really involve me in the prep (I do my best work when I have enough time to thoroughly prep a film in pre-production) – scouting locations together, discussing the storyboards. Most important, I love the work they do. People sometimes say to me, "you've got such a great list of credits – you're so lucky." But frankly, if I don't feel a film is worth doing, I turn it down. I'd rather leave the industry than do a violent action picture which makes me think, "this is not what I want to say to an audience." OK, I'm only the cameraman, but the film's got my name on it and I'm putting my life in it. I know one has to earn a living, but I think a lot of people compromise too much too early. What happens is that you build a reputation for doing a certain kind of film. In L.A. especially, you are what you've done – not what you'd like to do. People look at your credits; they don't give a damn about your talent. So if you start your career doing action movies, that's what you're going to be offered. My roundabout advice to an aspiring cinematographer would be, try to figure out the kind of film you really want to do, and stick to it. Compromise as little as you possibly can.

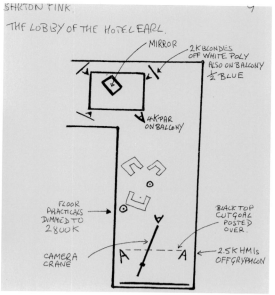

BARTON FINK.
THE LOBBY OF THE HOTEL EARL.

MIRROR

2K BLONDES OFF WHITE POLY
ALSO ON BALCONY ½ BLUE

4K PAR ON BALCONY

BLACK TOP CUT GOAL POSTED OVER.

FLOOR PRACTICALS DIMMED TO 2800K

CAMERA CRANE

2.5K HMIs OFF GRYPHALON

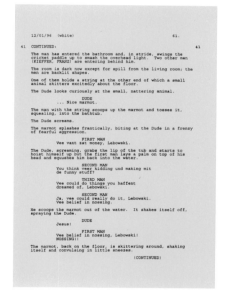

12/01/96 (white)   61.

41   CONTINUED: 41

The man has entered the bathroom and, in stride, swings the
cricket paddle up to smash the overhead light. Two other men
(KIEFFER, FRANZ) are entering behind him.

The room is dark now except for spill from the living room; the
men are backlit shapes.

One of them holds a string at the other end of which a small
animal skitters excitedly about the floor.

The Dude looks curiously at the small, nattering animal.

                    DUDE
              ... Nice marmot.

The man with the string scoops up the marmot and tosses it,
squealing, into the bathtub.

The Dude screams.

The marmot splashes frantically, biting at the Dude in a frenzy
of fearful aggression.

                    FIRST MAN
              Vee vant zat money, Lebowski.

The Dude, screaming, grabs the lip of the tub and starts to
hoist himself up but the first man lays a palm on top of his
head and squashes him back into the water.

                    SECOND MAN
              You think veer kidding und making mit
              de funny stuff?

                    THIRD MAN
              Vee could do things you haffent
              dreamed of, Lebowski.

                    SECOND MAN
              Ja, vee could really do it, Lebowski.
              Vee belief in nossing.

He scoops the marmot out of the water. It shakes itself off,
spraying the Dude.

                    DUDE
              Jesus!

                    FIRST MAN
              Vee belief in nossing, Lebowski!
              NOSSING!!

The marmot, back on the floor, is skittering around, shaking
itself and convulsing in little sneezes.

                                              (CONTINUED)

'THE BIG LEBOWSKI'   SCENE 41
                                      SET-UP 5

5. Med. Close on the Marmot at the end of his lead.

'THE BIG LEBOWSKI'   SCENE 41
                                      SET-UP 6

6. Pull on the bathtub as Dieter throws the marmot in.

'THE BIG LEBOWSKI'   SCENE 41
                                      SET-UP 6A

6a. Reverse for Marmot in and out--also hold for POV thrashing with
    marmot-on-a-stick.

'THE BIG LEBOWSKI'   SCENE 41
                                      SET-UP 7

7. POP IN closer on the tub for thrashing with the marmot.

Working with the Coen Brothers is for Deakins a truly collaborative process, and he
is very involved in the location-scouting and storyboarding process. *(top right)*
Barton Fink (1991), with lighting plan for the hotel lobby with a dramatic shaft of
sunlight effect: "A very different, upfront style of shooting for me: the camera is
almost like a character, drawing you through the film." *(above, lower left)* **The
Hudsucker Proxy** (1994): "Because the story was such a pastiche of '40s screwball
comedy, I felt it would be too much if we had lit it in that style; so I went right against
it and used colour to soften it and make it more contemporary, despite the period
setting." *(above, top left)* **Fargo** (1996): "The whole concept was that this was a true
story, so the camera was restrained, observational." *(above & right)* Script and storyboard for the 'marmot sequence' of **The Big Lebowski** (1998).

(above, left) **Dead Man Walking** (1995): "The visual evolution of Sean and Susan's relationship was structured so the barrier between them seemed to dissolve as they grew close. First we used wider lenses so Sean was less visible through the wire and used hard frontal light, like the sun coming out from a cloud, to make the wire screen even more present. Later we shot with increasingly long lenses, tracking in to reveal Sean and using small sections of mesh of a different gauge, reducing the interference. Later, when they talk through glass, wire would have been 'truer' to the actual events but the openness of the glass and the use of reflections was a better dramatic statement and a good transition to the point before Sean's execution where they can physically touch."

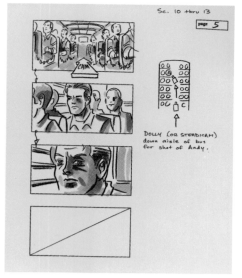

Sc. 10 thru 13
page 5

DOLLY (OR STEADICAM)
down aisle of bus
for shot of ANDY.

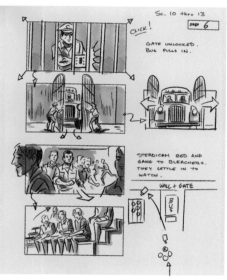

Sc. 10 thru 13
page 6

CLICK!

GATE UNLOCKED.
BUS PULLS IN.

STEADICAM RED AND
GANG TO BLEACHERS.
THEY SETTLE IN TO
WATCH.

WALL + GATE

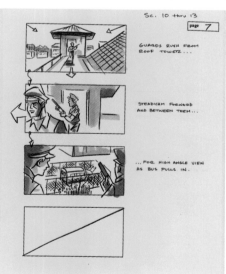

Sc. 10 thru 13
page 7

GUARDS RUSH FROM
ROOF TOWER...

STEADICAM FORWARD
AND BETWEEN THEM...

...FOR HIGH ANGLE VIEW
AS BUS PULLS IN.

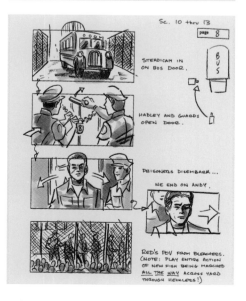

Sc. 10 thru 13
page 8

STEADICAM IN
ON BUS DOOR.

HADLEY AND GUARDS
OPEN DOOR.

PRISONERS DISEMBARK...
WE END ON ANDY.

RED'S POV FROM BLEACHERS.
(NOTE: PLAY ENTIRE ACTION
OF NEW FISH BEING MARCHED
ALL THE WAY ACROSS YARD
THROUGH HECKLERS!)

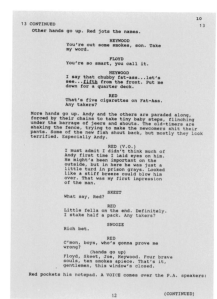

10 CONTINUED   10

     RED emerges into fading daylight, slouches low-key through the
     activity, worn cap on his head, exchanging hellos and doing
     minor business. He's an important man here.

                    RED (V.O.)
               There's a con like me in every prison
               in America, I guess. I'm the guy who
               can get it for you. Cigarettes, a
               bag of reefer if you're partial, a
               bottle of brandy to celebrate your
               kid's high school graduation. Damn
               near anything, within reason.

     He slips somebody a pack of smokes, smooth sleight-of-hand.

                    RED (V.O.)
               Yes sir, I'm a regular Sears &
               Roebuck.

     TWO SHORT SIREN BLASTS issue from the main tower, drawing
     everybody's attention to the loading dock. The outer gate
     swings open...revealing a gray prison bus outside.

                    RED (V.O.)
               So when Andy Dufresne came to me in
               1949 and asked me to smuggle Rita
               Hayworth into the prison for him, I
               told him no problem. And it wasn't.

                    CON
               Fresh fish! Fresh fish today!

     Red is joined by HEYWOOD, SKEET, FLOYD, JIGGER, ERNIE, SNOOZE.
     Most cons crowd to the fence to gawk and jeer, but Red and his
     group mount the bleachers and settle in comfortably.

11   INT - PRISON BUS - DUSK (1947)   11

     Andy sits in back, wearing steel collar and chains.

                    RED (V.O.)
               Andy came to Shawshank Prison in
               early 1947 for murdering his wife
               and the fella she was bangin'.

     The bus lurches forward, RUMBLES through the gates. Andy gazes
     around, swallowed by prison walls.

                    RED (V.O.)
               On the outside, he'd been vice-
               president of a large Portland bank.
               Good work for a man as young as he
               was, when you consider how
               conservative banks were back then.

                              10

13 CONTINUED   10
                                                               13
     Other hands go up. Red jots the names.

                    HEYWOOD
               You're out some smokes, son. Take
               my word.

                    FLOYD
               You're so smart, you call it.

                    HEYWOOD
               I say that chubby fat-ass...let's
               see...fifth from the front. Put me
               down for a quarter deck.

                    RED
               That's five cigarettes on Fat-Ass.
               Any takers?

     More hands go up. Andy and the others are paraded along,
     forced by their chains to take tiny baby steps, flinching
     under the barrage of jeers and shouts. The old-timers are
     shaking the fence, trying to make the newcomers shit their
     pants. Some of the new fish shout back, but mostly they look
     terrified. Especially Andy.

                    RED (V.O.)
               I must admit I didn't think much of
               Andy first time I laid eyes on him.
               He might'a been important on the
               outside, but in here he was just a
               little turd in prison grays. Looked
               like a stiff breeze could blow him
               over. That was my first impression
               of the man.

                    SKEET
               What say, Red?

                    RED
               Little fella on the end. Definitely.
               I stake half a pack. Any takers?

                    SNOOZE
               Rich bet.

                    RED
               C'mon, boys, who's gonna prove me
               wrong?
                    (hands go up)
               Floyd, Skeet, Joe, Heywood. Four brave
               souls, ten smokes apiece. That's it,
               gentlemen, this window's closed.

     Red pockets his notepad. A VOICE comes over the P.A. speakers:

                              12   (CONTINUED)

12   EXT - PRISON YARD - DUSK (1947)   12

                    TOWER GUARD
               All clear!

     GUARDS approach the bus with carbines. The door jerks open.
     The new fish disembark, chained together single-file, blinking
     sourly at their surroundings. Andy stumbles against the MAN in
     front of him, almost drags him down.
     BYRON HADLEY, captain of the guard, slams his baton into
     Andy's back. Andy goes to his knees, gasping in pain. JEERS
     and SHOUTS from the spectators.

                    HADLEY
               On your feet before I fuck you up
               so bad you never walk again.

13   ON THE BLEACHERS   13

                    RED
               There they are, boys. The Human
               Charm Bracelet.

                    HEYWOOD
               Never seen such a sorry-lookin'
               heap of maggot shit in my life.

               Comin' from you, Heywood, you being
               so pretty and all...

                    FLOYD
               Takin' bets today, Red?

                    RED
                    (pulls notepad and pencil)
               Bear Catholic? Pope shit in the woods?
               Smokes or coin, bettor's choice.

                    FLOYD
               Smokes. Put me down for two.

                    RED
               High roller. Who's your horse?

                    FLOYD
               That gangly sack of shit, third
               from the front. He'll be the first.

                    HEYWOOD
               Bullshit. I'll take that action.

                    ERNIE
               Me too.

                              11   (CONTINUED)

13 CONTINUED   11
                                                               13
                    VOICE (amplified)
               Return to your cellblocks for
               evening count.

14   INT - ADMITTING AREA - DUSK (1947)   14

     The new fish are marched in. Guards unlock the shackles. The
     chains drop away, rattling to the stone floor.

                    HADLEY
               Eyes front.

     WARDEN SAMUEL NORTON strolls forth, a colorless man in a gray
     suit and a church pin in his lapel. He looks like he could
     piss ice water. He appraises the newcomers with flinty eyes.

                    NORTON
               This is Mr. Hadley, captain of the
               guard. I am Mr. Norton, the warden.
               You are sinners and scum, that's
               why they sent you to me. Rule
               number one: no blaspheming. I'll
               not have the Lord's name taken in
               vain in my prison. The other rules
               you'll figure out as you go along.
               Any questions?

                    JIGGER
               When do we eat?

     Cued by Norton's glance, Hadley steps up to the con and screams
     right in his face:

                    HADLEY
               YOU EAT WHEN WE SAY YOU EAT! YOU
               PISS WHEN WE SAY YOU PISS! YOU SHIT
               WHEN WE SAY YOU SHIT! YOU SLEEP
               WHEN WE SAY YOU SLEEP! YOU MAGGOT-
               DICK MOTHERFUCKER!

     Hadley rams the tip of his club into the con's belly. The
     man falls to his knees, gasping and clutching himself.
     Hadley takes his place at Norton's side again. Softly:

                    NORTON
               Any other questions?
                    (there are none)
               I believe in two things. Discipline
               and the Bible. Here, you'll receive
               both.
                    (holds up a Bible)
               Put your faith in the Lord. Your
               ass belongs to me. Welcome to
               Shawshank.

                              13   (CONTINUED)

(above, & far left) **The Shawshank Redemption** (1994): Deakins was involved with the storyboarding process from day one with director Frank Darabont (above right, with Deakins) and artist Peter von Sholley. (left) "The inmate arriving sequence was carefully storyboarded and we pretty well stuck to it." Deakins says of his work on the film: "Probably the most consistent film I've done in terms of its look; it had a unity of style and feeling which pleased me more than anything else I've done to date."

biography

Born in Lisbon, Eduardo Serra studied engineering before political activities against Salazar's Fascist dictatorship forced him to leave Portugal. A passionate film-lover from an early age, Serra became a student in the prestigious Vaugirard film school (now Ecole Louis Lumière) in Paris (amongst his fellow students was D.P. Philippe Rousselot). He also took a degree in History of Art and Archaeology at the Sorbonne

eduardo serra

interview

before becoming a camera assistant to Pierre Lhomme, whom Serra regards as being the father of modern French cinematography and a great influence on his own work. Since becoming a D.P. in 1980, Serra has shot over 35 feature films. His collaboration with Patrice Leconte has produced five films, including **The Hairdresser's Husband** (1990), **Tango** (1992), **Le Parfum d'Yvonne** (1993), and **Les Grands Ducs** (1995). He also shot Vincent Ward's epic romance, **Map of the Human Heart** (1991), Michel Blanc's **Grosse Fatigue** (1993), Peter Chelsom's **Funny Bones** (1994), and Claude Chabrol's **Rien Ne Va Plus** (1996). His imaginative and sensitive use of colour has enabled two films to transcend period, literary sources: **Jude** (1996, directed by Michael Winterbottom) and **The Wings of the Dove** (directed by Iain Softley) for which Serra was Academy Award-nominated and won a BAFTA in 1998. In 1997, he shot **What Dreams May Come** for Vincent Ward; in 1998, new films with Leconte and Chabrol in France.

I feel very much a part of the family of people who refer to natural light – an attitude usually thought of as modern in the world of film-making, but which is deeply rooted in art history. Until the Renaissance, painting represented the world on a symbolic level; but with the emergence of humanism and a new way of relating to the world, painting aspired to be true to nature and sought to reproduce perspective in order to create a rational sense of space. Light revealed this space, and particular attention was paid to its nature – to where it came from and also, more and more, to how it modelled the subject's features. (If you compare an early Renaissance portrait to a late Rembrandt one, you understand how light circled around the viewer and subject – changing from an idealised, almost frontal light, to a dramatic three-quarter back-light). This treatment of light is the contemporary cinematographer's proper heritage – but it is only relatively recently that we have been able to claim it. For much of this century, the prevailing aesthetic has been determined by the influence of theatrical lighting (where the actor is illuminated by beams of light) and also by the technical shortcomings of the medium. Because we needed a lot of light to register an image on film, it was difficult to work with, for example, practical lamps or bounced light (the photographic style that evolved gave us those magical shots of Marlene Dietrich in **Shanghai Express**). But that era has gone. Such 'magic' necessitated an inflexible, stylised screen-acting technique. Actors would have to struggle to maintain an eyeline in the face of blinding light sources, while hitting one position – from which they could not move – for optimum lighting. The look was also achieved with heavy make-up – a sculptured mask of ideal beauty. Today's sharper lenses and fine-grain colour emulsions require very light make-up. Just as the contemporary screen actor's craft has become rooted in naturalism, we as cinematographers – supported by more responsive and flexible technology – are at last connected with an earlier period in art history (even if we don't consciously realise it).

My starting point is always the space we are shooting in. I am very careful in my lighting not to disrupt the architecture of a set or location, but rather to respect the logic of the space. So if light would naturally enter through a window, I'll avoid having a light source coming from another angle that would confuse or disrupt that logic. I also try never to put in any more light than is needed. If we can shoot without artificial lighting, good, it is often the best choice. Because I try to avoid the theatrical convention of beams of light, I prefer to use bounced or diffused lights, which give me better

modelling while being 'friendly' to the actors. I always think of the actors; I like them to feel comfortable, to have a degree of freedom, so that if they miss a mark, it doesn't ruin the shot. Working with one big light source facilitates this freedom. If you work with, say, ten small projectors coming from every angle, you soon find shadows multiplying across the set like cancerous cells. My approach also means that I can work fast, so the momentum of the director and the actors isn't broken. I try to make everything I do simple, quick and inexpensive. It's almost a moral imperative for me – films cost a lot of money, and I hate the idea of spending any more money than is necessary.

I have always been interested in unconventional lights, especially fluorescent lights – they produce a large source, but they are not blinding. They are cool and quiet, and they don't throw shadows on to the back walls. You can assemble them to any size or shape. I knew from film school that something akin to the fluorescent tube was widely used on silent films, but this high-pressure mercury lamp was unsuitable for modern emulsions. In 1980, when I started working as a D.P., the poor quality of fluorescent tubes kept them away from film sets. I first used tubes to light an entire set in 1983 – but I had to ship them over from the U.S. Since then, the quality of the tubes you can buy in any shop around the corner has improved with amazing rapidity. Today, such tubes are better than HMIs (the standard lights used in filming exteriors). When I photographed **Le Mari de la Coiffeuse (The Hairdresser's Husband)**, the producer urged me to use the space lights commonly used to combine the strong light of the

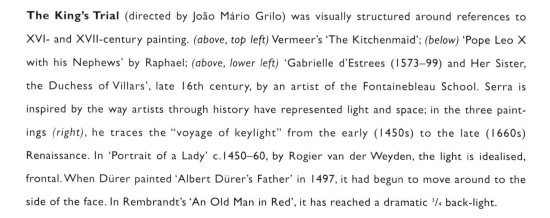

The King's Trial (directed by João Mário Grilo) was visually structured around references to XVI- and XVII-century painting. *(above, top left)* Vermeer's 'The Kitchenmaid'; *(below)* 'Pope Leo X with his Nephews' by Raphael; *(above, lower left)* 'Gabrielle d'Estrees (1573–99) and Her Sister, the Duchess of Villars', late 16th century, by an artist of the Fontainebleau School. Serra is inspired by the way artists through history have represented light and space; in the three paintings *(right)*, he traces the "voyage of keylight" from the early (1450s) to the late (1660s) Renaissance. In 'Portrait of a Lady' c.1450–60, by Rogier van der Weyden, the light is idealised, frontal. When Dürer painted 'Albert Dürer's Father' in 1497, it had begun to move around to the side of the face. In Rembrandt's 'An Old Man in Red', it has reached a dramatic $^3/_4$ back-light.

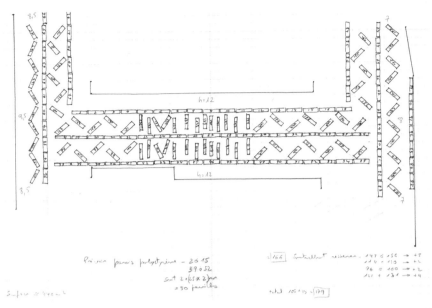

cinematography

The Hairdresser's Husband (1990): Serra was influenced by the light in Joel Meyerowitz's photographs of Cape Cod *(top left)*. Seeking to reproduce on a studio set the soft, even, shadowless light which drops from the sky, Serra decided to use fluorescents. It was the first time they had been used for this purpose, even though banks of fluorescent-like mercury lights were used for silent films like Fritz Lang's **Metropolis** *(above, right)*. Serra: "It was a really great moment when we switched them on for the first time." *(above)* Serra's lighting diagram and the production stills show how the fluorescents were arranged over the street of the hairdressing salon.

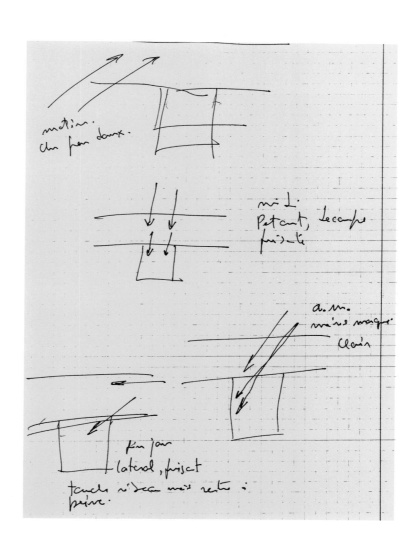

Serra's diagram (and accompanying stills) *(above)*, show the positions of the light source he used to simulate the sun at different times of day in relation to the hairdressing salon: the soft early morning light; the strong midday light; the less contrasty, bright afternoon light; and the slanting end-of-day light which strikes the front of the salon but does not really penetrate inside. Part of Serra's – and director Leconte's – philosophy is that, in the studio, you have to let things go out of control just as they would on location; hence the overexposed quality of the midday/afternoon scenes in the film.

Map of the Human Heart (1991): to make the bombing scenes in the film authentic, Serra avoided conventional film lights: "I didn't have a single projector, just fire, and flares, and welding equipment." While researching the film's Inuit background, Serra was inspired by the period photographs of the French explorer, Paul-Emile Victor, which recorded Eskimo life. He used the image *(above)* showing a hut interior, illuminated by a lamp containing reindeer oil on a bed of moss, as a reference for the scene *(lower left)*.

sun with the soft light coming from the canopy of the sky. But I didn't feel that they would produce the kind of light I wanted. I finally decided to use 400 fluorescent tubes which gave me a soft, even light with no shadows. To my knowledge, this had never been done before. It was regarded as something of a gamble – so the moment when we switched them on was very exciting.

There are a lot of long-established rules and received wisdoms in cinematography. For example, I was taught that if you shoot at night, you should use a blue back-light on the street. After shooting three or four features, I began to think, "wait a minute, why am I doing this? It's not how I want the scene to look..." I killed the back-light, and tried to do something more appropriate for the film. I also never liked the conventional way of lighting fire-lit scenes with flickering electric light – it always seemed artificial to me. So whenever I need to have firelight, I illuminate the action with real fire – flares, torches, gas fire, welding equipment. The bombing scenes in **Map of the Human Heart** were lit entirely by fire. Likewise, the foreground action in the Venice carnival scenes shot for **The Wings of the Dove** (for the very wide shots, I had to use some artificial light in the backgrounds). It's important to acknowledge that some of the established rules and traditions belong to previous eras. Black-and-white required back-light for separation. Technicolor required light everywhere! Today, however, with the fast colour stocks, we no longer have the same technical problems – and yet, one finds that certain traditions become ingrained in the industry. So as a cinematographer, you really have to assert yourself if you want to have any control over the industrial machine. Early in my career, I remember shooting in a studio where the production designer assumed I'd need catwalks from which to hang lights over the set (the standard approach). No sooner had he rigged them, than the gaffer was hanging a panoply of lights on them – and it was so easy to switch them on! As a result, I found myself working with lighting that was not at all what I had in mind for the scene. In the U.S., especially, they're so used to doing things a certain way (and doing them so well) that the machine can run quite happily without the D.P.; so if you want to impose your will on the machine, it requires some effort – and you cannot afford to be wrong.

When I'm choosing projects, who is directing is always a more important consideration than the screenplay; this approach is common in France, where we tend to attach more importance to the vision of a film-maker – to the way a story will be visually translated into a film – rather than to the script itself. In America, the written word plays a much more fundamental role in the film-making process. Working with Patrice Leconte (for whom I've shot five films) was complete joy. He knows exactly what he wants, and he'll often express it very succinctly in just one sentence. While we were preparing **The Hairdresser's Husband**, he described the atmosphere of the film with these words: "It's summer, the south of France, all the light comes through the window; have in mind the moment just before perspiration begins to appear on the skin." Clear, simple, evocative direction. Because he knows exactly what kind of film he is making and is always very honest, he provides a strong framework for everyone to

cinematography

JUDE STOCK BREAKDOWN
THIS LIST DATED 29.9.95

SCENES			STOCK AND PROCESS		
OPENING/TITLES	1	TO 8	KODAK PLUS-X	(5231)	NORMAL PROCESS
MARYGREEN	9	TO 34	FUJI F-500	(8514)	PULLED ONE STOP
	35	TO 41A	FUJI F-500	(8514)	NORMAL PROCESS
CHRISTMINSTER	42	TO 90E	KODAK 500T	(5298)	NORMAL PROCESS
MELCHESTER	91	TO 125	FUJI F-125	(8530)	NORMAL PROCESS
			FUJI F-500	(8514)	NORMAL PROCESS
SHASTON	126	TO 137	KODAK 100-T	(5248)	NORMAL PROCESS
			KODAK 500-T	(5298)	NORMAL PROCESS
ALBRICKHAM	137A	TO 147	KODAK 500-T	(5298)	NORMAL PROCESS
	147A	TO 163	KODAK 500-T	(5298)	BLEACH BYPASS
CHRISTMINSTER (2)	164	TO 202	KODAK 500-T	(5298)	BLEACH BYPASS & 2 ADDED STAGES

STOCK BREAKDOWN FOR WHOLE SHOOT

TYPE	% OF FILM	% 1000'S/400'S	TAKE TO DURHAM/EDINB
KODAK PLUS-X (5231)	4	--/100	10,000 Ft
KODAK 100-T (7248)	4	80/20	5,000 Ft
KODAK 500-T (5298)	62	90/10	25,000 Ft
FUJI F-125 (8530)	9	85/15	10,000 Ft
FUJI F-500 (8514)	21	85/15	25,000 Ft

Jude (1996): Serra used different stocks and printing processes, combined with his lighting and composition, to evoke the atmosphere appropriate to each stage of the developing story, from its black-and-white prologue and summery 'watercolour' first act (in Marygreen), to the dark, tragic conclusion, where he used bleach by-pass to give a strong monochrome feeling to the photography.

work within, to take risks. Shooting for someone like Vincent Ward is very different. It's exciting, because Vincent is a visionary; he has a visual arts background and is not at all a traditional film director. Vincent ignores the conventions of film-making and builds the structure entirely from his own extremely visual imagination. Claude Chabrol, meanwhile, has no interest in modern film technology. He avoids tight close-ups and uses only medium-range lenses to choreograph the relations between characters. His restrained style evokes, to me, the pre-war American film, particularly those of Lubitsch.

When you shoot a commercial, the image is the message. On a feature film, the story is the message. I cannot work on a film by just walking on to a set and relying on the inspiration of the moment to decide how I photograph it. Before shooting begins, I like to build a lighting structure in my mind that will make visible the dramatic structure of the script. The best example in my work is Jude, the narrative of which unfolded over a long period of time and contained very different emotional and dramatic moods. The director Michael Winterbottom and I discussed how to approach each 'chapter' in the story, in terms of light and colour. The opening of the film – Jude as a child – is shot in black-and-white. If you shoot on colour negative and print it to black-and-white (which is the usual and easiest route), you only get colourless images – like when you turn the colour switch down on a TV set. But to have real black-and-white photography you have to use its tools, and mainly its extended filtration possibilities. For young Jude finding his first wife, we opted for a soft,

romantic look. I shot on Fuji film, which is softer than Kodak. Filters were used to give the images warmth. I 'pulled' the film in the developing process – the opposite to pushing it, so instead of processing for a longer time and getting more speed, you process less and lose contrast and speed. This technique, used with direct sunlight, gives a transparent look – as close to watercolour as we can get on film (as I had previously found when shooting **Le Parfum d'Yvonne**). As the narrative mood of **Jude** became progressively darker, I introduced Kodak, cooler filtration and side-lighting, which was more dramatic than the even light used in the opening section of the film. Towards the climax of the film, where the story becomes charged with intense emotion and despair, I began to light from three-quarters back and to use bleach by-pass in the labs (to introduce an element of black-and-white into the print). This gave the faces a feeling of stark drama. The look of the last sequences is almost monochromatic – there's very little colour in the images – which, of course, relates to the opening black-and-white sequences.

Jude contains some of my best work, but it also unfortunately illustrates how fragile and transitory the cinematographer's work can be. Usually, I try to control every part of the image's evolution. I direct the grading; I supervise the processing of the inter-negative and inter-positive; I view the release print. I also always try to oversee the film's video transfer; but often, by the time that this happens, I will have moved on to another project and may be unavailable. The danger is that if the transfer is done without the director or cinematographer present, the colourist has to work without any knowledge of

The visual look of **The Wings of the Dove** (1997) was arrived at through discussions between Serra, director Iain Softley and designer John Beard about what London and Venice, the two main locations in the story, represented in dramatic terms. London was depicted as colder, bluer in tone, where as Venice had a warmer, almost 'Oriental' look – a key reference was the painting of a Venetian fishmarket *(above)*, 'Pescheria Vecchia a Venezia' by Ettore Tito. For the carnival sequence, Serra employed fire-lit sources – torches and fire bars – apart from a few wide shots which required some artificial lighting. He also used the silver retaining process to secure rich blacks. *(far right)* Previsualisations for Vincent Ward's **What Dreams May Come** (1997). Computer-created by the art department, they simulate camera positions and movements, thus helping to decide how live action shots will be combined with computer-generated images that complete or extend the main set, seen in the accompanying photographs (with plan of the basic lighting set-up).

the requirements of specific scenes. So if he sees a cold blue image, or a warm orange image, he will adjust the levels to make it appear 'normal'. At present, there is no neutral setting as there is for printing in film laboratories (although some manufacturers and cinematographers' associations are working to change that). To my deep regret, neither Michael Winterbottom nor myself was able to attend the video transfer of **Jude** – and as a result, everything we worked so hard to achieve was nullified by the film's video release (which of course is when a large part of the audience sees a film).

Two principles inform everything I do. The first is, always question the rules which are presented to you. Some are good; others aren't (although they may have been at some earlier stage in the evolution of film technology). Secondly, never accept to become involved in any project that you suspect you may be ashamed of. Whatever you choose to do, you must do your best; so if you don't think a project deserves your best – all your commitment and talent and energy – then avoid it.

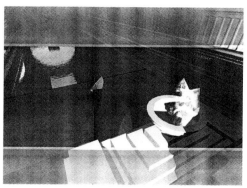

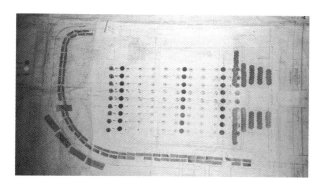

biography

Born in Poland in 1959, Janusz Kaminski arrived in the U.S. as a political refugee in 1981. He studied film at Columbia College in Chicago before moving to L.A., where he was accepted on to the American Film Institute's prestigious post-graduate programme as a cinematography student. In 1991, he shot **Wildflower**, directed by Diane Keaton and starring Patricia Arquette. Although destined for television, Kaminski

janusz kaminski

photographed it as though it were a theatrical feature. His efforts came to the attention of Steven Spielberg, and the rest is the stuff of Hollywood legend. Kaminski was assigned to **Schindler's List** (1993), his stunning, visceral black-and-white photography won an Oscar (and also the BAFTA for cinematography) and launched a collaboration with Spielberg that, after four films, suggests that we are witnessing the emergence of one of the great director/cinematographer part-nerships. Between his work with Spielberg on **Schindler's List** and **The Lost World: Jurassic Park** (1997), Kaminski shot **How To Make an American Quilt** (1995), for Jocelyn Moorhouse and **Jerry Maguire** (1996), for Cameron Crowe, building a body of work which shows a remarkable ability to adapt his sensitivity and style to the requirements of vastly differing stories. His partnership with Spielberg has contin-ued with **Amistad** (1997) and **Saving Private Ryan** (1998).

interview

What makes a cinematographer put the camera here rather than over there? What makes him light a particular scene from the left rather than the right? All one's experience of life subconsciously informs every creative decision one makes. That's what makes each individual cinematographer different. I think what shaped me visually was my experience of growing up in Poland – the grimness and oppression of life under a Communist regime. One wasn't allowed to go abroad; so movies automatically became a way of travel for me, showing us what the world beyond was like. My picture of life in the U.S. was formed by movies like **Easy Rider**, **The Graduate** and **Midnight Cowboy**, but when I arrived in New York in 1981, I encountered a radically different way of life – a country in the midst of enormous economic boom where people seemed to be obsessed with self-image. As a political refugee in this alien world, I came to feel a certain nostalgia for what I had left behind, for my childhood in eastern Europe; and also for the romantic view of America I

(left) Images from 'A Vanished World', Roman Vishniac's collection of photographs of Jewish life in Poland before the rise of Nazism. "I was so impressed by the pictures; he took them by himself, with no lights, and he created these amazing, timeless images. I love their realism: people in windows, in doorways, against snow in black traditional clothes." This naturalism formed the basis of the visual approach for **Schindler's List** (1993), translated into hand-held, documentary realism. *(right)* Pages from Kaminski's personal notebook with his preparatory notes and comments and results of filter tests for black-and-white shooting. Although the film was designed to be shot in black and white, a second camera shot around 100 scenes in colour, in order to dissolve between the two. Ultimately, however, the film's prologue, epilogue, and the red coat worn by a Jewish girl in the ghetto were the only colour images that remained.

— try to put dark object in
the frame, dark against bright
will help to create contrast

— don't be flashy for the sake
of being flashy

— make realistic photography, but
not a documentary style

— be stylish but not music-video
style

— be careful with faces
against sky — modify the
faces
— put light in the frame —
create flares in the lens with
duve fogs. —

Technical Informations

— a misty sky does not photograph
as dark as clear blue sky
I can't darken an overcast
sky by using filters

— the sky near the sun is less
blue and less affected than
the surrounding sky.

— a yellow filter blocks some of
blue light darkening the
shadows and stressing the
texture on the snow

— orange and light red will make
the skin whiter and suppress
the blemishes, evens up the sky

— to wash out the blue sky and
increase the haze effect use
blue filter

Filter tests for Black &
white photography
Based on my tests I choose
s this stop compensation

FILTERS

Type & color		Lens opening
3	Light yellow	1/2 stop
8	yellow	1 stop
12	Deep yellow	1 1/4 stop
15	Deep yellow	1 1/3 stop
21	orange	1 2/3 stop
23A	Light red	2 1/4 stop
25	red	3 stop
29	Deep red	4 stops
56	Light green	4
58	green	2 2/3
96		3 stops

had grown up with. I was also conscious that my status as an outsider enabled me to see my adopted country with fresh eyes, very objectively.

Once I had made up my mind to be a cinematographer, I never had any doubt that I would succeed. I worked really hard in film school; at weekends, when other students would go and hang out, I'd be asking around: "Do you want me to shoot your movie? Do you need a cinematographer?" Apparently, I became a legend around the school; nobody had ever worked so hard. So after five years of film school, I had close to forty 20-minute films; and my demo reel got me my first job. I think going to film school is essential – you learn about technique and theory, the history of cinema. You're surrounded by film-makers of the future and, as you shoot more and more, you start to think of yourself as a cameraman.

The first thing that attracts me to a project is the storyline. I care for the story much more than the lighting. There's always the temptation to create visually stunning images, but ultimately, my greatest concern is to stay true to the drama of the scene. Look at Philippe Rousselot (a cinematographer whose work I admire tremendously) – his lighting in **The People Vs. Larry Flynt** is completely unobtrusive. Or the way Roger Deakins photographed **Fargo** – it's so realistic, it barely feels lit. In both cases, the cinematography totally serves the story. It takes a lot more confidence, a lot more bravery, to shoot something like that than to create pictorially beautiful shots. I always try to use minimal lighting in order to give the director and the actors more freedom. The actors

are the primary communicators of the story, and if you start using a lot of lights, you restrict their space. I always try to leave at least 160 degrees open for the actors to move around in. My friend and camera operator, Mitch Dubin, will sometimes make me increase this latitude to 270 degrees because he has a great suggestion for how the camera should move (thanks, buddy...). I try to accommodate him because he's an amazing artist who shares my respect for the story and the actors, and is concerned with the dramatic intent of every shot.

I like to have a strong sense of light in a scene; I hate it when things are flatly lit. I'm the kind of cinematographer who lights in such a way that when you walk on to the set, you always know what the source of the light is. It's also important for the actors to know where the light comes from and what the camera is doing. I also use light to support character development. In **How To Make an American Quilt**, the story of Samantha Mathison, revealed in flashback, goes from romance and optimism to disillusion. I tried to echo this journey, starting with warm, lush colours, then depicting the character in a bluer, more shadowy environment to evoke her disappointment as the years pass.

I think every cinematographer needs to have a particular movie, or a particular collaboration with a director, to really blossom. For me, that happened when I began to work with Steven Spielberg on **Schindler's List**. We met soon after I photographed **Wildflower**, a television movie directed by Diane Keaton. Steven liked the way I'd photographed it, but I

While seeking to avoid the clichés of period drama, Kaminski was influenced by Goya's paintings, such as 'A Prison Scene, 1793–94' *(above, top right)*, for the look of **Amistad** (1997), and also by Philippe Rousselot's photography on **Queen Margot** and **Interview With a Vampire**. "My goal was to achieve beauty without sentimentality. I didn't want the photography to be lyrical, or nostalgic, or romantic: I wanted it to be raw." *(below)* An extract from Kaminski's annotated script with his shooting notes.

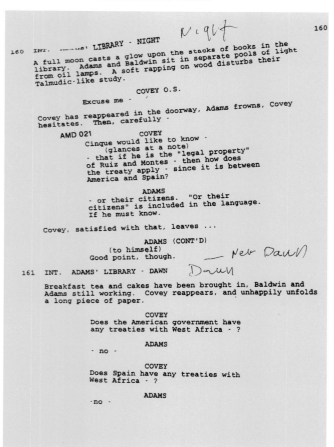

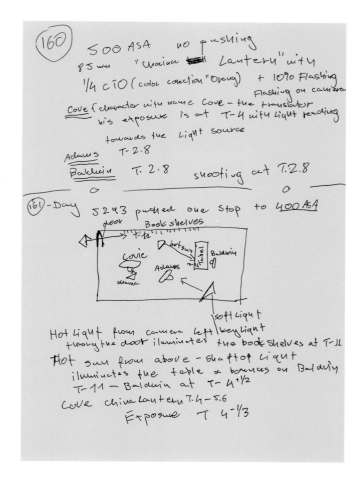

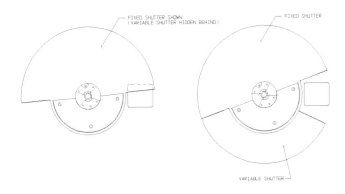

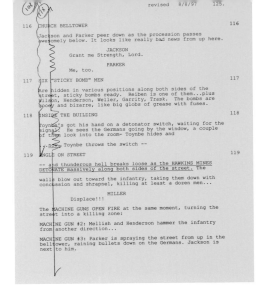

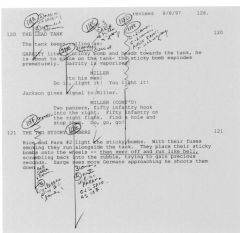

Robert Capa's photograph, 'D-Day Landings, Normandy, June 6th, 1944' *(above, centre)*, was a key influence for **Saving Private Ryan** (1998), 90% of which was shot hand-held. The immediacy and vivid but ghostly impact of Capa's photograph was achieved in cinematographic terms by altering the camera's shutter angle *(see diagrams, top left)*. Conventionally, shooting 24 frames per second with a 180° angle produces the illusion of movement. Kaminski played with the shutter angle in tests: "At 90°, movement became staccato, giving a strobed effect. At 45°, the image is sped up, but the detail is incredibly crisp – all the particles flying through the air after an explosion become frozen." *(right)* Script and continuity notes detail camera set-ups for combat scenes. *(far right)* 'Liberation of France by the Allied Forces. Paris. Les Champs Élysées. 1944. The triumphal parade celebrating the liberation of the city' by Robert Capa.

know that what really impressed him was the fact that we had shot it in 22 days! Steven likes to work fast. He hates waiting for the lighting, a sentiment I share. I will always sacrifice perfect lighting for the sake of maintaining energy on set. If the actors have to wait for two hours while the director of photography lights the set, it's too long, they lose the momentum. If you can work fast, it creates a sense of continuity, it means the director and the actors can work more from their intuition.

After our first meeting, Steven assigned me to shoot a pilot for Amblin, his company. He wanted to see if **Wildflower** was a fluke, if I was capable of maintaining high standards on a tight schedule. Fortunately I passed my test – and was asked to shoot **Schindler's List**. Our collaboration is a cinematographer's dream. Steven is an amazing, amazing film-maker. He knows how to please the audience, not because he tries to, but because he is like one of them. He makes films to please himself. He is masterful when it comes to blocking a scene in one shot. He understands actors, is always able to take the script to another level. He gives me tremendous freedom – although he often has wonderful suggestions for dramatic lighting (for example, using a strobe lighting effect as the sole light source for an entire scene in **Amistad**). I think what I give him is more freedom (because I work fast) and more flexibility in terms of lighting, allowing him a greater range of options with the actors and the way the camera can move. I think I also bring a slightly rawer sensibility to the cinematography in his films; before we started working together, Steven was known for the way he always used back-

light which automatically romanticises a scene, makes everything pretty and sentimental. He also used to work a lot from storyboards; now he is more spontaneous. We both enjoy working on instinct, making spur-of-the-moment decisions.

Before you start shooting a movie, it's important to establish in theory its visual style – to have some general idea of how you want it to look. With **Schindler's List**, Roman Vishniac's timeless photographs of the Jewish community in eastern Europe were an important influence. The idea was to make the film as naturalistic as possible, like a documentary, to give the events a feeling of urgency. The camera became a participant in the action – for example, there's a scene where Itzhak Stern (Ben Kingsley) is confronted by a Nazi screaming for his identification papers. The hand-held camera follows Stern's hands going from pocket to pocket, the agitated camera-movement sharing his rising panic as he realises he's forgotten the papers. This approach was further developed when Steven and I began working on **Saving Private Ryan**. Influenced by the immediacy of Robert Capa's war photographs, and newsreel footage of the Normandy landings, we wanted to put the audience into battle with the soldiers. **Schindler's List** was maybe 50 per cent shot with hand-held camera, **Saving Private Ryan** was 90 per cent – whole scenes were filmed using camera point of view; running, falling, getting up and running again. We also experimented with a variety of techniques to heighten the immediacy of the images – altering the shutter angle; stripping the protective coating from the lenses so that the light would bounce around and make them much more prone

(right) "With **The Lost World** (1997), I wanted to give the film a darker, more intimidating atmosphere than its predecessor and most other summer blockbusters, which tend to have little visual interest. Sometimes, however, a story demands a more conventional approach. The cinematography of **How To Make an American Quilt** (1995) *(above, top left)*, for example, influenced by hand-painted photographs in 'Life' magazines of the 1940s, reflected the romantic, nostalgic atmosphere of the story (in retrospect, however, I think my lighting on this picture was ultimately too sentimental). Conversely, there are times when you try to work against cliché; I didn't want **Jerry Maguire** (1996), *(above, lower left)* to look like high-gloss Hollywood. Rather than the back-light you often see in romantic comedy, I wanted a subtler directional light (I was influenced in this by Giuseppe Rotunno's work on **Carnal Knowledge**)."

to flaring; using various printing processes to evoke the news-reel feeling. When I came to shoot **Amistad**, I tried to avoid the temptation to follow the kind of sumptuous cinematography, with rich lighting, usually associated with period pictures, especially as I knew I was going to be shooting beautiful faces and fantastic production and costume design. But the movie's subject is not romantic; it's a harsh, emotional story about suffering – and so the cinematography had to support that. For example, I was worried that the natural warmth of the candlelight and torch-light would make the prison seem like a friendly environment, so I drained some of the colour out when I timed these scenes in the lab. This gave the firelight a pale white tone.

Although I will have theorised about the general look of a film beforehand, in practise, things inevitably rarely happen quite as you expect. In the first week of shooting, you soon see which of your ideas work; and you may have to modify them in the light of the reality of making the film. I also think it's important to remember that visual consistency is essential – you can't suddenly start using very long lenses if you've been using wide lenses (unless, of course, you want the jarring effect this creates). At the same time, it can become monotonous if you don't occasionally temper that consistency. I deliberately gave some scenes in **Saving Private Ryan** a warm feeling to alleviate the bleakness of the rest of the film. Likewise, in **Amistad** we used the scenes involving the Queen of Spain to go for a warmer, more golden look which counterpointed the overall mood of the film, with sunlight bouncing off the table to illuminate the rich, velvet costumes.

I often think cinematographers get too little credit for what we contribute to a film. We are considered as being 'below the line' – which makes us little more than technicians, on paper. But a really talented cinematographer is not just a technician, he's an artist. You have to bring to the job your life's experience, the way you see the world, your knowledge of art, as well as your mastery of the science and technology of motion pictures. When you start out as a cinematographer, shoot as much as you can. It almost doesn't matter whether it's video, Super-8 or 16mm, the aim is to learn how to tell stories with a camera, through the lighting and blocking. Learn through your mistakes. Become faster – the more you shoot, the more confidence you'll have, the quicker you'll learn to work. And this is the time to be flashy, because you've got to get yourself noticed. Hopefully, if you start early enough, you won't have too many financial obligations. (Once you have a family, for example, it becomes harder; so try to stay without responsibilities while you're establishing yourself!) If you want to be a cinematographer, it's more than likely that your first paid work will be as a technician – a camera assistant, a grip, a gaffer. But don't get trapped by the earnings, because you can find that pretty soon you'll be making good money doing that, and suddenly you're 35 or 40 and you suddenly realise, "my God, I'm still an assistant". If that's what you want, fine, but if your ambition is to be a cinematographer, then keep your attention on that goal.

biography

Since shooting **Delicatessen** (1991, directed by Jean-Pierre Jeunet and Marc Caro), Darius Khondji has emerged as one of the most innovative and distinctive cinematographers working today. Each movie he shoots has its own particular visual style, but all have in common an extraordinary sensitivity and boldness in the way they use colour and light, space and movement. While he believes firmly that his job is to serve

darius khondji

the director, there is no doubt that his own vision and passion for the cinema makes every film he shoots compelling viewing. Like an actor preparing for a role, he researches the background to a film before thinking about how to apply and combine each technical element at his disposal – lights, film stocks, lenses, format, printing techniques – to bring the film to life visually. Splitting his professional life between Europe and the U.S., Khondji continued his collaboration with Jeunet and Caro with **The City of Lost Children** (1995), before shooting **Seven** (1995), for David Fincher, **Stealing Beauty** (1996), for Bernardo Bertolucci, **Evita** (1997), for Alan Parker (for which Khondji received an Oscar nomination), **Alien Resurrection** (1997), for Jeunet again and **In Dreams** (1998), for Neil Jordan.

interview

As a boy, I was immersed in film. My father was a distributor, buying films in Europe to show in Tehran, where we lived. I'm told that while I was still a baby, my nanny would often take me in my pram to the cinema. Later, when my family moved to Paris, there were always film stills and posters around the house. I became fascinated by them. Aged 12, I'd developed a passion for horror movies. My brother was working in England and he would send me pictures from Hammer films. Around this time, I bought a second-hand 8mm camera and started to make my own 'Dracula' films. My sister then began to take my film education in hand. Every weekend, she would drag me to the Cinémathèque Française. The first movie I saw there was Nicholas Ray's **Johnny Guitar**. I remember vividly the incredible emotion I felt – not only because of the film, but also just being in the Cinémathèque. Obviously, I'd been in cinemas before, but never had I experienced the feeling of being part of an audience bound together by a common passion. It was astonishing: the film would start, and everyone would clap and cheer. My sister explained to me that film was an international language, and how if you loved movies you became part of a 'family' that transcended national and cultural boundaries. From then on, I must have seen about ten movies a week. I knew by now that I wanted to work in film. My ambition was to direct, but as I watched more films, I became increasingly aware of their visual impact. Silent films were my greatest source of inspiration (and still are). I learned how, when cinema began, the same person directed and photographed the action, but then the job became separated into the two roles of director and cinematographer. I started to look out for the work of my favourite cameramen: Billy Bitzer, who worked with D.W. Griffith; Gregg Toland – **Citizen Kane** was the most powerful film I'd ever seen, but Toland also achieved a stunning American equivalent of Italian neo-realism in **The Grapes of Wrath**; and Vittorio Storaro. I remember seeing **The Conformist** for the first time. A period movie – but like a totally abstract piece of art. Watching these masters, I began to realise that what they did was to project stories through images.

I went on to study film at New York University, where I was taught by the great Haig Manoogian (Martin Scorsese, a former student, dedicated **Raging Bull** to him). Returning to France was very difficult. The film industry was like a wall in front of me, almost impossible to penetrate. I shot some shorts for friends, and looked for work as a camera assistant. I was lucky enough to be taken on by Bruno Nuytten, France's greatest cinematographer in the '70s. When he saw one of my short films, he told me: "You don't need to be an assistant.

You have to start lighting. Go. Now..." Shooting pop videos and commercials was, for me, the best possible training for a career in feature films. I am not a technician; I knew nothing about sensitometry or optics or physics or chemistry. I would just read the script for the promo or commercial, and try to imagine how I could turn the written ideas into images. I shot tests to experiment with the lighting, to see how far I could push or pull the negative, to discover different ways of processing the film. I drove my producers mad with all the testing – but that's how I learned about what I could do with the medium. Meanwhile, any ambition I still had to direct finally disappeared as I came to realise how much I enjoyed collaborating with directors to create the look of a film. That's why the most important thing that influences my decision to work on a feature is who the director is. When I was first offered **Alien Resurrection** to shoot, I turned it down – the studio did not have a director attached. But then the job was given to one of my best friends, Jean-Pierre Jeunet, for whom I had shot **Delicatessen** and **The City of Lost Children**; luckily, it was offered to me again. Similarly, when I was asked to do **Evita**, I wasn't sure that I wanted to work on a musical; but then I met Alan Parker and his passion made me forget my objections. I see my job as helping the director to visualise his film. This is a very intense process, so my relationship with directors I work with is never just professional; often we become close friends during the course of our collaboration.

I don't feel I have a particular style. Each film I do has its own visual world. I try to discover what this is slowly, by

(left) Photographs from the era of pictorialism from a collection entitled 'Le Salon de Photographie': "The moment of art when painting and photography linked, at the end of the last century, beginning of this century — an area of imagery which is a permanent inspiration for me." *(above centre, from top to bottom)* 'Christina's World', 1948, by Andrew Wyeth and 'The Island of the Dead', 1880, by Arnold Böcklin: both powerful influences for Khondji, as are the paintings of Whistler, for example 'Nocturne, Blue and Gold: Valparaiso', 1866. *(above right, from top to bottom)* Scenes from some of the films which formed Khondji's sensibility at the Cinémathèque Française. D.W. Griffiths' **Intolerance** and **The Birth of a Nation**: "the first 20 or 30 years of cinema remain a very strong inspiration for me". Seeing **Citizen Kane** for the first time had a huge impact: "I remember the low angles and the music, the way we start creeping into this movie, pass the gates and enter the castle — almost like a horror film." Khondji first saw **The Conformist** aged 14: "I was totally captivated by the imagery."

2 SUITE
CLAPET: Ah! vous en convenez ? Y'a certainement mieux ailleurs...
LOUISON: Peut-être qu'au fond vous me trouvez antipathique ?
CLAPET: Moi ?
LOUISON: Ben oui, vous parlez comme si vous vouliez que je parte.

3 CLAPET: Oh non, au contraire, enfin ... c'est pas du tout ce que je voulais
dire... (changeant de sujet): vous reprenez du thé ?
LOUISON: euh oui, attendez...
Il s'envoie rapidement le thé froid récupéré, tend sa tasse, qui déborde
rapidement. Il en place une seconde dessous, qui déborde à son tour, puis
une troisième, provoquant ainsi un effet de fontaine. A ce moment, la
musique dérape, le disque est rayé.
CLAPET: Oh! ça arrive parfois...

4 Plan subjectif complètement flou du trajet qu'elle va devoir parcourir.

5 Elle se lève comme un somnambule, et se dirige vers l'instrument. Au
passage, elle heurte un objet sur un support, qui tombe.
LOUISON se précipite...

6 ... et l'attrape à l'instant où il va toucher le sol !

5 SUITE
Elle heurte le lampadaire qui tombe à son tour...

7 LOUISON l'attrape avec le pied...

41

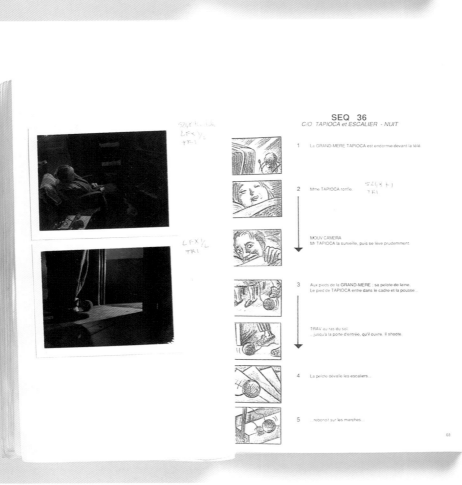

SEQ   36
C/O TAPIOCA et ESCALIER - NUIT

1 La GRAND-MERE TAPIOCA est endormie devant la télé.

2 Mme TAPIOCA ronfle.

MOUV CAMERA
Mr TAPIOCA la surveille, puis se lève prudemment.

3 Aux pieds de la GRAND-MERE : sa pelote de laine.
Le pied de TAPIOCA entre dans le cadre et la pousse...

TRAV au ras du sol.
... jusqu'à la porte d'entrée, qu'il ouvre. Il shoote.

4 La pelote dévale les escaliers...

5 ... rebondit sur les marches...

68

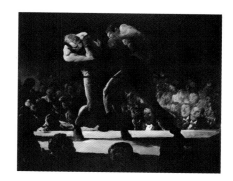

The look of **Delicatessen** (1991), was influenced by French poetic realist cinema of the 1930s – films such as Carne's **Quai des Brumes** and Vigo's **L'Atalante** *(left, third & fourth still from top)* – and also by the work of American realist painter George Bellows, in particular his boxing pictures, such as 'Club Night', 1907 *(above, right)*. Khondji used silver printing processes to 'sweat' the black-and-white image out of the colours. *(far left & below)* Pages from Khondji's workbook for the film, with director Marc Caro's story-boards and Khondji's notes and personal Polaroid shots. Much of the film was lit by Chinese lanterns, like the paper lanterns which Khondji remembered from childhood.

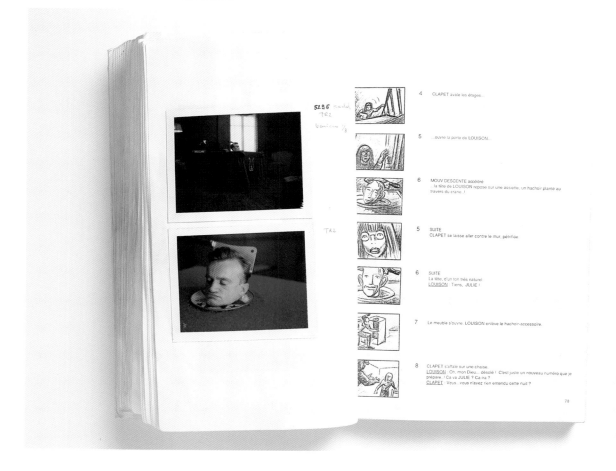

cinematography

The work of Expressionist painters like Otto Dix − (for example, 'Grosstadt' (Urban Debauchery),1927−28, (triptych), *(below)*) − influenced the visual approach for Khondji's second collaboration with directors Jeunet and Caro, **The City of Lost Children** (1995).

studying the screenplay, by talking to the director. Together, we discuss the look and feel of the film, often with the help of other references. On **Delicatessen**, we were very inspired by the atmosphere of French films of the 1930s. For **The City of Lost Children**, we looked at painters like Otto Dix and Egon Schiele. With **Evita**, Alan Parker and I studied the work of George Bellows, an American realist painter of the early 1900s, whose style was close to Impressionism. On **Seven**, two films became key influences: **Klute** (for its scary, stylised lighting) and **The French Connection** (for its hard-edged, almost documentary quality). American horror B-movies from the '40s were very influential in preparing **Alien Resurrection**, as well as the paintings of Francis Bacon, where you never know where the light is coming from – it seems to emanate from the characters and the walls.

When I first read the screenplay of a film, I am immediately looking for the main dramatic contrasts in the story, the psychological contrasts between the characters. For me, contrast is like another character in the film – a role which is played by the cinematography. In photographic terms, it can be difficult to achieve contrast when you are working in colour. Often, one's eye does not know where to look because there are too many colours. Orson Welles said of filming in black and white that it was like putting a magnifier on the actors, which separated them from their background. My aim is to achieve this kind of contrast using colour. To do this, I have to be able to control the colour in the image. I use printing techniques like ENR, which retains a percentage of the silver grains that are usually eliminated when colour film

is printed. This process makes the blacks more black, dramatically increasing contrast. I've used such techniques on every film I've shot, although I vary the degree of contrast according to each film's needs. To help me judge this, I do a lot of testing with the labs before shooting, and then always work with the same colour-timer in post-production, Yvan Lucas. He shares my passion for film and has a very sensual approach to colour. In addition to these printing techniques, I use the VariCon – a contrast-control system which is attached to the camera in front of the lens, and which allows you to flash the negative with colour tones as you shoot. This enables me to soften the contrast in certain scenes, and to play with the colours. For example, if I am lighting a scene with warm golden tones, I may not want the shadows to be as black as ENR tends to make them – so I flash the film with blue to give the shadows an ashy, charcoal quality, and push the negative a stop to saturate the remaining colours. Combining techniques like ENR and the VariCon gives me real control over colour and contrast. By playing with the balance of these ingredients, I can achieve a blend that is appropriate to the dramatic content of each individual story. On **Delicatessen**, for example, the blend was designed to create a colour version of the black-and-white 'poetic realism' in French cinema of the 1930s. On **Seven**, it served a very different purpose – to create a gritty, immediate atmosphere.

A lot of cinematographers will talk about Vermeer or Caravaggio as influences. I tend to be more inspired by pictures with less obvious lighting themes. One of my 'bibles' is Robert Frank's 'The Americans'. I take it with me wherever

I travel. The pure naturalism of these photographs is to me the essence of modernity. Ideally, I would love not to have to use lights, but just work with the natural lighting conditions as you find them. I love going on the location recce when we are preparing a film. Without the paraphernalia and pressures of the film shoot – the trucks, the equipment, the sea of people – you have a unique opportunity to get a real feeling for the environment, and its natural light. By contrast, a studio set is an entirely contrived world – every element is designed. When a set is being constructed, I like to visit it regularly to see it growing. As the space evolves, it provokes feelings in you, and you start to sense where you might place the camera and how to use light to reveal the space. It's very important to understand that the work of the cinematographer is only one part of the film's overall design. I work very closely with the production and costume designers and the make-up artist to achieve the director's concept. On **Alien Resurrection**, I was very inspired by Nigel Phelps' sets, and I was privileged to be able to collaborate with him so that the lighting and design could be blended into an organic whole. I'm not at all concerned with who has what idea in the creative process; sometimes a grip, a gaffer or a camera assistant will make a really great suggestion. Working on a film, there are so many responsibilities and pressures that it's tempting to shut yourself off – but you must remain open to other people's ideas.

Every technical decision you make has implications for the overall look of the film. I spend a lot of time with the director discussing how the camera will move and how individual shots are going to be cut together. On **Evita**, Alan Parker and I decided not to use too much camera movement, but to build the story through tableaux. The accumulation of compositions featuring masses of people – swept up by emotion, surging through the shot – is what gives the film its impression of incredible movement. By contrast, when I shot **Stealing Beauty**, Bernardo Bertolucci wanted the camera to be very mobile in order to reflect different characters' points of view. You always see the action unfold through a window, or from a doorway, spying on a character, or circling like a predator. Often the camera would track through 360 degrees within a scene. Although this approach can limit the lighting options of the cinematographer, it gives the director greater freedom in terms of how he tells the story with the camera. The impression of voyeurism conveyed by the camera in **Stealing Beauty** was essential to the nature of the story and the characterisation.

The choice of which lenses to use is also of critical importance. I tend to use two makes of lenses – Primos and Cookes. Each gives a very different texture. Primos provide a very sharp edge to the image, and so are very well-suited to contemporary dramas – urban, realistic stories or action movies (I used them on **Seven** and **Alien Resurrection**). Cooke lenses, my personal favourites, tend to provide a very round and beautiful look (which was perfect for **Delicatessen** and **Stealing Beauty**). On **Evita**, I used a combination of Cookes for the early part of Evita's life, and Zeiss lenses – which give a colder, harsher rendering of the image – for the later part of her life. The other major decision regarding lenses is what focal length to use. I try to make this reflect the

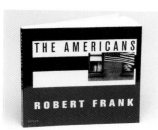

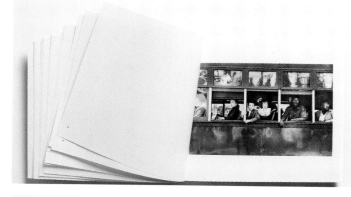

(left) The colour-noir look of **Seven** (1995), was influenced by Gordon Willis' stylised, sinister lighting on **Klute** (above) and Owen Roizman's gritty, hand-held work on **The French Connection**. But Khondji's key influence was Robert Frank's collection of photographs, 'The Americans' (above, top & centre) "the essence of modernity. I travel everywhere with this book. It's like a friend to me. Wherever I am, I just let it fall open on a page, and let the image work on me."

director's vision of the story. I don't like to mix wide and long lenses; I'll try to shoot the whole film using either one or the other. What the human eye sees is best represented by a 40–50mm lens in the 35mm format. On **Delicatessen**, our main lens was a 25mm; on **The City of Lost Children**, it was an 18mm. These wider lenses increase the depth of field; I feel it's a more modern way of looking at things. Long lenses tend to bring the background much closer to the actor, which can give a more claustrophobic effect. So the choice you make really affects how you play with the audience's sense of space, as does the format in which you decide to shoot. If you shoot with true anamorphic, as I did on **Evita**, it's very different to the crisp, dry look of Super 35 (which I used for **Seven** and **Alien Resurrection**). With anamorphic, you lose depth of field; the backgrounds take on a liquid quality – which was just right for the Impressionist quality I wanted for the film, much of which was shot through a glow of light and dust.

Although all these technical issues need to be fully considered when you prepare a film, you must also allow yourself to be influenced by what the actors do in rehearsal and on set. Sometimes, you may have to temporarily sacrifice the consistency of the look you are trying to achieve in order to give the actors the freedom they require, or to respond to something in their performance. Personally, I identify my work very closely with the leading actors. When I first try to imagine what a film should look like, I always see the story through the eyes of one of the main characters. On **Stealing Beauty**, I lit Liv Tyler with fluorescents, which I felt would lend her character a texture of modern America to bring into the Tuscan

setting. My key to **Alien Resurrection** was Ripley. She is an enlightened being – at once new-born and reborn in the story. I evoked this by lighting her so she looked translucent. On **Evita**, I came to share Madonna's passion for Eva Peron, and I wanted to reflect the character's incredible aura through the energy of the lighting on her face. Jonathan Pryce offered a different challenge. Researching the historical background, I learned that Juan Peron was a much more complex character than Eva. He had a very dual personality – apparently sympathetic and generous, but also clever, devious. I found myself lighting him so he was often half in darkness. Whenever I'm on set, I always feel like I'm one of the cast, and I want my lighting to interact with their performances. Something happens when you play with the light on people's faces and bodies. Cinematography makes you look beyond the surface; it makes you seek out the essence of a character. Often, I find there is an intimate exchange between the light and the subject. Morgan Freeman has a speech in **Seven** about his past, which he delivered in such a way that it made me want to take him from light into dark, dark into light.

To anybody who wants to be a cinematographer today, I would say don't spend too much time in film school. Travel. Seek out contrasts: go to the Sahara; go to the black-and-white landscapes of Iceland. Go to cities: New York; Venice. Open your eyes to the light in these places, watch how it bounces off the architecture, how it reveals the landscape. Take a train, or get in your car and drive. The most inspirational time for me is when I drive at night in my car with the music on, especially if it's raining. Take photographs. And watch movies. Watch a lot of movies.

For Khondji, the most important factor in working on a film is the director. *(above, left)* Alan Parker's passion and his desire to make **Evita** (1997) more than a slick vehicle for Madonna persuaded Khondji to shoot the film. *(below)* 'Cliff Dwellers' by George Bellows, an important reference for the street scenes in **Evita**. *(above, centre & top right)* **Stealing Beauty** (1996), brought him the opportunity to collaborate with Bernardo Bertolucci, whose work with Vittorio Storaro was such a formative influence for Khondji. *(right)* **Alien Resurrection** (1997) reunited him with director Jean-Pierre Jeunet.

glossary

CAMERA AND LIGHTING PERSONNEL

Director of photography, also referred to as D.P., cinematographer, lighting cameraman (or simply cameraman): Head of the camera department, primarily responsible for all the photographic elements of a film.

Camera operator: Works in close collaboration with the D.P. and the director to determine the camera's position and movement during a shot, which s/he physically executes.

Focus puller (1st camera assistant): Responsible for determining and maintaining the field of focus required by each shot.

Clapper loader (2nd camera assistant): Responsible for loading and unloading film stock and keeping records of each day's shooting so that the film laboratories know what to print. Also responsible for the clapperboard which identifies each shot and every take of the film; the 'clap' also provides the editor's assistants with the means of synchronising picture and sound.

Grip: Works with the D.P. and camera operator, and is responsible for how the camera is mounted and moved, for example, on a tripod, dolly or crane. For a tracking shot, the grip will lay tracks on which the dolly is pushed or pulled. On bigger budget films, which require a lot of complex camera movement, a team of grips will work under the key grip.

Gaffer: Head of the lighting department, works closely with the D.P. to determine how to execute the lighting required in each set or location. Responsible for hiring and supplying the lighting units and gels needed on the shoot.

Sparks: The electricians who control the power supply and rig the lights according to the gaffer/D.P.'s instructions.

SHOOTING TERMS

Blocking: The technical rehearsal in which the actors' positions in relation to the camera are plotted out.

Coverage: The way in which a group of shots is designed (by the director and D.P.) to cover all the action described in any one scene of the screenplay.

Magic hour: The term used to describe the twilight time of the early evening, which on film can make the sky appear deep blue. "That's the magic part", says Jack Cardiff. "The hour part is nonsense – it's more like a magic minute."

Marks: Positions, marked out by tape on the floor, given to the actors to enable them to achieve the camera/action blocking and to ensure they will be in the optimum place for focus and illumination.

Scene: A self-contained unit of action in one location, as laid out in the screenplay. A sequence of such units constitutes the dramatic action of the whole film.

Set-up: The position of the camera in relation to the action during a shot, designed to cover a portion of a scene. Each set-up is identified by a slate number on the clapperboard.

Storyboard: The action of a scene or sequence, broken down into a series of drawings like a comic strip.

Take: Each repeated attempt to capture successfully on film the intentions of the set-up.

THE CAMERA

Gate: The pressure plate constructed around the aperture, the rectangular opening which creates a frame for the light passing through it on to the film.

Magazine: The compartment into which rolls of film stock are loaded before being attached to the camera.

Matte box: A box which can be attached to the camera, making it possible to use a variety of devices – such as mattes and filters (*see page 205*) and contrast control systems, such as the VariCon (*see* Darius Khondji) – which affect the way the image is registered.

Motor: The mechanism which controls the rotation of the shutter and the transport of the film through the camera, usually at 24 fps (frames per second) to achieve the persistence of vision (which creates the illusion of movement when projected at 24 fps). Variable motors can 'overcrank' to 64 fps and higher, giving the effect of slow motion (projected at 24 fps), or 'undercrank' to as low as 2 fps, giving the effect of high speed (*see* Michael Chapman on **Raging Bull**).

Shutter: Disk with 180 degree cut-out which rotates, so that each frame passing the aperture is exposed to light. The size of the cut-out can be varied; a narrow shutter angle results in a strobing effect (*see* Janusz Kaminski on **Saving Private Ryan**).

Viewfinder: In modern cameras, the image is reflected from the shutter mirror into the viewfinder, so that the operator can see the exact image being filmed (*see* John Seale).

THE LENS

Depth of field: The area between the nearest and farthest point in front of a lens in which an actor or object can move and stay in focus – dependent on such factors as the speed and focal length of the lens, the f-stop and the amount of light illuminating the action.

Exposure: The quantity of light passing through the lens and on to the film over a given time, producing a latent image – perhaps the D.P.'s most important tool in defining the look of a film. For dramatic reasons, the D.P. may choose to use a degree of under- or overexposure to create an atmospheric sense of darkness or brightness (*see* Gordon Willis).

f-stop/t-stop: Units of measurement indicating the degree of opening of the lens diaphragm, determining how much light passes through the camera aperture (t-stops are more accurate). If any factors (such as changing light or variation in the speed of the camera motor) make the exposure unstable while filming, the f-stop may have to be altered manually (*see* Michael Chapman on **Raging Bull** and Robby Müller on **Breaking the Waves**).

Flaring: An effect created when the lens is pointed at a strong directional light source. Although regarded as a technical mistake, flaring is part of the modern cinematographer's vocabulary, which can be used to evoke a sense of immediacy (*see* Janusz Kaminski on **Saving Private Ryan**).

Focal length: The distance from the optical centre of the lens to the point just behind the lens where the image is in sharp focus, while the focus is set to infinity. Long focal lengths bring distant objects up close; short lengths push distant objects further away, and give a much wider angle. Because different focal lengths affect the viewer's sense of perspective in different ways, choice of focal length is a key factor in determining how best to render the dramatic action of a scene (*see* Darius Khondji).

Prime: Lens of fixed focal length.

Zoom: A lens of variable focal length, so that the magnification of the subject of a shot can be altered during filming. This allows an alteration in the sense of perspective between the subject and the background (unlike the tracking shot).

GRIP AND CAMERA-OPERATING TERMS

Crane: Allows the camera to climb to a vantage point high over the subject and to descend towards it – or vice-versa (*see* Roger Deakins on **Kundun**).

Dolly: A wheeled vehicle on which the camera is mounted for tracking shots (in which the camera moves towards or away from the subject).

Steadicam/Panaglide: Trade names for two camera-stabilising systems which allow the camera to be harnessed to the body and which include gyroscopic controls to ensure that the operator's movements do not create a jerky image (a danger with hand-held shooting). Steadicam shots are characterised by a floating, fluid sense of movement and camera mobility has been greatly increased since the system's introduction in 1975.

Pan/tilt: Camera movement on horizontal/vertical axis respectively, facilitated by geared heads (used for most 35mm films) which connect the camera to its mounting (on a tripod/dolly/crane), allowing the camera operator to move the camera by rotating wheels for each axis.

Track: Movement towards or away from an object by means of a dolly (*see* **Zoom**, *above*).

SCREEN FORMATS

Anamorphic: A wide-screen format based on lenses which optically squeeze the picture, which is then unsqueezed in the projector to produce a wider image whose aspect ratio is 2.35:1 (*see* Darius Khondji on **Evita**).

Aspect ratio: The ratio between the width and height of the frame. The industry standard, which was 1.37:1 until the 1950s, is today 1.85:1 (*see* John Seale on **The English Patient**).

Cinemascope: Trade name for one of the earliest wide-screen formats, introduced in the 1950s to give the cinema an edge over its new rival, television.

Super 35: A variable format system which ranges from 1.85:1 to 2.35:1.

FILM STOCK

EI/ASA: The sensitivity of film to light as rated numerically.

Emulsion: The light-sensitive coating on film negative, consisting of silver halide crystals suspended in gelatin. Black-and-white film stock contains one layer of emulsion; colour has several. The emulsion is fused on to an acetate base.

Exposure latitude: Refers to the emulsion's ability to produce acceptable images over a range of exposures.

Frame: A single picture on a strip of film.

Negative: Raw film stock, and also raw stock which has been exposed but not processed.

Sensitometry: The science of measuring a film emulsion's light sensitivity.

Speed: The emulsion's sensitivity to light expressed by the EI/ASA rating, enabling the D.P. to make important decisions as to which stocks to use in different lighting conditions.

FILTERS AND GELS

Diffusion filters: Used to scatter light and reduce image resolution – to soften hard edges.

Fog filters: Used to scatter light from the bright part of the image to the dark part, creating a foggy effect over the picture (*see* Jack Cardiff on **Black Narcissus**).

Graduated filters/grads: Filters with neutral density *(see below)* or colour on one part of the glass, graduating to clear glass.

Low-contrast filters: Used to reduce the contrast of a scene – useful when shooting in exteriors with heavy contrast.

Matte: An opaque mask placed in front of the lens to black out a portion of the image. Whatever part is blocked is later filled with another image element – such as a mountainous vista – which is shot separately (*see* Jack Cardiff on **Black Narcissus**).

Net: A hair-net used as a form of diffusion *(see above)*.

Neutral density filters: Colourless filters in a range of densities, used to reduce the amount of light entering the lens when the intensity is too great for the film stock or the required f-stop. Can be used in the camera or over windows.

Pola screen: Used to polarise light and eliminate reflections in glass, glare from a bright light source and flares (if used at certain angles). Is also used to deepen the colour in a blue sky and make the clouds 'pop' out (*see* John Seale on **The Hitcher**).

LIGHTS AND LIGHTING

Arc-light: A high-intensity source in which light is produced by discharge of electricity between two electrodes.

Available light: A term used for shooting without film lighting, using only the light available in the natural surroundings (*see* Haskell Wexler).

Back-light: Lighting a subject from behind (*see* Subrata Mitra and Eduardo Serra).

Barn-door: The metal shields hinged in front of a lamp to limit/shape the light it produces.

Bounce lighting: A technique in which light is directed on to a reflective surface, producing a softer, more shadowless effect (*see* Raoul Coutard and Subrata Mitra).

Brutes: A type of arc-light producing a high-intensity spot.

Colour temperature: The measurement of light's colour quality on the Kelvin scale.

Contrast: The difference in intensity between the brightest and darkest parts of the scene to be photographed (*see* Darius Khondji).

Cross-lighting: Lighting which comes from the side of the scene.

Eye-light: A small, hard light source placed close to the camera, used to pick out an actor's eyes (*see* Haskell Wexler).

Fill-light: Secondary lighting used to reveal more detail in shadow areas of the image; also reduces overall contrast.

Flag: Used to shield unwanted light from the lens, or to create shadows. When perforated, it creates shadow patterns and dappled light effects (referred to as a 'cookie').

Gel: A transparent filter placed in front of a light; different coloured gels can act as colour correction for daylight or tungsten; gels can also be used to colour the light for aesthetic effects.

High-key lighting: Lighting which gives an overall brightness to the image, obtained, for example, by a soft, diffused light source.

HMI: Daylight-coloured lights.

Inky-dink: A small, incandescent light source.

Keylight: The principal light source used to illuminate a scene.

Kicker: This serves a similar function to back-light *(see above)*,placed in a three-quarter-back position at a low angle behind the subject.

Low-key lighting: Describes a scene usually lit by one principal light source which casts shadows and only partially illuminates the whole image (as in the paintings of Caravaggio or Rembrandt).

Reflectors: A light-reflective surface, used chiefly for redirecting sunlight on to the scene in order to fill in shadows (*see* Jack Cardiff on **African Queen**).

Rim-light: A form of back-light placed so that the edges of a subject are framed by light. Used to separate the subject from the background.

Scrim: Fabric placed on a light to diffuse its intensity.

Soft light: Open reflector lights that produce soft and shadowless light (*see* Subrata Mitra).

Source light: Refers to light which is intended to come from a source in the image, e.g., a window, or a practical light source in the interior, such as a table lamp.

Space light: Used to provide a very big source of light. A number of space lights are often rigged at ten-feet intervals to provide fill-lighting over very large interior sets.

FILM PROCESSING AND THE LABORATORY

Answer print: The first complete print of a film delivered by the laboratory.

Bleaching: A stage in colour film processing when the metallic silver image is converted into halides, later removed in fixing.

Bleach by-pass: Generic name for a variety of techniques which make it possible to retain a certain amount of silver (usually lost in bleaching, *see above*) in the colour print or intermediate, thus adding a strong element of black and white to the original colour image (*see* Roger Deakins on **1984** and Eduardo Serra on **Jude**).

ENR: Trade name for the Technicolor printing process, named after laboratory technician Ernesto N. Rico, who pioneered it with D.P. Vittorio Storaro. As in bleach by-pass *(see above)*, ENR retains the silver, resulting in a high-contrast image with rich blacks. With ENR, the amount of silver retained can be controlled, which makes the process more flexible than the bleach by-pass (*see* Darius Khondji).

Flashing: A laboratory process in which the negative is exposed to light before shooting, reducing the contrast of the stock and resulting in an image which appears slightly desaturated (*see* Haskell Wexler on **Bound For Glory**).

Grading or timing: The laboratory operation wherein printer light intensity and colour filters are selected to optimise the density and colour rendition of the original footage.

Rushes/dailies: The first prints produced from the exposed negative, processed overnight by the labs and delivered to the film's cutting-rooms for viewing by the crew.

Saturation: A colour when it is reproduced in its purest and most vivid state.

picture credits

Courtesy of The Kobal Collection: 19 **The Red Shoes**, Rank; 22 **War and Peace**, Paramount; **African Queen**, United Artists; 26 **The Man in The White Suit**, Ealing; **The Lavender Hill Mob**, Ealing; 26, 27 **Kind Hearts and Coronets**, Ealing; 31 **Julia**, 20th Century Fox; **The Great Gatsby**, Paramount; 34 **Raiders of the Lost Ark**, Lucasfilm Ltd./Paramount; 36, 39 **Persona**, Svensk Filmindustri; 39 **Through A Glass Darkly**, Svensk Filmindustri; **Winter Light**, Svensk Filmindustri/Nora Film; **The Silence**, Svensk Filmindustri; 40 **En Passion**, Svensk Filmindustri; **Cries and Whispers**, Cinematograph/Svenska Filminstitutet; **Fanny and Alexander**, Svensk/Filminstitut/ Gaumont/Tobis; 43 **The Unbearable Lightness of Being**, SAUL ZAENTZ Company; 44 **Sleepless in Seattle**, TRI-STAR; 45 **Pretty Baby**, Paramount; 46 **Crimes and Misdemeanors**, Orion; 48, 59 **The Householder**, Merchant Ivory; 51 **Rashomon**, Daiei Films; **Oliver Twist**, Cineguild; **The River**, United Artists; **Bitter Rice**, Lux/De Laurentiis; **Bicycle Thieves**, Produzione De Sica; **The Rose Tattoo**, Paramount; 52 **Apu Trilogy: Pather Panchali**, Govt. of West Bengal; 55 **Apu Trilogy: Aparajito**, Epic; **Apu Trilogy: Apur Sansar**, Satyajit Ray Films; 56 **Charulata**, R.D. Bansal; 59 **Shakespeare Wallah** and **Bombay Talkie**, Merchant Ivory; **The Guru**, Arcadia/Merchant Ivory; 60, 66 **A Bout de Souffle**, SNC; 65 **Lola**, Rome-Paris Films/Unidex; 67 **Alphaville**, Chaumiane/Film Studio; **Pierrot le Fou**, Rome-Paris/De Laurentiis/Beauregard; **Week-end**, Copernic/Comacico/Lira/Ascot; 69 **Jules et Jim**, Films du Carrosse/Sedif; 70 **Tirez sur la Pianiste**, Films de la Pleiade; 72, 74 **Who's Afraid of Virginia Woolf?**, Warner Bros.; 76 **One Flew Over The Cuckoo's Nest**, United Artists/Fantasy Films; 78 **The Thomas Crown Affair**, United Artists; **In the Heat of the Night**, Mirisch/United Artists; **American Graffiti**, Lucasfilm/Coppola Co/Universal; 81 **The Secret of Roan Inish**, Skerry/Jones/Newman; **Matewan**, Red Dog/Cinecom; **Bound for Glory**, United Artists; 82, 89 **Paper Moon**, Paramount; 86 **Easy Rider**, Columbia/Colour Origination by KHBB; 90 **New York, New York**, United Artists; **Shampoo**, Columbia; **Five Easy Pieces**, Columbia; 92 **Copycat**, New Regency; **My Best Friend's Wedding**, Tri-Star; **Heart Beat**, Orion/Further Prods.; **Frances**, Universal; 94, 99 **Gandhi**, Indo-British/Int Film Investors; 96 **Women in Love**, United Artists; 97 **The Rainbow**, Vestron; 100 **Sunday, Bloody Sunday**, United Artists; 101 **Eleni**, Warner Bros.; **The Wind and The Lion**, Columbia; 104 **Dreamchild**, Pennies from Heaven/Thorn EMI; 109 **The American Friend**, Road Movies/Films Du Losange/W. Wenders; 112 **Breaking the Waves**, Zentropa; 114 **Mystery Train**, MTI/Orion; **Down By Law**, Island; **Korzcak**, Perspektywa/Regina Ziegler Filmproduktion; 116, 119 **The Godfather**, Paramount; 120 **The Godfather Part II**, Paramount; 121 **The Godfather Part III**, Paramount; 122 **The Purple Rose of Cairo**, Orion; **A Midsummer Night's Sex Comedy**, Orion; **Broadway Danny Rose**, Orion Pictures; **Zelig**, Orion/Warner Bros.; 124 **All the President's Men**, Warner Bros.; **Pennies from Heaven**, MGM; **Klute**, Warner Bros.; 128, 129 **Taxi Driver**, Columbia; 130 **Raging Bull**, United Artists; 131 **L'Atalante**, Nounez/Gaumont; **On the Waterfront**, Columbia; 133 **Jaws**, Universal; **The Last Detail**, Columbia; **The White Dawn**, Paramount; 134 **Invasion of the Body Snatchers**, United Artists; **The Fugitive**, Warner Bros.; **Dead Men Don't Wear Plaid**, Universal; 136, 146 **The English Patient**, Tiger Moth/Miramax; 141 **Witness**, Paramount; 143 **Dead Poet's Society**, Touchstone; **Children of a Lesser God**, Paramount; **Lorenzo's Oil**, Universal; 144 **Gorillas in the Mist**, Warner Bros.; **The Mosquito Coast**, SAUL ZAENTZ Company; 150, 152 **The Piano**, Jan Champion Prods/CIBY 2000; 156 **An Angel At My Table**, Hibiscus Films/Sharmill Films; **Once Were Warriors**, New Zealand Film Comm.; **The Perez Family**, Samuel Goldwyn Company; **Lone Star**, Castle Rock; 161 **Kameradschaft**, NERO; **Nosferatu**, PRANA-FILM GMBH, Berlin; **Fat City**, Columbia; **Doctor Strangelove**Hawk Films Prod/Columbia; **Alexander Nevsky**, MOSFILM; **L'Avventura**, Cino del Duca/PCE/LYRE; **Hour of the Wolf**, Svensk Filmindustri/United Artists; 164 **Mountains of the Moon**, Carolco/Indieprod; 168 **The Shawshank Redemption**, Castle Rock Entertainment; 175 **The Hairdresser's Husband**, Lambart/TFI/Investimage; 184, 185 **Schindler's List**, Universal; 190 **How to make an American Quilt**, Universal/Amblin; **Jerry Maguire**, Columbia Tri Star; **The Lost World: Jurassic Park**, Universal/Amblin; 195 **Intolerance**, Wark Producing Company; **The Birth of a Nation**, Epic; **Citizen Kane**, RKO; **The Conformist**, Mars/Marianne/Maran; 197 **Delicatessen**, Constellation/UGC/Hachette Premiere; **Quai des Brumes**, Cine Alliance/Pathe; **L'Atalante**, Nounez/Gaumont; 201 **Seven**, New Line Cinema. Photography © Peter Sorel; 203 **Evita**, Cinergi Pictures; **Stealing Beauty**, Fiction Cinematografica; **Alien Resurrection**, 20th Century Fox;

Courtesy of The Ronald Grant Archive: 12, 19 **The Red Shoes**; 21 **Black Narcissus**; **A Matter of Life and Death**; 22 **The Prince and The Showgirl**; 28 **Freud: A Secret Passion**; 37 **Star 80**; 43 **The Unbearable Lightness of Being**; 44 **The Postman Always Rings Twice**; 45 **The Tenant**; 46 **Another Woman**; 47 **The Sacrifice**, (Sven Nykvist & Andrei Tarkovsky); 51 **Louisiana Story**; 74 **America, America**; 76 **One Flew Over The Cuckoo's Nest**; 106, 109 **Paris, Texas**; 109 **Kings of the Road**; **Alice in the Cities**; 110 **To Live and Die in L.A.**; 119 **The Godfather**; 120 **The Godfather Part II**; 126, 129 **Taxi Driver**; 156 **An Angel At My Table**; **The Perez Family**; 164 **Kundun** © Touchstone Pictures; 192, 198 **The City of Lost Children**, Entertainment Film; 201 **Seven**, New Line Cinema; **Klute**; 203 **Alien Resurrection**, 20th Century Fox;

Courtesy of BFI Stills, Posters and Designs: 19 **The Red Shoes** © Carlton International Media Limited; 21 **A Matter of Life and Death** © Carlton International Media Limited; 26 Ealing Studios and 27 **Kind Hearts and Coronets** © Copyright by Canal + Image UK Ltd.; 28 **Freud: A Secret Passion** Copyright © 1998 by Universal City Studios, Inc. Courtesy of Universal Studios Publishing Rights, a division of Universal Studios Licensing, Inc. All Rights Reserved; 66 **A Bout de Souffle** © Copyright by SNC; 102 **On Golden Pond** © Polygram/Pictorial Press; 130 **Raging Bull** © United Artists;

Courtesy of Polygram/Pictorial Press Ltd.: 76 **One Flew Over The Cuckoo's Nest**; 78 **The Thomas Crown Affair**; 102 **On Golden Pond** script pages and stills; 148, 154 **Portrait of a Lady**; 158, 168 **Dead Man Walking**; 159, 167 **Fargo**; 163 **1984**; 167 **The Hudsucker Proxy**; **Barton Fink**; 176 **Map of the Human Heart**; 178 **Jude**;

Courtesy of The Movie Store Collection: 76 **One Flew Over The Cuckoo's Nest**; 78 **In the Heat of the Night**; 81 **The Secret of Roan Inish**; 114 **Dead Man**; 122 **Manhattan**; **Annie Hall**; 124 **Klute**; 133 **The Last Detail**; 130 **Raging Bull**; 140, 141 **Witness**; 164 **Kundun**; 187 **Amistad**;

Courtesy of IPOL Inc. International Press Online: 46 **Another Woman**, Brian Hamill/IPOL Inc.; 110 **The Tango Lesson**, IPOL Inc.; 117 **Manhattan**, Brian Hamill/IPOL Inc.; 122 **Manhattan**, Brian Hamill/IPOL Inc.; **Zelig**, Brian Hamill/IPOL Inc.; 123 Woody Allen/Gordon Willis on movie set, Brian Hamill/IPOL Inc.; Portrait shot from set of **Annie Hall**, Brian Hamill/IPOL Inc;

Courtesy of The Bridgeman Art Library: 16 'The Supper at Emmaus' by Michelangelo Merisi da Caravaggio (1571–1610) National Gallery, London/Bridgeman Art Library, London; 'Self Portrait', 1629 by Harmensz van Rijn Rembrandt (1606–69) Mauritshuis, The Hague/Bridgeman Art Library, London; 'The Virgin of the Rocks (with the infant St. John adoring the Infant Christ accompanied by an Angel)' c.1508 (oil on panel) by Leonardo da Vinci (1452–1519) National Gallery, London/Bridgeman Art Library, London; 17 'Lady writing a letter with her Maid', 1671 by Jan Vermeer (1632–75) Beit Collection, Co. Wicklow, Ireland/Bridgeman Art Library, London; 'Nave Nave Moe (Sacred Spring)', 1894 by Paul Gauguin (1848–1903) Hermitage, St. Petersburg/Bridgeman Art Library, London; 100 'St Jerome in his study by Antonello da Messina' (1430–79), National Gallery, London/Bridgeman Art Library, London; 140 'Woman Weighing Gold' by Jan Vermeer (1632–75) National Gallery of Art, Washington DC/Bridgeman Art Library, London; 160 'The Trinity', c1577/79 by El Greco (Domenico Theotocopuli) (1541–1614), Prado, Madrid/Bridgeman Art Library, London; 'The Nightmare' by Henry Fuseli (1741–1825), Detroit Institute of Arts, Michigan/Bridgeman Art Library, London; 'The Silent Statue, (Ariadne)', 1913 (oil on canvas) by Giorgio de Chirico (1888–1978), Kunstsammlung Nordrhein-Westfalen, Dusseldorf, Germany/Bridgeman Art Library, London/Peter Willi © DACS 1998; 'The First Book of Urizen; Man floating upside down', 1794 (colour-printed relief etching) by William Blake (1757–1827), Private Collection/Bridgeman Art Library, London; 'Summer Night', 1890 by Winslow Homer (1836–1910), Musee d'Orsay, Paris, France/Bridgeman Art Library, London; 173 'Pope Leo X with his nephews' by Sanzio of Urbino Raphael (1483–1520) Galleria degli Uffizi, Florence, Italy/Bridgeman Art Library, London; 'Gabrielle d'Estrees (1573-99) and her sister, the Duchess of Villars', late 16th century (oil on panel) by Fontainbleau School (16th century) Louvre, Paris, France/Giraudon/Bridgeman Art Library, London; 'Portrait of a Lady', c.1450–60 (oil on panel) by Rogier van der Weyden (1399–1465) National Gallery, London/Bridgeman Art Library, London; 'Albrecht Dürer's Father', 1497 (panel) by Albrecht Dürer (1471–1528) National Gallery, London/Bridgeman Art Library, London; 'An Old Man in Red' by Harmensz van Rijn Rembrandt (1606–69) Hermitage, St. Petersburg/Bridgeman Art Gallery, London; 187 'A Prison Scene', 1793–94 by Francisco Jose de Goya y Lucientes (1746–1828) Bowes Museum, Co. Durham, UK/Bridgeman Art Library, London; 195 'The Island of the Dead', 1880 (oil on canvas) by Arnold Böcklin (1827–1901) Kunstmuseum, Basle/Peter Willi/Bridgeman Art Library, London; 'Nocturne, Blue and Gold: Valparaiso', 1866 by James Abbot McNeill Whistler (1834–1903), FREER GALLERY, Smithsonian Institution, Washington/Bridgeman Art Library, London; 198 'Grosstadt', (Urban Debauchery), 1927–28, (triptych), (oil on canvas) by Otto Dix (1891–1969), Galerie der Stadt, Stuttgart/Bridgeman Art Library, London © DACS 1998;

2 **The Unbearable Lightness of Being** © Copyright by Saul Zaentz; 6 **Pather Panchali**, courtesy of the Satyajit Ray Archive, Nandan, Calcutta and Sandip Ray; 16 Rembrandt's 'The Nightwatch', courtesy of the Rijksmuseum, Amsterdam; 17 Vincent Van Gogh, 'The Night Café', 1888, courtesy of Yale University Art Gallery, Bequest of Stephen Carlton Clark, B.A. 1903; 28 'Une leçon clinique à la Saltpétrière', by A. Brouillet, 1887, courtesy of Assistance Hôpitaux Publique de Paris; 29 'Park Greeting, 24th June 1939' and 'Danzig Synagogue, circa 1939' © Copyright by Hulton Getty; 43 **The Unbearable Lightness of Being**, script and stills © Copyright by Saul Zaentz; 49 Portrait shot, 52, 53, 54, 55 **Pather Panchali**, **Aparajito**, **Apur Sansar**; and 56, 57 **Devi**, **Mahanagar**, **Charulata**, all courtesy of the Satyajit Ray Archive, Nandan, Calcutta and Sandip Ray; 51 **Monsieur Vincent**, image courtesy of BIFI © Canal + Image International; 55 Satyajit Ray and Subrata Mitra, photography © Marc Riboud; 63, 67 images courtesy of Production Bela, Paris; 63 **Cinema, Cinema** documentary, images courtesy of Wall to Wall Television Ltd. and Channel 4 Film Studios; 67 **Une Femme est Une Femme**, courtesy of BIFI © Copyright by Canal + Image International; 70 **La Marieé etait en Noir**, courtesy of BIFI and MGM Consumer Products; 83 Photography © Tamas Mack; 85 'Hungary's Last Battle For Freedom', courtesy of The Hulton Getty Picture Collection Ltd.; 'Hungarian Revolution, 1956', courtesy of The Hulton-Deutsch Collection; 93 **Copycat** © 1995 Copyright by Monarchy Enterprises, photography by Melissa Moseley; 96 **Women in Love**, courtesy of MGM Consumer Products; 97 **The Rainbow**, script pages and notes courtesy of Live International USA; 107, 112, 113 **Breaking the Waves**, courtesy of Zentropa Productions, photography © Rolf Konow; 112 **Breaking the Waves**, chapter openers courtesy of Zentropa Productions, Per Kirkeby, Lars von Trier, Robby Müller; 109 **Until the End of the World** © M. Pelletier/SYGMA; 114, 115 **Korzcak**, courtesy of Regina Ziegler Filmproduktion, photography © Renata Pajchel; 124 Edward Hopper, American, 1882–1967, 'Nighthawks', oil on canvas, 1942, 84.1 x 152.4cm, Friends of the American Art Collection, 1942.51: photograph © 1997, The Art Institute of Chicago. All Rights Reserved; 127 Portrait shot © 1995 Paramount Pictures: photography © Ron Phillips; 128, 129 **Taxi Driver** © Copyright 1976 Columbia Pictures Industries, Inc. All Rights Reserved. Courtesy of Columbia Pictures; 130 'The Critic' Nov. 22, 1943 and 'Murder at the Feast of San Gennaro' Sept. 22, 1939 by Weegee (Arthur Fellig) © 1994, International Center of Photography, New York, Bequest of Wilma Wilcox; 137, 144, 145 **The Mosquito Coast**, photography © Francois Duhamel; 138 **The American President** and **The Firm**, photography © Francois Duhamel; 144 **Gorillas in the Mist**, Photography © Murray Close; 147 **The Paper**, sketch taken from an article by John Seale in 'International Photographer' published by International Photographers Guild; 149, 154, 155 **Portrait of a Lady**, photography © Lulu Zezza; 152, 153 **The Piano**, script pages and image grabs courtesy of CIBY 2000/Jan Chapman Prods, and sketches courtesy of Stuart Dryburgh and Jane Campion; 160 Vincent van Gogh 1853–1890) 'The Potato Eaters'. Oil on canvas, 1885. Courtesy of Amsterdam, Van Gogh Museum (Vincent Van Gogh Foundation); Hopper, Edward (1882–1967) 'From Williamsburg Bridge'. Oil on canvas. Courtesy of The Metropolitan Museum of Art, George A. Hearn Fund, 1937, (37.44). Photograph © 1989 The Metropolitan Museum of Art; 'Whalers' by J. M. Turner, courtesy of the Tate Gallery, London; Munch, Edvard. 'The Storm', 1893. Oil on Canvas. Courtesy of The Museum of Modern Art, New York. Gift of Mr and Mrs H. Irgens Larsen and acquired through the Lillie P. Bliss and Abby Aldrich Rockefeller Funds. Photograph © 1998 The Museum of Modern Art, New York; 161 'Beatrice Cenci (May Prinsep), Albumen 1867' by Julia Margaret Cameron and 'New York, 1916, Photogravure, From Camera Work No. 48' by Paul Strand, both courtesy of The Royal Photographic Society Picture Library, Bath, England; Henri Cartier-Bresson, 'India, Cremation of Gandhi, 1947' © Henri Cartier-Bresson/Magnum Photos; Don McCullin, 'Father and Child wounded when US Marines dropped hand genades into their shelter, Hue, Vietnam, 1968' © Don McCullin/Magnum Photos; W. Eugene Smith, 'Pacific War end 2 Sept 1945' © Smith W. Eugene/Magnum Photos; Henri Cartier-Bresson, 'Mexico, Calle Cuatemoczin, 1934' © Henri Cartier-Bresson/Magnum Photos; Bruce Davidson, 'Black Americans, 1962–1965, New York City 1962' © Bruce Davidson/Magnum Photos; **Culloden** © BBC 1964; 'Two Iranian women passing in front of a poster of the Ayatollah Khomeini', Tehran 1979, courtesy of Marc Riboud; 164 **Kundun** © SYGMA; 167 **The Big Lebowski**, script page and storyboards © Polygram Filmed Entertainment, Inc. Courtesy of Polygram Films, Joel and Etahn Coen, and Faber and Faber Ltd.; 169 **The Shawshank Redemption**, script pages and storyboards © Frank Darabont/Castle Rock Entertainment; 170, 174, 175 **The Hairdresser's Husband** © Benoit Barbier/SYGMA; 171 Portrait shot of Eduardo Serra, photography © J. M. Leroy; 173 'The Kitchenmaid' by J. Vermeer, courtesy of the Rijksmuseum, Amsterdam; **The King's Trial**, image grabs, courtesy of Paulo Branco; 174 'Porch, Provincetown, 1977', 'Ballston Beach, Truro, 1976' and 'Wilson Cottage, Wellfleet, 1976', photography © Joel Meyerowitz; **Metropolis/Lang** © Transit Films, Munich, Germany; 176 **Map of the Human Heart** © Polygram; Picture taken from 'Eskimo' by Paul-Emile Victor © Paul-Emile Victor. Courtesy of Jean-Christopher Victor; 180 **The Wings of the Dove** © Miramax; 'Pescheria vecchia a Venezia' by Ettore Tito © National Gallery of Modern Art, Rome; 181 **What Dreams May Come** © Polygram Film International; 182, 183 Portrait shot, 186, 187 **Amistad**, script page and stills © 1997 Dreamworks LLC. Photography © Andrew Cooper; 184 Pages from 'A Vanished World', published by the Penguin Group © 1975 by Roman Vishniac; 187 **Amistad** © SYGMA; 188 Technical drawings courtesy of Panavision USA; **Saving Private Ryan** script pages and still © 1998 TM Dreamworks LLC; 188, 189 'D-Day Landing, Normandy, June 6th 1944' and 'Liberation of France by the Allied Forces, Paris, Les Champs Élysées, 1944. The triumphal parade celebrating the liberation of the city' © Robert Capa/Magnum Photo Ltd.; 190 **The Lost World: Jurassic Park** TM & © 1997 Universal Studios, Inc. and Amblin Entertainment, Inc.; 193 Portrait shot, photography © Francois Duhamel; 195 'A Street in Algiers', 1905 by Frederick Holland Day, 'Grand Roue', 1900–05 by Pierre Dubreuil, 'Mélancolie', 1910–15 by Paul Haviland, 'Forêt innondée', 1908 by Antonin Personnaz, and 'Sans Titre', 1907 by Gustave Marissiaux, 'Le Salon de Photographie: Les écoles pictorialistes en Europe et aux Etats-Unis vers 1900'; Wyeth, Andrew. 'Christina's World' (1948). Tempera on gessoed panel, 32 1/4 x 47 3/4 inches (81.9 x 121.3 cm). The Museum of Modern Art, New York. Purchase. Photograph © 1998 The Museum of Modern Art, New York; 197 Bellows, George (American, 1882–1925) 'Club Night', John Hay Whitney Collection, © 1997 Board of Trustees, National Gallery of Art, Washington, 1907, oil on canvas, 1.092 x 1.350 (43 x 53 1/8); 201 Pages from Robert Frank's 'The Americans', (© 1958 Robert Frank/introduction © 1959 by Jack Kerouac); 203 Los Angeles County Museum of Art, 'Cliff Dwellers', 1913, by George Bellows, United States, 1882–1925. Courtesy of Los Angeles County Museum of Art, Los Angeles County Fund © 1997 Museum Associates, Los Angeles County Museum of Art. All Rights Reserved.

index

cinematography